I0584992

HBO's *Girls* and the Awkward Politics of Gender, Race, and Privilege

HBO's *Girls* and the Awkward Politics of Gender, Race, and Privilege

Edited by Elwood Watson, Jennifer Mitchell, and Marc Edward Shaw

LEXINGTON BOOKS
Lanham • Boulder • New York • London

Published by Lexington Books
An imprint of The Rowman & Littlefield Publishing Group, Inc.
4501 Forbes Boulevard, Suite 200, Lanham, Maryland 20706
www.rowman.com

Unit A, Whitacre Mews, 26-34 Stannary Street, London SE11 4AB

Copyright © 2015 by Lexington Books

All rights reserved. No part of this book may be reproduced in any form or by any
electronic or mechanical means, including information storage and retrieval systems,
without written permission from the publisher, except by a reviewer who may quote
passages in a review.

British Library Cataloguing in Publication Information Available

Library of Congress Cataloging-in-Publication Data

ISBN 978-1-4985-1261-9 (cloth)
ISBN 978-1-4985-1262-6 (electronic)
ISBN 978-1-4985-2299-1 (pbk)

TABLE OF CONTENTS

Introduction

Reading Into Girls, *Writing What We Read*

Dear Readers, thank you for taking the time to focus on our collection. You bought the book or checked it out from the library; or maybe, like Hannah Horvath's first writing contract, you are taking the e-book route. As this collection goes to print, the fourth season has just completed. Lena Dunham and company wrote Hannah and company some exciting new chapters: Hannah's attending-then-leaving the Iowa Writers' Workshop; her teaching English; Adam's breaking-up-then-missing his relationship with her; Hannah's new man; Hannah's father seeking a man (Elijah read Tad's homosexuality back in season 1). And that's just the first of the four *Girls*. What's clear is that things stay the same and everything changes; and, the possibilities are endless for the future now. (We are personally lobbying for a spin-off series, *Shoshanna! Shinjuku!*)

Over the four seasons, *Girls* is often a program about writing and reading: discovering Hannah's personal diary writings, then reading them aloud at the Questionable Goods gig; writing an app to prevent ex-dialing; studying and applying *Listen Ladies: A Tough Love Approach to The Tough Game of Love*; attending a group reading to help your writing; hate-reading *Listen Ladies: A Tough Love Approach to The Tough Game of Love*; discovering Adam's love of books; rediscovering Obsessive Compulsive Disorder because writing is hard (do not read that last sentence seven more times); taking cocaine to write about it; feeling like a sellout writing for GQ sponsors; having to attend the celebration after reading *Leave Me Alone*; reading too much online about medical issues; writing songs; reading *Gawker* and *Jezebel* to learn about an editor's death (as editors we thought, an especially sick plot twist).

Our collection reads and writes about *Girls* too. Each of our writers reads *Girls* in a distinct way. Like you, we are viewers, fans, spectators; but, to rewrite an idea from Jill Dolan's *Feminist Spectator as Critic*, we all read or spectate from our own distinct, subjective place in the living room.[1] We might see things differently from our loveseats than you do from yours. In a seminal work about reading, reader response criticism to be precise, Hans Robert Jauss argues that:

> In the triangle of author [Lena Dunham and company], work [*Girls*] and reading public [all of us] the latter is no passive part, no chain of mere reactions, but even history-making energy. The historical life of a literary work is unthinkable without the active participation of its audience. For it is only through the process of its communication that the work reaches the changing horizon of experience in a continuity in which the continual change occurs from simple reception to critical understanding, from passive to active reception, from recognized aesthetic norms to a new production which surpasses them.[2]

Since Dunham channels novelist Gustave Flaubert in the pilot episode, it is fair for us to use literary critical terms here. In Jauss's "continuity" we move with our collection from simple reception to active, critical understanding. This book tries to pinpoint how or how not Dunham and her collaborators surpass aesthetic norms into uncharted dramatic territory. How has *Girls*, in Jauss's words, made a "horizon change"?

What makes *Girls* a divisive or—to use the word in our title—*awkward* show? One answer might be that Dunham writes her world in the present without any strong alternative dramatic premise. Seeing *Girls* alongside others in the HBO program-scape, the young adults in Brooklyn have only each other as co-stars—no dragons, Atlantic City bootleggers, angels, apocalyptic vanishings, or vampires to spice the narrative. And in placing *Girls* in a familiar naturalistic reality, Dunham opens herself to others responding, "that is not my reality." The difference in realities predicates awkward truths. One other reason is that the *Girls* camera shows us explicit detail, not just in the sex scenes but in lingering longer or including moments that might make us uncomfortable: Hannah's parents have sex in the shower or Adam pees on Hannah. It is here that the comparison with Flaubert that Hannah makes in the pilot seems most fitting. When Flaubert went to trial for obscenity in *Madame Bovary* in 1857, according to Hans Robert Jauss, one issue that arose that changed his readers "horizon of expectation" was that Flaubert's "impersonal narrative form forces his readers not only to perceive things differently 'photographically exact' according to the judgment of the time— but it also forced them into an alienating insecurity about their judgment."[3] Readers of novels at that time were used to being told how to feel by the narrator, but Flaubert allowed a gap between the material and his audience. Dunham often forces us into a similar "alienating insecurity" about how we should feel about her characters.

The essays in this collection explore the awkward realities of *Girls* and evaluate why reviews have attacked its politics, lack of racial diversity, style, self-indulgence, lack of likable characters, complex representations of sex, and Dunham's own agenda, body, and writing. The show has spawned a cottage industry of op-ed pieces and academic conference panels about the work ethic, dating habits, sex lives, and other habits of older Millennials. Good, bad, brash, brave, racist, sexist, elitist, narcissistic, self-indulgent, immature, juvenile, groundbreaking, hip—are a few of the terms aimed at the series. Such wide-ranging descriptions and perceptions of *Girls* are a testament to the show's significance. By sparking outrage and adoration, the show iterates its place in the history of pioneering popular culture. Regardless, *Girls* refuses to shy away from representing experiences and characters that viewers find unsettling. From the show's blatant whiteness to its willingness to allow frank sexual experience, there is always something controversial to discuss the next day.

And, like Hannah, we writers feel our own anxieties as we create. After all, so much has been written about *Girls*, what else is there to write? From its debut in April 2012 virtually every mainstream print and Internet publication including the *New York Times*, *Entertainment Weekly*, *Cosmopolitan*, *Salon*, *Slate*, *Jezebel*, the *Atlantic*, the *New Yorker*, the *National Review*, the *New Republic*, the *Village Voice*, *Grantland* and *Rolling Stone*, has regularly covered the program. In a way, we feel a variation of the anxiety of influence. Harold Bloom argues that writers today worry about being influenced by the masters of the past.[4] So many people have opined about *Girls* (not all of them literary masters), what can we add? We don't want to be the Marnie lip-sync equivalent of criticism. Good news: we have curated a collection worth reading.

This anthology works to consider the broader implications of some of these issues, including, of course, questions of gender and racial politics; human indifference; class; sexuality; friendships among Millennials; white privilege; body image; parental attitudes; third wave feminism; male emasculation and immaturity; hipster, indie and urban music as it relates to Generation Y; Generation X perspectives of the series; image and identity; and the series' treatment of classical and contemporary literature and popular culture. This collection synthesizes and analyzes many of the most pressing issues that have surfaced in the show through its third season.

THE ESSAYS

The first chapter in this collection traces the connection between *Girls* and its television ancestors. In "She's Just Not That Into You: Dating, Damage, and Gender," Jennifer Mitchell approaches the dating trials chronicled in *Girls* in conjunction with dating "guides" and earlier representations of dating in New York City. In order to explore *Girls*'s representations of love and sex, Mitchell puts the show in conversation with some of the clichés that comprise the "dating" narratives that precede *Girls*—including *Friends* and *Sex and the City*. Through this comparison, Mitchell argues that, unlike its television ancestors, in its first two seasons, *Girls* presents damage not as an obstacle to overcome but as a foundational part of Hannah's and Adam's personal struggles and romantic exchanges.

Jocelyn Bailey and Maria San Filippo explore representations of gendered experience in "'The Body Police': Lena Dunham, Susan Bordo, and HBO's *Girls*" and "Owning Her Abjection: Lena Dunham's Feminist Politics of Embodiment." The outcry against Lena Dunham's body, and how it exposes the state of women's representation in visual media has been an explosive topic. Through television critics such as Tim Molloy of *TheWrap.com*, websites such as Jezebel.com, and longtime shock jock Howard Stern, the media has demonstrated itself to be resistant to bodies that defy the conventions of its own making. Bailey uses the 1993 work of Susan Bordo, *Unbearable Weight*, which examined the deep effects of a media culture gone mad for thinness. Though Bordo's analysis is twenty years old, her discussion of the "contained" female body still rings true. By examining *Girls* and its surrounding discourse in light of Bordo's work, Bailey demonstrates how Dunham's unruly body rebels against media conventions—and how the public response reveals that little has changed since Bordo's analysis of the 1990s. In short, though her body is a statistically average size and shape, there is currently no body in the media more exceptional or subversive than Lena's.

San Filippo argues that by displaying yet defetishizing female nudity, Dunham makes visible body types that are rarely screened and positions them in a way that accentuates women's embodied subjectivity, rather than sexual objectivity. More than simply recontouring the gaze and its desired object from the normative scope policed by mainstream cinema and porn, Dunham pushes further to explore and affirm women's bodies and desires for their most "unladylike" characteristics, elsewhere on screen rendered abject if not effaced completely. This chapter discusses Dunham's body politics through the lens of Julia Kristeva's formulation of *abjection* as a hetero patriarchal tool for coercing female bodies into regulated social subjects, alienating women from their bodies and one another. San Filippo further argues that over the first three seasons of the series, Dunham has established *Girls* as a feminist precedent for physical and sexual exhibitionism, performing acts relegated to the private sphere (from bathrooming to binging to sex) brought into the public and politicized. In so doing, Dunham re-envisions female embodied subjectivity as self-determining, women-loving, body-positive, pro-sex, and—to borrow an advertising slogan—contoured for her pleasure.

The question of "her pleasure" is, in many ways, the focus of Yael Levy's piece "Girls' Issues: The Feminist Politics of *Girls*'s Celebration of the 'Trivial,'" which delineates the way in which *Girls* represents feminine performance and evokes feminist resistance to the hegemonic division between that which is considered trivial (often congruent with "the feminine") and that which is considered culturally significant. By analyzing the show's treatment of the theme of death in two specific episodes—season 1's "Leave Me Alone" and season 3's "Dead Inside"—Levy argues that *Girls* offers a "feminist-inspired reworking of what counts as legitimate public discussion," given the considerable attention that the series dedicates to all too often marginalized and trivialized issues that pertain to women's lives.

Representations of gender identity, most specifically masculine identity, are the focal point of the chapter written by Marc Edward Shaw, "Falling from Pedestals: Dunham's Cracked *Girls* and Boys." Shaw responds to actor James Franco's essay on *Girls* by analyzing a recent commercial starring Franco—"The Fall"—as an example of dominant corporate masculinity. Shaw then draws contrasts between traditional masculinity/gender and Dunham's men and women in *Girls*—where the author does not mind letting her characters get damaged as they fall from their "pedestals" (via George Bernard Shaw). A textual analysis of the relating masculinities and femininities in one episode, "Welcome to Bushwick: aka The Crackcident" (episode 1.7) demonstrates how Dunham's characters evolve in relation to one another.

Music can become a crucial part of any television series no matter how extensively or minimally it is utilized. In "Capitalizing on Post-Hipster Cool: The Music That Makes *Girls*," Hank Willenbrink articulates how music operates in *Girls* by focusing on how song choices relate to the ascendance and identity of hipster culture. The use of music in *Girls* offers insights into how social standing is accrued in hipster culture. While the show has created hits out of previously unknown songs and artists, the characters that make music in *Girls* are regularly derided by their peers. While independent culture of the late 1990s stressed a do-it-yourself aesthetic, hipster culture prizes a consumer-based ideology whereby one's taste, which is often ironic, determines social standing.

Tom Pace's "Generation X Archetypes in HBO's *Girls*," critiques social status and generational identity in the show. While *Girls* is clearly defined as unquestionably Millennial in its spirit, Dunham and the shows' writers have used numerous images and archetypes from 1990s Generation X culture and media to create a show that is ultimately more complex and interesting than anything else from that earlier period. This is evident in the fact that virtually all the characters embody similar traits that were ascribed to Generation Xers during the 1990s. Pace astutely addresses several of these archetypes, including the male slacker, the reliance on friends, and a general distrust of adults. He also analyzes season 2's controversial episode, "One Man's Trash," in which Hannah spends a weekend with a forty-two-year-old Gen-X doctor played by renaissance actor Patrick Wilson, getting a glimpse of what her life could be like once she gets through the difficulty of her twenties.

Laura Witherington's "Reading *Girls*: Diegesis and Distinction" deftly examines the cultural act of reading and the implication of texts as props and as inter-textual extensions to the meaning of scenes and understanding of characters. While many of the characters are dysfunctional to some, most of them are also well educated and can be seen reading upscale newspapers and magazines and frequently making references to classic texts and highbrow authors when finding themselves in various situations. Witherington looks at how the sexualized mystification of symbols by authors and philosophers such as Pierre Bourdieu and Jean Baudrillard and others contribute to the fetishization of reading and books.

In his essay, Lena Dunham: The Awkward/Ambiguous Politics of White Millennial Feminism," Elwood Watson tackles one of the most pressing issues surrounding the series: race. Even before its premiere in the spring of 2012, *Girls* and its major star, twenty something wunderkind Lena Dunham, came under attack for what seemed to be the program's lack of racial and ethnic diversity as well as Dunham and her staff's response to the criticism. After the premiere of the series' first episode, the criticism intensified tenfold. The manner in which Ms. Dunham and her producers responded to the controversy was a messy combination of arrogance, confusion, and candor. Watson further examines the hypocrisy of Lena Dunham, her supporters, detractors, the show's producers, and how all camps—Dunham, her advocates, critics, the show's writers and occasional interlopers—need to be taken to task on how they have clumsily and awkwardly handled the issue of race.

The intersection of race, class, and performance is examined in the final essay of the collection. In "Marnye on the Ones and Twos: Appropriating Race, Criticizing Class in *Girls*," Lloyd Isaac Vayo focuses on Marnie's performance of Kanye West's song "Stronger." Seemingly a minor moment, Marnie's performance, at once a cover of "Stronger" and a remix, alters the tone and content of the song and stands as a moment of self-awareness for the series. Marnie's performance engages in a problematic appropriation and repurposing of West's song, removing it from the mouth of an African-American artist and placing it in the mouth of an especially white young New Yorker. That appropriation is also flawed in that Marnie selectively quotes from the song, taking lines out of context and changing the song's meaning, if only through a gender reversal and her conversion of a rap song into a torch song. Yet, at the same time, Marnie performs a critique of class and privilege, adopting the perspective of the cultural Other (West) as a means of attacking Charlie's class status and according privilege. Marnie, via West, ridicules Charlie's celebration and, by proxy, his app (meant to prevent jilted lovers from contacting their exes), challenging the swift success of the app company as akin to the boom and bust cycle of Internet start-ups in the late 1990s.

With four seasons of episodes that have garnered national attention, the show has yet to conclude the trajectories of its primary characters. The essays in this collection analyze the social, artistic, and political implications of a thought-provoking series right in the midst of its success. As Lena Dunham continues to be a cultural presence—as viewers and readers alike continue to discuss her life, work, and writing—so, too, the show will surely continue to work through many of the issues covered in this collection. We editors, as such, anticipate this book's participation in an ongoing (sometimes awkward, but always necessary) conversation about gender, race, and privilege within popular culture.

NOTES

1. Jill Dolan, *Feminist Spectator as Critic*, University of Michigan Press, 1988.
2. Hans Robert Jauss, "Literary History as a Challenge to Literary Theory," *New Literary History* 2.1, 7-37. 8, parentheses added.
3. Ibid., 35.
4. Harold Bloom, *The Anxiety of Influence*, Oxford University Press, 1973.

Chapter One

She's Just Not That Into You: Dating, Damage, and Gender

Jennifer Mitchell

The beginning of *He's Just Not that Into You* (2009) theorizes the tragic history of mixed signals within a romantic framework. After a young boy pushes a young girl down, her mother tries to make her feel better with the following explanation: "Do you know why that little boy did those things and said those things? It's because he likes you. That little boy is doing those terrible things because he's got a crush on you."[1] For Ginnifer Goodwin's character, this narrative is "the beginning of our problem" because it sets young, single, straight girls up to "think that if a guy acts like a total jerk he likes you."[2] This sentiment that men are jerks and that women misinterpret their fairly straightforward negative behavior as something indirectly positive, of course, echoes that of the book by Greg Behrendt and Liz Tuccilo on which the movie is based. Whereas the book works to assure women that they are *never* the exception, most of the movie's intersecting story lines reiterate the traditional fairy tale mythology where the "heroine" is, without question, the exception to all romantic rules and regulations. Ultimately, the "he's just not that into you" mantra that underscores the entirety of the book is only applicable to one or two of the major plotlines of the film.

The introductory segment of the film reinforces the opposition between men and women in virtually all things related to love, dating, romance, and sex. For the characters in the movie, their respective partners in question are indicative of "types" of men, and, as a result, types of relationships. The dating drama chronicled throughout—a mix of bad Myspace encounters, adultery, casual sex, misinterpreted signals, ultimatums, among others—is a testament to the demand for "real" stories that address the spectrum of damage that one encounters whilst attempting to date. *He's Just Not That Into You*, of course, is neither the first nor the last popular attempt at making a point about the complex and dynamic nature of heterosexual dating.

Focusing on the more nuanced and, one might argue, messier portraits of damage, HBO's *Girls* is a reaction to cultural portraits of "damage"—both in terms of sex and in terms of dating—that have been chronicled over the last two decades. Television shows about friendship and dating that take place in New York City like *Friends* (1994–2004) and *Sex and the City* (1998–2004) each break down "damage" into two distinct categories: romantic deal breaker or fixer-upper.[3] The shows' protagonists encounter a variety of dating "nightmares" deemed as such precisely because of the revelation of the insurmountable damage accompanying their partners. From horrifying doppelgangers to incompatible sexual proclivities, such damage proves itself impossible to overcome. As a result, the successful pairings—ultimately heteronormative, straight, all white couples—speak to the notion that romantic success comes from overcoming all that dating nonsense with someone whose damage is malleable and, well, surmountable. Thus Ross and Rachel find their way back to each other, with five of the six friends happily paired off by the series finale. When Carrie ultimately ends up with Big, she is the last of her foursome to end up in a long-term committed relationship by the end of the series.[4] Over the course of their runs, the characters on these shows eventually end up in their thirties or forties (or even fifties), but in the case of *Friends*, viewers follow closely the dating lives of twenty somethings for much of the series. Contrarily, in its first two seasons, *Girls* presents damage not as an obstacle to overcome but as a foundational part of Hannah's and Adam's personal struggles and romantic exchanges, presenting viewers with a whole new dating paradigm—one that is telling in its frankness.

In particular, all three shows attempt to convey the harsh, absurd, comical, and distressing "realities" of what it means to actually attempt to date in New York City. The significance of geography here cannot be overstated, especially when Sarah Jessica Parker of *Sex and the City* thanked New York as the "fifth lady" on the series during her 2002 Golden Globe Award acceptance speech. The proliferation of New York City as the setting for dating drama is a testament to its singularity. Indeed, if one does a Google search about dating in New York, one will stumble across all sorts of funny and somewhat depressing articles with catchy titles such as, "Ask a Native New Yorker: Why Is the NYC Dating Scene so Rough?" Native New Yorker, John Del Signore, provides a telling response to this question:

> You say you're looking for "Interesting, attractive, not insane people." Take it from a native: in thirty-seven years I have never met a person in this city that embodied all three of these qualities at once. Perhaps this is possible in a

simpler town—Minneapolis, maybe, or Vancouver. But you chose New York, a city so expensive that it drives the sane mad just trying to make rent, tempts the attractive with cronuts until they become morbidly obese, and forces all the interesting people to discuss real estate and careers until they kill everyone with boredom.[5]

Del Signore identifies the specific "type" of person attracted to New York as fundamentally lacking. In other words, "normal" single people interested in finding "normal" partners do not choose to live in New York City. Similarly, in "5 Reasons Dating in NYC Is Exhausting," Madison Moore identifies the geographically specific proliferation of "weirdos":

> The Chances Of Them Being A Major Weirdo Are High: Everybody has some kind of ratchetness in their mind-closet. I don't think there's a single human being out there who doesn't have issues. New York is an expensive city to live in, which means people work eighty hours a week and drink and do other stuff to relax, but it also means that they have developed some kind of weird neuroses that you will either have to learn to deal with or run away from. Just remember to be fair, though, because you have your own shit, too. Nobody's perfect.[6]

There is an explicit connection being made between New York as "a city so expensive" that it is impossible to stay sane (or, to simply be sane) and those who are willing to sacrifice their sanity in order to live there. These articles, representative of dozens more like them, use a mix of humor and melancholy to cultivate camaraderie amongst those who believe they have been wronged by the harshness of the dating scene in the city. The thematic undercurrent of both articles is clear—in New York, "normal" is impossible.

As such, television shows that focus on heterosexual dating—which, for the purposes of this chapter, I consider anything that ranges from a traditional date in which one party asks another out on an actual date to contemporary hook-ups in which one party has some form of sexual interactions with another—pay particular attention to the not-so-normal. For the "not so normal" dating behaviors that I am going to discuss, I adopt the term "damage," using the *Oxford English Dictionary*'s definition: "Loss or detriment caused by hurt or injury affecting estate, condition, or circumstances; A disadvantage, inconvenience, trouble; A matter for regret, a misfortune, 'a pity.'"[7] Damage, then, becomes the umbrella term under which all sorts of dating and sexual demons can be categorized. From Chandler's willingness to disregard potential partners for "big nostrils"[8] to Harry's problematic tea bag situation,[9] the spectrum of damage ranges from the absurd and impossible to the traditional and forgivable. What both *Friends* and *Sex and the City* have in common, however, is that those two ends of the spectrum reinforce the notion that prospective partners are either *too* damaged or in need of some fixing up. *Girls*, on the other hand, presents a third—and far more interesting—possibility: that damage is itself a foundational part of the romantic package, chronicling the ways in which damage is simultaneously ubiquitous and attractive.

When Dates Meant, Well, Dates

Monica, Ross, Rachel, Chandler, Joey, and Phoebe all navigated the slippery slope of dating whilst young, straight, white, and in New York City during the mid 1990s. Their dating stories, the comedic backbone of the series, are filled with a slew of dating mishaps and misdemeanors. The first season, in fact, chronicles what may be considered the most fleeting of these issues. In "The One with the Stoned Guy," Ross's "hot" date with Celia becomes simply too hot for him. Mid-make-out, Celia says, "Talk to me."[10] Ross's response, "um, a weird thing happened to me on the train this morning . . . ," reveals his fundamental inability to understand exactly what Celia is asking of him. Finally, after she demands something "hot," Ross blurts out "vulva."[11] Of course, there is no ensuing sex, but rather resigned cuddling. Accordingly, Ross spends the next few segments of the episode asking Joey, *Friends*'s resident ladies' man, for advice. Ultimately, Ross attempts to face his fear and chronicles his wholehearted second attempt at dirty talk: "I was the James Michener of dirty talk. It was the most elaborate filth you have *ever* heard. I mean, there were different characters, plot lines, themes, a motif . . . at one point there were villagers."[12] Despite this rather elaborate recollection, Ross and Celia spend this date cuddling as well. Here, Celia's "damage" is barely that; yet, her predilection for dirty talk is particularly mock-able precisely because Ross cannot possibly adapt to it. *Sex and the City* tackles this same subject when Miranda sleeps with someone who loves dirty talk. In "The Awful Truth," she, somewhat channeling the usually verbose Ross, explains that, "sex is not a time to chat."[13]

In "The One with the Ick Factor," Monica inadvertently sleeps with a high school student. Prior to what she hopes will be the first time that they have sex, Ethan reveals his virginity, romantically declaring, "I've kinda been waiting for the right person."[14] The sex that follows, apparently, is remarkable for both Monica and Ethan. Yet, it inspires Monica to reveal a little something about herself: "Listen, uh, you told me something that was really difficult for you. And I, I—I figured if you could be honest, then I can too . . . Um, okay, here it goes. I'm not twenty-two. I'm, I'm twenty-five . . . and thirteen months."[15] It turns out that Monica undershot her age to seem more compatible with young Ethan, who, inspired by Monica's candor and declaration that "that shouldn't change anything . . . [because] what the hell does it matter how old we are," reveals even more about himself:

Ethan: Uh, listen um, as long as we're telling stuff, uh, I have another one for you. I'm a little younger than I said.

Monica: You're not a senior?

Ethan: Oh, I'm a senior . . . in high school. [16]

Thus, the titular "Ick Factor" surfaces. Despite the fact that what Monica shaved off of her age is roughly equivalent to what Ethan added onto his—and despite the fact that *both* of their lies made what happened between them in bed illegal, Monica places the blame almost entirely on Ethan and his adolescence. Her post-confessional freak out comprises much of the humor in this aspect of the episode:

Monica: What we did was wrong. Oh god, I just had sex with somebody that wasn't alive during the Bicentennial.

Ethan: I just had sex.

Monica: Ethan, focus. How could you not tell me?

Ethan: Well, you never told me how old you were.

Monica: Well, that's different. My lie didn't make one of us a felon in forty-eight states. [17]

The "damage" that viewers can locate here, a basic lie about something fundamentally unchangeable about oneself, is something that resurfaces in subsequent decades with the proliferation of online dating: think height, weight, body shape, level of education, alcohol and cigarette consumption, desire for children, among others. In this early *Friends* episode, though, the obstacle to dating happiness is unquestionably insurmountable.

These two examples are indicative of the various tracts of damage that surface on the show. Celia's dirty talk is indicative of a general sexual incompatibility that could, elsewhere, be overcome—and that, for Adam and Hannah in *Girls*, would actually signify sexual compatibility—whereas Ethan's youth is a straightforward deal-breaker—as, potentially, Hannah's admission to graduate school could be. In the show, both minor characters are ditched in favor of, first, more comedic damage, and second, more permanent commitment. After ten seasons, Ross ends up with Rachel, fulfilling their destiny as "the show's emotional core" and Monica finds true love across the hall with Chandler. [18]

More nuanced "damage" surfaces throughout the series, which provides viewers with overt condemnations of particular sexual and dating choices. Chandler falls for a mysterious woman named Aurora in "The One with the Butt" and is initially smitten by her foreign intrigue. He explains, "she's Italian, and she pronounces my name 'Chand-lerr'. 'Chand-lerr.'"[19] Her appeal only grows when, in brief flashbacks to their date, she explains her romantic situation:

> Chandler: So explain something to me here. What kind of a relationship do you imagine us having if you already have a husband and a boyfriend?
>
> Aurora: I suppose mainly sexual.[20]

While Monica and the other friends presume that this revelation means the end for Chandler and Aurora, Chandler is clear about the appeal of such a scenario:

> Monica: Didn't you listen to the story? I mean, this is twisted! How could you get involved with a woman like this?
>
> Chandler: Well, y'know, I had some trouble with it at first, too, but the way I look at it is, I get all the good stuff: all the fun, all the talking, all the sex, and none of the responsibility. I mean, this is every guy's fantasy![21]

All those involved in a relationship with Aurora are aware of her circumstances, yet Monica adamantly maintains that the dynamic Aurora describes is "twisted." As Chandler continues to "date" Aurora, he becomes torn between the fantasy of getting "all the good stuff" and the reality of having to share a woman for whom he is developing feelings. That tension reaches its climax in the final encounter between Chandler and Aurora, when they both finally acknowledge his reservations:

> Aurora: Why can't we just have what we have now? Why can't we just talk, and laugh, and make love, without feeling obligated to one another . . . and up until tonight I thought that's what you wanted, too.
>
> Chandler: Well, y'know, part of me wants that, but it's like I'm two guys, y'know? I mean, one guy's going "Shut up! This is great!" But there's this other guy. Actually it's the same guy that wells up every time that Grinch's heart grows three sizes and breaks that measuring device . . . And he's saying, y'know, "This is too hard! Get out! Get out!"[22]

Of course, when this episode is put in conversation with the future trajectory of Chandler and Monica, it is clear that *Friends* sides with Monica—Aurora and all the subversive, alternative sexual and romantic dynamics that she represents are "twisted." Even the versions of what has been seen as extreme sexual objectification in *Girls* are primarily framed in terms of partnerships; aside from Jessa and Marnie's momentary threesome, "twisted" sexual encounters exist between two parties.[23] Thus, the safe, traditional, heteronormative romantic narrative plays itself out in a proposal, a marriage, and babies for Chandler and Monica by the time the series ends. The same is, somewhat remarkably, true of Phoebe as the show progresses. In "The One with the Boob Job," Ross is surprised to see that Phoebe is more traditional than her dating history would suggest. After boyfriend Mike asks her to move in with him, Phoebe tells her friends, who have already revealed their own personal interest in or commitment to marriage:

Monica: I hear wedding bells.

Phoebe: Monica, slow down! Ok? I'm just excited to be living with him. You know I mean, I don't know, Can I see someday being married to Mike? Sure! Yeah. Y'know. I can picture myself walking down the aisle in a wedding dress that highlights my breasts in an obvious yet classy way. But do I want that house in Connecticut . . . you know, near the good schools where Mike and I can send Sophie and Mike Junior. Oh my god I do.

Ross: Phoebe, I had no idea you were so conventional.

Phoebe: I know! I guess I am! Oh my god! Load up the Volvo I want to be a soccer mom![24]

Free spirit Phoebe is probably least likely to get married given her atypical adolescence. Yet, just when Mike makes it clear that he has no interest in marriage, Phoebe comes to terms with the fact that she actually does and the two break up. Mike's "damage" is fairly conventional, a man afraid of marriage, and when faced with a competing suitor willing to offer Phoebe that traditional commitment, Mike overcomes his "damage" and their reconciliation ensues. *Friends* embraces a fairy tale mythology, with five of the six main characters paired off monogamously by the final episode. Thus, for romantic fulfillment of the most traditional kind, damage needs to be overcome or recast—as it becomes a relic of formerly single days.

When Dates, Well, Meant Sex

Because *Friends* aired on primetime network television, the "damage" that it chronicled was certainly tame by comparison. Without the nudity, explicit language, and actual sex scenes that are a commonplace element in *Sex and the City* and *Girls*, *Friends* can only go so far in terms of its coverage of the sexually and/or emotionally quirky. In their introduction to *Reading Sex and the City*, Kim Akass and Janet McCabe define the show as, "four women talking candidly about sex and relationships."[25] Such candidness—what Dana Heller explains as "its unapologetic frankness with respect to matters of heterosexual sex and female sexuality" (151)[26]—is somewhat indebted to the freedoms that accompany HBO. Because of this limited-holds-barred framework, *Sex and the City* seeks to chronicle the realities of an older bracket of friends attempting to find love and/or orgasms. Within that narrative framework, Carrie, Samantha, Charlotte, and Miranda all go through their fair share of dating drama. From suitors who secretly tape their sexual conquests[27] to gym instructors who "brand" their conquests[28] to unadulterated exhibitionists,[29] the men that are portrayed on the show are indicative of the vast array of damage that could be ascribed to a sexual partner.

From the first episode of the series, in which Carrie interrogates the concept of "having sex like a man," the foursome of successful women become representative of the various dating tendencies and female archetypes available to young women in New York City.[30] Alexandra Silver-Fagan explains, "Ask any New York City woman if they consider themselves a Carrie, Charlotte, Miranda or Samantha and you'll have an answer before you blink. We NYC women, a subspecies of the traditional female, have looked towards *Sex and the City* for guidance and comfort in the miseries of dating."[31] Silver-Fagan's identification of the NYC woman as a "subspecies of the traditional female" is particularly apt when considering the ways in which the show highlights the singularity of dating in New York.

That being said, the show itself tackles questions that are a cornerstone of many television shows and films that focus on love and courtship. In "Just Say Yes," after finding a "bad" engagement ring in Aiden's duffel bag, Carrie mulls over the big question that underscores much of the fourth season of the show: "How do you know when it's right?"[32] Torn between Aiden and Big in multiple seasons, Carrie poses a question that, while applicable to the dating scene in New York City, has much broader reach than, say, the prevalence of Manolo Blanik shoes, the possibility of first "date" trips to Brazil, and the horror that is potentially moving to Brooklyn. Knowing when it's right is the theory underneath the series. For many of the characters, the question of timing is incredibly relevant to the possibility of a happily-ever-after. Carrie tries to date Big monogamously numerous times unsuccessfully before their ultimate wedding bells (which, of course, ring not without complication in the first film based on the series) while Miranda and Steve attempt monogamous coupling several times before really committing to one another. Throughout this quest for partnered monogamy, all four women have their fair share of dating mishaps both inside and outside of the bedroom. Damage in *Sex and the City*—for Carrie and her great love affair with Big, Charlotte and her failed first "ideal" marriage but successful "quirky" second, and Miranda with her initially questionable choice of Steve the bartender—is, yet again, a hurdle. To overcome said hurdle is a sign of the impending success of the straight, monogamous relationship. Even Samantha, with her marginalized doctrine of non-monogamy, wraps up the television show in a monogamous, committed relationship. *Sex and the City* takes as its subject four successful women and focuses on the trials inherent in finding suitable partners—romantic and sexual—for them. Of course, the difference in age, experience, and ensuing economic and career trajectories between those four women and the younger, messier foursome on *Girls*, is telling. While *Sex and the City* itself certainly articulates the reality of needing to revisit damage in order to gauge circumstantial compatibility, it too suggests that certain types of damage are workable—Steve's rough around the edges working class mentality proves attractive despite Miranda's educated reservations—whereas some types of damage are permanent—regardless of how much Samantha falls for Richard, she cannot "cure" him of his cheating impulses.

When Dates, Mean, Well, Nothing

In the age of OKCupid and group texts, where more and more people are not only meeting online but willing to admit that fact, it appears that dating—as television and film have captured it for decades—no longer exists. Gone are the days when Big's car would pull up to Carrie's brownstone prior to a late, swanky dinner reservation. Gone are the days when Joey could utter, "How you doin'?" in Central Park and have a dinner date for the following night. As such, television shows and movies that focus on dating are forced to adapt accordingly. Indeed, *How I Met Your Mother*'s romantic lead, Ted, still wants the fairy tale in which he takes girls out on dates, but acknowledges that that isn't the only course of action. *Girls* is even more explicit in its acknowledgment of the shift in dating culture and its implications. In "The End of Courtship?" Alex Williams argues that traditional courtship and dating is no longer relevant in the realities of dating in New York City.[33] Accordingly, Williams cites *Girls* because "none of the main characters paired off in a manner that might count as courtship even a decade ago." In response, Mary C. Hickey, writes, "if the cast on *Girls* is any indication, more people are hooking up a little more casually—and getting naked more quickly—than most of us did when we were that age. But to me, the overall experience of the twenty something dating scene seems very much the same. Experimentation. Guilt. Jealousy. Hurt. Confusion."[34]

Like Williams suggests, dating might have changed its proverbial stripes—the combination of dinner, movie, and anxious kiss seems to have been replaced by group trivia night and subsequent no-strings sex. And, like Hickey suggests, the underlying emotional roller coaster of dating eerily remains the same. Yet, what *Girls* does far differently than its television predecessors is pay more explicit attention to the foundational role that damage plays in the contemporary dating game. Instead of the fleeting damage of incompatible, even wacky sexual proclivities or behavioral tendencies that need to be rectified in order for a relationship to progress, the damage exposed on *Girls* is, at least in the first two seasons of the show, more honest. Hannah's primary love/sex interest, Adam, is more complex than Big or Aiden, Chandler or Ross. Critics have argued that he's "disgusting"[35] and "vile,"[36] citing everything from his sexual proclivities to his general demeanor to condemn him. Crystal Bell responds aggressively to one of the early notorious scenes in which "Adam pulled a Nicole Kidman and peed on Hannah in the shower"—an encounter that she describes as "too repulsive for words." While Hannah is horrified, this scene is most certainly not a deal breaker, which is likely how it would have been cast had *Friends* dabbled in golden showers and which is certainly how it was cast when *Sex and the City* attempted to approach it in "Politically Erect."

While peeing in the shower is a singular instance in their sex lives on the show, other representations of sex between Hannah and Adam are equally awkward and fascinating. As L.V. Anderson explains, *Girls* is honest in its portrayal of bad sex, a facet of dating in New York City that often goes unrepresented:

> Most TV and film sex scenes still involve two people undulating their bodies against each other as slowly as humanly possible and gazing nonstop into each other's eyes—except when their lids flutter shut as they climax simultaneously. On the other end of the straight sex-scene spectrum lies, of course, hardcore porn, in which the women are always climaxing, sometimes for hours at a stretch, as men penetrate and manipulate their bodies in all sorts of ferocious ways, until we finally reach the money shot. Rarely do we see anything between these two fantasies—one neutered, one embellished, both purporting to show people having a great time in the sack.[37]

As most straight, sexually active twenty something girls attempting to date in New York City can attest, bad sex—whether the byproduct of incompatibility, inexperience, the influence of various substances, among other reasons—is simply part of the dating game. It is precisely the "bad" sex of *Girls* that Anderson is interested in, when the show focuses on "real life" and its accompanying "physically uncomfortable, emotionally complicated, politically imbalanced" bad sex.[38] Early sex between Adam and Hannah reiterates Hannah's somewhat painful inexperience. While both Ross and Miranda are reluctant to talk dirty in the sack, Hannah's verboseness heightens the awkwardness of the scene; after Adam asks whether he should come on Hannah's "Face? Tummy? Those little tits of yours?" Hannah longwindedly responds: "It seems like you want to come on my tits, so I think you should come on my tits, because I want you to come, and it seems like you're going to do it."[39] As such, much of this early sex ends with an orgasm on Adam's behalf but not Hannah's. In that regard, Adam seems to understand his own sexual desires and demands much more than Hannah understands hers.

Indeed, that process of discovery, which happens both within and outside of her experiences with Adam, is, for many viewers, a part of the show's appeal. Emily Nussbaum explains that such early encounters "presented sex as a rough draft, a failed negotiation, at once hilarious and real."[40] Even though Nussbaum credits *Girls* as a "show about life lived as a rough draft—something well intentioned, possibly promising, but definitely begging for cruel critiques," reality and hilarity are not presented as necessarily part and parcel of the same whole.[41] In "On All Fours" toward the end of the second season of the show, Adam and post-Hannah "girlfriend" Natalia have sex for the first time and it is, most certainly, not hilarious. She explains, "I'm ready to have sex now . . . You've been really nice all week. We can do it, if you want." This somewhat hesitant set-up is undercut by how direct Natalia is about her sexual no-nos: "I don't like to be on top that much. Or soft touching, because it tickles me and takes me out of the moment. But everything else is OK . . . "[42] That clarity is something that Adam explicitly appreciates and their interactions here are lighthearted and straightforward. After this somewhat idyllic scene, the two go to a party during which Adam falls off the wagon, and they return to his apartment where he tells Natalia to "get on all fours" and crawl into his bedroom. Amanda Hess chronicles the scene as it unfolds:

> Adam grabs her from the floor, throws her on the bed, and explains: "I want to fuck you from behind, hit the walls with you." *She consents, numbly.* He removes her underwear and goes down on her. She does not consent. "No. Look, I didn't take a shower today," she says. "It's fine, relax," he tells her. He begins fucking her from behind. He asks her to confirm that she likes his apartment, that she likes the way he looks, and that she really likes him. *She consents, limply.* Then, he pulls out and masturbates over her. "No, no, no, no, not on my dress!" she says. She pulls off her top, grimaces, and looks away. He comes on her chest. "I don't think I like that," she says, when he's done. "I, like, really didn't like that."[43] (Emphasis added)

This scene reveals a lot about its two participants. First, under the influence of alcohol Adam is even more aggressive in bed than the elaborate fantasies of his that we see in the first season of *Girls*. Second, the directness that both Natalia and Adam have previously acknowledged as crucial—Adam says, "I like how clear you are with me" and Natalia responds with, "What other way is there?"—is clearly only applicable to talking and not doing. In this scene Adam is alarmingly direct with his desires, yet regardless of Natalia's previous celebration of clarity and directness, she does not seem to enjoy the sex that follows at all.

With critics asking whether the sex acts captured constitute rape, the coverage garnered by "On All Fours" is remarkably varied. Joe Flint declares it "a violent and hard-to-watch scene."[44] Jace Lacob pushes that claim even further:

> The semen that Adam deposits on Natalia's chest is not meant to titillate or arouse. It's meant to shock the viewer into opening their eyes, to see the damage that Adam perpetuates here, one based upon countless male fantasies enacted in porn. But while other cable shows might use sex and female nudity as window dressing, *Girls* strives for something both deeper and darker here, a revelation that there are repercussions to physical intimacy, that Natalia's humiliation and debasement are not sexy, but painful.[45]

This scene is certainly complicated and it provides crucial insight into the depths of what viewers can consider Adam's sexual damage. While both *Friends* and *Sex and the City* are not shy about discussing sexual incompatibility, especially in terms of comic relief, the seriousness with which this scene is treated emphasizes its significance. Although Natalia is unhappy with this sexual encounter—and the extent of her unhappiness is poignantly covered in the first episode of the third season—viewers are invited to consider Hannah as potentially more willing to engage in it. The season 3 opener sets up that comparison directly, with Natalia describing Adam as "an off-the-wagon Neanderthal sociopath" and yelling at both Hannah and Adam, "I hope you two just enjoy your urine-soaked life fucking like the two feral animals that you both know you are."[46]

Natalia's judgment here echoes much of the criticism of Adam and his sexual desires. Sarah Caldwell, in "Girls: How Are We Supposed to Feel about Adam," posits: "In the book of Hannah's life, Adam would be the guy she was with before she became the self-actualized woman she was meant to be. He was the guy who tried to debase Hannah by making her act out scenes from porn movies he had watched."[47] Whereas many viewers of the show are quick to condemn Adam, his arc with Natalia retroactively solidifies much of what has been building since the first episode of the show: Hannah and Adam are, in fact, compatible; rather than assuming that Adam dominates Hannah, we learn that Hannah is equally interested in the types of fantasies that Adam instigates. Indeed, as Adam and Hannah become more and more conventional throughout the third season of *Girls*, it is Hannah who wishes to revive the elements of their sex life that involve "humiliation and debasement." In "Role-Play," Hannah dons a blonde wig and impersonates the wife of a businessman to entice Adam back to their early sexual encounters. Yet, her plan backfires as she switches roles mid-fantasy and Adam angrily criticizes her illogical narrative choices:

> Hannah: What? I was trying to do something you'd like. Like have sex the way that we used to. Why are you getting so mad at me?
>
> Adam: What do you mean the way we used to? You don't like the way we do it now?
>
> Hannah: Well, do you? You used to have all these ideas about me being like a little street slut or like an orphan with a disease or you said I was like a woman with a baby's body or something. I was just trying to do it the way that we used to, the way that sex always was for us.[48]

While Hannah wants to rekindle the creative, narrative fire that once underscored their sexual encounters, Adam is upset that she even thinks their old dynamic is applicable to their current relationship. When she tries to justify her choices by claiming that she "was just doing sex the way [Adam] wanted to," Adam replies: "You have an old idea of who I am. Sex was the thing that kept me from drinking. That's why I fucked women I met in bars or whatever . . . But then, we fell in love. And then I just wanted to have sex with just you as us. Just fuck and be sweet . . . or whatever."[49] This interaction, perhaps the climactic moment between Adam and Hannah in season 3, reveals that Hannah is actually far less interested in "being sweet or whatever" and that her initial interest in Adam had much to do with the crazy "ideas" that Adam brought into the bedroom.[50]

This particular interaction actually speaks to the ways in which *Girls* is explicitly rejecting not only the television tradition of recuperating damage that both *Friends* and *Sex and the City* participate in, but is also rejecting the traditional fairy tale component that Adam momentarily represents here. The final episode of season 2 of *Girls* involves Adam literally coming to Hannah's rescue, running from his section of Brooklyn to hers, in order to protect her—the ultimate Prince Charming gesture. Caldwell, asking about Adam's likeability, compares that moment to the traditional romantic comedy narrative: "So, about that rom-com ending? I get that almost everyone has fantasized about a guy running to see them. But still, is the idea of him forcibly breaking down her door to then hold her in his arms like she's a baby really all that romantic? Isn't it just him being the dominant person again? Is that the only kind of relationship he can actually thrive in?"[51] Caldwell reads Hannah as entirely dependent on Adam's big, dominant personality—as molding herself accordingly. Of course, even Hannah admits to this malleability. Yet, the dynamic between the two of them is far more multidimensional and is more significantly based on a kind of mutual recognition. When Ross ends up with Rachel, and Monica and Chandler get together, and Phoebe realizes she wants a traditional marriage, viewers are satiated by the notion that these characters end up with partners who understand them as audience members do. Rachel and Ross evolve past their "on a break" damage; Chandler grows past his immaturity; Phoebe comes to terms with her conventional desires. The cast of *Sex and the City* explicitly follows similar trajectories. Big overcomes his fear of commitment; Samantha gets over her fear of intimacy; Charlotte abandons her unreasonably high standards; and Miranda, well, moves to Brooklyn. In this regard, the partnerships that survive are neatly packaged reminders that conventional monogamy requires both the discarding of insurmountable damage in conjunction with the treatment of moderate, quirky damage.

Girls, however, suggests that the type of recognition ultimately sought in these other television shows does not simply erase or soften damage; rather, such damage proves itself to be a foundational element in attraction, desire, and compatibility. Hannah is not interested in Adam in spite of his sexual proclivities, brooding temper, or general unpredictability[52]—all of which constitute various incarnations of the types of "damage" that I have been writing about here—and she is certainly not interested in him vis-à-vis a desire to cure him of those proclivities, as "Role-Play" articulates. Rather, Hannah is interested in Adam *because* of his damage. Indeed, for the early seasons of the show, their compatibility is contingent upon the appeal of such damage. The end of season 3, of course, leaves viewers on the precipice of the unknown, wondering what will happen to Hannah and Adam's relationship with the looming possibility of graduate school in Iowa and a great acting career. As such, it would be foolish to speculate that *Girls* will maintain its nuanced and formative presentation of damage, though I certainly hope that the show resists the powerful magnetism of the fairy tale trajectory to which its predecessors most certainly succumbed.

NOTES

1. *He's Just Not That Into You*, Dir. Ken Kwapis, New Line Cinema, 2009.
2. Ibid.
3. Given more time and space, this conversation could be extended to include other shows like *How I Met Your Mother* (2005–2014), *Felicity* (1998–2002), *Will and Grace* (1998–2006), and even *What I Like About You* (2002–2006).

4. The *Sex and the City* films attempt to reconcile this strange, heteronormative neatness. Miranda and Steve have marital problems, though their relationship ultimately survives those tests. And Samantha, whose commitment to Smith seems romantic at the end of the series, finally ends up realizing that she enjoys life more when she is single. See *Sex and the City* and *Sex and the City 2*, Dir. Michael Patrick King, 2008 and 2010.

5. John Del Signore, "Ask a Native New Yorker: Why is the NYC Dating Scene So Rough?" *Gothamist*, 23 August 2013. Accessed 3 January 2014.

6. Madison Moore, "5 Reasons Dating in New York City is Exhausting," *Thought Catalog*, 26 November 2013. Accessed 3 January 2014.

7. "Damage," *Oxford English Dictionary*. Accessed 3 January 2014.

8. "The One where Mr. Heckles Dies," *Friends*, NBC, 5 October 1995.

9. "A Woman's Right to Shoes," *Sex and the City*, HBO, 17 April 2003.

10. "The One with the Stoned Guy," *Friends*, NBC, 16 February 1995.

11. Ibid.

12. Ibid.

13. "The Awful Truth," *Sex and the City*, HBO, 13 June 1999.

14. "The One with the Ick Factor," *Friends*, NBC, 4 May 1994.

15. Ibid.

16. Ibid.

17. Ibid.

18. Josef Adalian, "How *Friends* Decided to Pair Off Monica and Chandler," *Vulture*, 20 November 2013. Accessed 18 August 2014.

19. "The One with the Butt," *Friends*, NBC, 27 October 1994. Much could be written on the presentation of "otherness" in all of the shows in question. The judgment about Aurora's choices that ensues throughout the episode is itself a judgment on "alien" romantic ways. Aurora, from a strangely exoticized land, parallels other foreign prospects in the series, each of whom is discarded in favor of more traditional American values. See "The One After the Superbowl" with Jean-Claude Van Damme, for example.

20. Ibid.

21. Ibid.

22. Ibid.

23. "Weirdos Need Girlfriends, Too," *Girls*, HBO, 3 June 2012.

24. "The One with the Boob Job," *Friends*, NBC, 20 February 2003.

25. Kim Akass and Janet McCabe, eds, *Reading Sex and the City*, (London: I.B. Tauris, 2003).

26. Dana Heller, "Sex and the Series: Paris, New York, and Post-National Romance," *American Studies* 46.2 (2005): 145–69.

27. "Models and Mortals," *Sex and the City*, HBO, 14 June 1998.

28. "The Cheating Curve," *Sex and the City*, HBO, 11 July 1999.

29. "La Douleur Exquisite," *Sex and the City*, HBO, 22 August 1999.

30. "Sex and the City," *Sex and the City*, HBO, 6 June 1998.

31. Alexandra Silver-Fagan, "Dating in New York: Right Swipe or Left," *Huffington Post*, 18 September 2013, Accessed 6 January 2014. Silver-Fagan explains "unfortunately, the '90s hit show is a bit outdated for the dating scene of today and for the generation of undergrad/post-grads gallivanting around Manhattan."

32. "Just Say Yes," *Sex and the City*, HBO, 12 August 2001.

33. Alex Williams, "The End of Courtship?" *New York Times*, 11 January 2013, Accessed 6 January 2014.

34. Mary C Hickey, "HBO's *Girls*: The Millenial Dating Scene," *AARP Blog*, 14 January 2013, Accessed 3 January 2013.

35. Crystal Bell, "'Girls' Recap: The Golden Shower Incident in 'Weirdos Need Girlfriends Too.'" *Huffington Post*, 3 June 2012. Accessed 19 August 2014.

36. Eileen Jones, "The Horror of HBO's Girls," *The Exiled*, 26 April 2012. Accessed 19 August 2014.

37. L. V. Anderson, "Girls: Bad Sex Made Great," *Slate*. Accessed 19 June 2014.

38. Ibid.

39. "Vagina Panic," *Girls*, HBO, 22 April 2012.

40. Emily Nussbaum, "It's Different for 'Girls,'" *New York Magazine*, 25 March 2012. Accessed 19 August 2014.

41. Ibid.

42. "On All Fours," *Girls*, HBO, 10 March 2013.

43. Amanda Hess, "Was That a Rape Scene in Girls?" *Slate*, 11 March 2013. Accessed 3 January 2014.

44. Joe Flint, "Climax of Scene in HBO's 'Girls' a Shocker," *LA Times*, 11 March 2013. Accessed 6 January 2014.

45. Jace Lacob, "'Girls': Graphic Content, Objectification, and That Scene," *The Daily Beast*, 12 March 2013. Accessed 6 January 2014.

46. "Females Only," *Girls*, HBO, 12 January 2014.

47. Sarah Caldwell, "Girls: How Are We Supposed to Feel about Adam?" *Entertainment Weekly*, 18 March 2013. Accessed 3 January 2014.

48. "Role-Play," *Girls*, HBO, 9 March 2013.

49. Ibid.

50. There is a conversation to be staged here between this notion of sexual damage and the trajectory of the *Fifty Shades of Grey* trilogy. Christian Grey's BDSM fantasies are traced explicitly back to two "bad" women in his life: his mother—the "crack whore"—and his first dominatrix, dubbed "Mrs. Robinson" by narrator Ana. The three books chronicle Christian overcoming the demons that underscore his alternative sexual proclivities in much the same was as Adam momentarily identifies his previous fantasies as coping mechanisms meant to distract him from his addiction to alcohol. While in the books, Ana primarily works to expose Christian to the root of his damage, *Girls* presents Hannah as encouraging Adam to reclaim the type of sex that was initially a crucial part of their relationship.

51. Caldwell, "Girls: How are we Supposed to Feel about Adam?"

52. What proves problematic, though, is the way in which Adam-in-the-bedroom—whatever "damage" viewers are compelled to assign him—is, at the end of season 2, presented as potentially parallel to Hannah's OCD. Indeed, Willa Paskin, in "Why Girls Got So Dark" makes that connection clear: "The two episodes before the finale toggled between Hannah's OCD and Adam's uncomfortable sex choices." That connection suggests that Adam's "rape-y" intercourse with Natalia and Hannah's OCD are meant to be read as parallel. Trying to treat Adam's sex drive and Hannah's disorder in the same way begs serious questions about cultural treatment of any form of deviance. See Willa Paskin, "Why Girls Got So Dark," *Salon*, 17 March 2013. Accessed 6 January 2014.

BIBLIOGRAPHY

Adalian, Josef. "How *Friends* Decided to Pair Off Monica and Chandler." *Vulture*. 20 November 2013. Accessed 18 August 2014.

Akass, Kim and Janet McCabe, eds. *Reading Sex and the City*. London: I.B. Tauris, 2003.

Anderson, L. V. "Girls: Bad Sex Made Great." *Slate*.

"The Awful Truth." *Sex and the City*. HBO. 13 June 1999. Television.

Behrent, Greg and Liz Truccilo. *He's Just Not That Into You*. New York: Gallery Books, 2009.

Bell, Crystal. "'Girls' Recap: The Golden Shower Incident in 'Weirdos Need Girlfriends Too.'" *Huffington Post*. 3 June 2012. Accessed 19 August 2014.

"Boy, Girl, Boy, Girl . . . " *Sex and the City*. HBO. 25 June 2000. Television.

Caldwell, Sarah. "Girls: How Are We Supposed to Feel about Adam?" *Entertainment Weekly*. 18 March 2013. Accessed 3 January 2014.

"Damage." *Oxford English Dictionary*. Accessed 3 January 2014.

Del Signore, John. "Ask a Native New Yorker: Why Is the NYC Dating Scene so Rough?" *Gothamist*. 23 August 2013. Accessed 3 January 2014.

Flint, Joe. "Climax of Scene in HBO's 'Girls' a Shocker." *LA Times*. 11 March 2013. Accessed 6 January 2014.

"Games People Play." *Sex and the City*. HBO. 29 August 1999. Television.

Heller, Dana. "Sex and the Series: Paris, New York, and Post-National Romance." *American Studies* 46.2 (2005): 145-69.

Hermes, Joke. "Television and Its Viewers in Post-Feminist Dialogue Internet-Mediated Response to 'Ally McBeal' and 'Sex and the City.'" *Etnofoor* 1/2 (2002): 194-211.

He's Just Not That Into You. Dir. Ken Kwapis. New Line Cinema, 2009. Film.

Hess, Amanda. "Was That a Rape Scene in Girls?" *Slate.* 11 March 2013. Accessed 3 January 2014.

Hickey, Mary C. "HBO's Girls: The Millenial Dating Scene." *AARP Blog.* 14 January 2013. Accessed 3 January 2013.

Jones, Eileen. "The Horror of HBO's Girls." *The Exiled.* 26 April 2012. Accessed 19 August 2014.

"Just Say Yes." *Sex and the City.* HBO. 12 August 2001.

Lacob, Jace. "'Girls': Graphic Content, Objectification, and That Scene." *The Daily Beast.* 12 March 2013. Accessed 6 January 2014.

Moore, Madison. "5 Reasons Dating in New York City is Exhausting." *Thought Catalog.* 26 November 2013. Accessed 3 January 2014.

Nussbaum, Emily. "It's Different for 'Girls.'" *New York Magazine.* 25 March 2012. Accessed 19 August 2014.

"Oh Come All Ye Faithful." *Sex and the City.* HBO. 23 August 1998. Television.

"On All Fours." *Girls.* HBO. 10 March 2013. Television.

"The One After the Superbowl." *Friends.* NBC. 28 January 1996. Television.

"The One with the Boob Job." *Friends.* NBC. 20 February 2003. Television.

"The One with the Butt." *Friends.* NBC. 27 October 1994. Television.

"The One with the Ick Factor." *Friends.* NBC. 4 May 1994. Television.

"The One Where Mr. Heckles Dies." *Friends.* NBC. 5 October 1995. Television.

"The One with Russ." *Friends.* NBC. 4 January 1996. Television.

"The One with the Stoned Guy." *Friends.* NBC. 16 February 1995. Television.

Paskin, Willa. "Why Girls Got So Dark." *Salon.* 17 March 2013. Accessed 6 January 2014.

"Role-Play." *Girls.* HBO. 9 March 2013. Television.

Silver-Fagan, Alexandra. "Dating in New York: Right Swipe or Left." *Huffington Post.* 18 September 2013. Accessed 6 January 2014.

"Together." *Girls.* HBO. 17 March 2013. Television. (2.10).

"Weirdos Need Girlfriends Too." *Girls.* HBO. 3 June 2012. Television.

Williams, Alex. "The End of Courtship?" *New York Times.* 11 January 2013. Accessed 6 January 2014.

"A Woman's Right to Shoes." *Sex and the City.* HBO. 17 April 2003. Television.

Chapter Two

"The Body Police": Lena Dunham, Susan Bordo, and HBO's *Girls*

Jocelyn L. Bailey

On January 7, 2013, just days before the second season premiere of *Girls*, radio and television personality Howard Stern took to the airwaves to explain his distaste for the show. Referring to Lena Dunham as a "fat girl," Stern compared seeing Dunham's nude body on-screen to being raped. "It's like— I don't want to see that," he complained; "[but] good for her. It's hard for little fat chicks to get anything going."[1] Less than a week later, *Girls* won two Golden Globe Awards; and on January 16, Dunham called in to Stern's show to address his criticism. As Stern fumbled around for excuses and purported to suddenly be a fan of *Girls*, Dunham firmly but kindly asserted: "I'm not that fat, Howard." Stern then flipped the conversation by suggesting that Dunham "play[s] up the fat thing" for comedic purposes, conceded that Dunham is "not obese or anything," and quickly changed the subject to other questions pertaining to the series and Dunham's personal life—including when he will see the other female characters naked on the show, whether or not Dunham has had anal sex, and whether Dunham is intimidated that her boyfriend used to date Scarlett Johansson. Dunham humorously and deftly avoided answering Stern's questions.[2]

More than two years after the first episode of HBO's *Girls*, Dunham's body, aside from her body of work, remains a popular topic for public discussion. At a Television Critics Association press panel preceding the most recent season, TV journalist Tim Molloy of *TheWrap.com* pointedly asked Lena Dunham why her character, Hannah Horvath, is frequently nude in some episodes of the show. According to Molloy's transcription of his question, he said, "I don't get the purpose of all the nudity on the show. By you particularly. I feel like I'm walking into a trap where you say no one complains about the nudity on *Game of Thrones*, but I get why they're doing it. [HBO is] doing it to be salacious. To titillate people. And your character is often naked at random times for no reason."[3] Dunham succinctly replied that sometimes nudity reflects reality, and that if Molloy wasn't interested in looking at her body, that was his "problem." Producers Jenni Konner and Judd Apatow called Molloy's query misogynistic and offensive; and a clueless Molloy attempted to clarify himself to Apatow after the press panel by arguing he simply hoped to understand the creative value or purpose of Dunham's nudity. Molloy subsequently published his defense on *TheWrap.com*, but he never seemed to acknowledge or understand the issue with his comment—namely, the implication that Lena's body could not be considered interesting or provocative when compared to the nude bodies present in other cable series. Katie McDonough of *Salon.com* perfectly located the subtext of Molloy's question when, in a follow-up article to Molloy's, she asked, "What is the point of a naked woman if not to give heterosexual male journalists erections?"[4]

Though the nudity and frank sexual content present in all three seasons of *Girls* have certainly contributed to the buzz surrounding the show, the discussion regarding Lena's body in particular has provided rich opportunity for postmodern audiences to decide *which* types of bodies are appropriate for display. If television viewers—as represented by critics like Molloy—are not surprised by slender, tanned, large-breasted, surgically-enhanced female bodies on comparable series, why does Lena's body have the potential to shock, distract, or even offend? In a culture where pornographic images are readily available to anyone with cable television or Internet access, what is so controversial about one woman's body? That Dunham's body in particular is persistently under discussion is indicative of a broad cultural verdict that some bodies are still not suitable for viewing.

This chapter will explore the outcry against Lena Dunham's body, and how it exposes the state of women's representation in visual media. Amid comments like Molloy's, Howard Stern's insults regarding Dunham's appearance, and Jezebel.com's bizarre offer to pay for Dunham's un-retouched *Vogue* photographs, the media has demonstrated itself resistant to and confused by bodies that defy its own manufactured conventions. These media conversations reveal a set of cultural rules that celebrate the exposure and objectification of certain female bodies, while simultaneously arraigning women with "unconventional" bodies who take the public stage. Even more complicated is the often-conflicted pseudofeminist media culture that condemns body-shaming while demonstrating its own bizarre preoccupation with physical appearance and a woman's right (or requirement?) to "be sexy."

In order to evaluate these discourses, I will refer to feminist critic Susan Bordo's 1993 work *Unbearable Weight* and her cultural examination of the female body appearing in visual media. Though twenty years old, Bordo's analysis of a culture gone mad for thinness still resonates with contemporary readers who find that little has changed in the field of female representation. Bordo recognizes that there is much at stake with media constructions, as they tend to seep into culture at large by establishing injurious boundaries that put the body at risk. "Culture not only has taught women to be insecure, constantly monitoring themselves for signs of imperfection, constantly engaged in physical 'improvement,'" she argues, "it also is constantly teaching women (and, let us not forget, men as well) how to *see* bodies."[5] Examining *Girls* as a text and its accompanying media discourse in light of Bordo's work demonstrates how Dunham's unruly body rebels against pervasive, long-lasting American media conventions. Though it may be statistically average in size and shape, there is nothing more exceptional or subversive in contemporary media than Lena Dunham's body. Second, I will examine how the body is discussed and represented in *Girls*, and how these representations normalize the female body and its processes. Though the female body is a familiar television object, the blunt—and often awkward—depictions of the body on *Girls* present subversive, unglamorous, realistic interpretations of the experiences of female embodiment. In short, *Girls'* depictions of the female body as an unruly, uncontained, and dominant space celebrate women's subjectivity.

Why Bodies Matter

Academia recognizes the importance of bodies as locations for identity components: gender, sexuality, race, health and disability, and so forth. As such, bodies can be social signifiers. No body is the same as any other body, yet we tend to classify them and categorize certain bodies as *Other*. Theorist Richard Harvey Brown asserts that "Bodies/selves are principal fields of political, economic, and cultural activity, dominant tropes through which the tensions and crises of society are represented."[6] As such, the body is a stage as much as it is an actor. We cannot live without our bodies, yet we are not *just* our bodies. The body matters because it physically contains the "self"; it experiences pain and emotion; it enables thought; and because of its multiplex nature demands discursive exploration.

Entering discussions of the body is tricky because one can easily overemphasize or de-emphasize the body's significance. Its importance is well understood as the location of human existence—personality, intellect, sexuality, race, physical processes, and so forth. In short, when human bodies are at stake, life is at stake; any efforts to trivialize the bodily aspect of existence and experience may have literal, physical consequences. Focusing on the body alone, however, may inadvertently downplay the personhood, the wholeness of the subject. Though the body is an object, it is *simultaneously* a subject. In discussing Lena Dunham's body—both as a literal body and as a media representation—I hope to cautiously maintain this balance by defending her subjectivity in spite of a culture that often treats bodies as objects. Lena's body's representation is important as a site for discussion, but neither her selfhood nor her physical body ought to suffer from the discursive process.

The female body—both physically and in representation—is especially susceptible to these problematic conversations, as it has historically been a site fraught with tension. In the introduction to the tenth anniversary edition of *Unbearable Weight*, Susan Bordo reminds us that though different historical contexts produce differing frameworks for interpreting bodies, the *female* body in particular has long been associated with the bodily, or negative, aspect of the self. If Aristotle conceived of *the self* as both soul and body, and that the "not-body is the highest, the best, the noblest, the closest to God," then he likewise conceived of the physical body as the lesser, weaker component.[7] Though dualism as a philosophical framework is far too nuanced to fully examine here, Bordo recognizes that within Aristotelian ideology femaleness is frequently equated with the body and we may ask ourselves how this ideology appears within our own historical moment: "For if, whatever the specific historical content of the duality, *the body* is the negative term, and if woman *is* the body, then women *are* that negativity, whatever it may be."[8] How do women and their representations in contemporary culture bear witness to this ancient binary?

The female body's propensity to change—to grow and shrink, to bleed and secrete—has also historically been deemed a social threat. In their comprehensive study *The Curse: A Cultural History of Menstruation*, critics Delaney, Lupton, and Toth examine how menstruation has been perceived as both natural and supernatural—resulting in a series of contextual responses that have othered the biological processes associated with femaleness. Delaney, Lupton, and Toth explore many potential origins of this taboo, but they conclude that "the taboos were probably enforced by men, who connected this mysterious phenomenon with the cycles of the moon, the seasons, the rhythm of the tides, the disappearance of the sun in nightly darkness and who feared such cosmic power in the apparent control of a member of their own species."[9] Fear of the fluid, uncontainable female body may lead to social suppression or stigma; or perhaps it merely leads to alternate images of women as bordered, contained entities. If there is nothing frightening about menstrual blood, why is something as ubiquitous as a woman's period rarely depicted or even discussed on television?

Censoring menstruation is not the only method of containment used by modern media. Viewers expect the female bodies on display to be thin, tight, and taut—devoid of lumps, bumps, and cellulite. Bordo's analysis of the "contained" female body still rings true when she asserts that "*any* softness or bulge comes to be seen as unsightly—as disgusting, disorderly, 'fat'" when depicted in visual media;[10] most exceptions to this rule appear in the forms of extreme weight-loss shows or reality specials depicting its subjects/objects as repulsive, subhuman cases who cannot help themselves. In both scenarios, and broadly in visual media, fatness is presented as a problem to be fixed. Fatness becomes the subject of the show rather than the people themselves, and anything deemed "fat" cannot exist without its accompanying value judgment. In short, media represents bodies as either adequate, or in the process of becoming adequate—and there is very little in-between.

As Dunham herself pointed out to Howard Stern, she is not fat; but that does not prevent professional critics or online commenters from focusing upon her body's shape, size, and attractiveness rather than her work. That Dunham's body does not conform to the rule of containment makes her especially controversial due to her frequent nude scenes, and her character's general indifference to the "three or four" extra pounds she carries around her middle.[11] After the February 2013 episode "One Man's Trash"—in which Hannah meets a handsome older doctor and spends two days of sexual pleasure with him[12]—the Internet exploded with assertions that a woman who looks like Hannah Horvath (Lena Dunham) could never merit the sexual attention of a man as classically attractive as Patrick Wilson's character. David Haglund and Daniel Engber of Slate.com asked if "One Man's Trash" was "the worst episode of *Girls* ever?" primarily because they found the match implausible. Engber wrote,

> I felt trapped by my unwillingness to buy into the central premise. Narcissistic, childish men sleep with beautiful women all the time in movies and on TV, so why should this coupling be so difficult to fathom? I think it's because Hannah is especially and assertively ugly in this episode. She's rude ("what did you do?" she asks Joshua, referring to his broken marriage), self-centered ("I'm too smart and too sensitive,") sexually ungenerous ("no, make me come") and defiantly ungraceful (naked ping-pong).[13]

Haglund and Engber fished for ways to understand their own confusion, even claiming that they could perhaps see a guy as good-looking as Patrick Wilson hooking up *once* with Hannah (Lena), but certainly not multiple times in two days. They wondered if the episode's premise was intended to subvert the "standard dorky guy and hot babe narrative," but not without locating some "aggression" in Dunham's revision.[14] What that aggression is, they do not

quite explain, but considering the remark comes immediately after a comment about Dunham's nudity, readers can wonder if Haglund and Engber see
Dunham's body as the aggressor.

Such rationalizations are signs of a culture without imagination, of viewers whose interpretations of bodies are so predictable that a kink in their
system—in this case, a subversive female image—poses a potential threat to
their framework. Haglund's and Engber's observations of "One Man's
Trash" are not all wrong, but they are overshadowed by an inability, unwillingness, or even fear of seeing Hannah as a sexual subject. When Hannah
boldly engages in and asks for sexual pleasure in "One Man's Trash," it may
be the first time her character has verbalized *her* desires; and yet Haglund,
protecting his territory, considers the move "sexually ungenerous." Dunham's "defiantly ungraceful" body is upsetting, as it exposes an unarticulated
fear of the uncontained female.

As barometers, these responses (and others) to *Girls* testify to how little
culture has evolved since Bordo's research of the 1990s. Thin and fat bodies
still carry particular cultural associations and provoke predictable responses,
and media imagery is still dominantly male-centric in subject. Dr. Stacy L.
Smith of USC Annenberg recently published data that studied speaking roles
in four hundred popular films between 1990 and 2006, and her team counted
2.71 male speakers for every 1 female speaker—a statistic that does not
surprise us, considering the ratio of male-to-female directors/writers/produc-
ers (behind-the-scenes creators) is 5:1. [15] Television data may be more promising, but such statistics demonstrate that men principally manage the narratives we absorb on the large and small screens. Lena Dunham's position as a
writer, director, and actor on *Girls* is noteworthy in light of these statistics,
but it is even more remarkable as a catalyst for discussion, argumentation,
and cultural re-imagination. The provocative tendency of Dunham's show
has proven that we still need new narratives and new images—representations of women that candidly mimic the experiences of many women whose
realities do not resemble the ones we usually see on TV.

Girls as Text

As a television show, *Girls* occupies a fascinating genre location between
comedy and drama. Perhaps one of the show's most interesting narrative
trademarks is its tendency to move from hilarity to seriousness within a
scene, and its refusal to treat any subject as wholly humorous or dramatic.
This convergence entertains us but also mimics reality by refusing to completely belittle or revere certain subjects. The result is often awkward—
someplace between funny and painful—but so is the adult body. If *Girls* is a
bildungsroman for twentysomething women, one of the show's strengths is
its honest portrayal of women growing into their embodied selves. *Girls*

exposes the complicated process of adult womanhood, as its subjects grapple with relationships, social pressures and expectations, and the biological experiences of maturity.

Though it may merit criticism of all sorts, *Girls* grants subjectivity to the female body. Women are the primary subjects of *Girls*, and the issues of embodiment preoccupy many of the show's story lines. Topics including mental health, sexual preference, pregnancy and abortion, drug abuse, and self-perception dominate the episodes, affording viewers—especially women—the opportunity to engage discussions of the female body that are not often candidly undertaken in contemporary media. Perhaps one of the reasons *Girls* generates conversations and strong feelings is because it asks questions without easy answers, providing spaces for fraught discourses and alternate narratives. Even though critiques regarding the show's primarily white, economically-advantaged set of characters are well-made and arguably valid, Hannah Horvath's claim to be *"a* voice of *a* generation"[16] is exactly that: just one narrative among many, seeking to create resonance within a broader set of women. Though not all women relate to Hannah's socioeconomic, educational, or racial backgrounds, many *can* still relate to the common-ground bodily topics that are issues for them. Without minimizing the need for locating and emphasizing racial differences within female culture, Bordo argues that women—as a diverse group—must search for common narratives in order to harness their collective power. She writes, "Feminist theory—even the work of white, upper-class, heterosexual women—is not located at the *center* of cultural power. The axes whose intersections form the cultural locations of feminist authors give some of us positions of privilege, certainly; but all women, *as* women, also occupy subordinate positions, positions in which they feel ignored or denigrated."[17] Dunham's status as a white, heterosexual, upper-class woman positions her in a comparatively privileged location—which, to some feminists, may disqualify her narrative; but she is still a woman combating power structures that rarely grant women authority over media imagery.

Though this chapter will not attempt to defend or even define Lena Dunham's particular brand of feminism, and though the narcissistic characters of *Girls* seem at times uninterested in the project of female connection or collectivity, one can argue that *Girls*—by consciously paying attention to issues of the female body—provides opportunity for these moments of association. If common biology and experience are the moving parts within a feminist paradigm, and if we cannot sympathize with her characters' experiences with race or class, Dunham's narrative at least supplies space for women to see themselves within her characters' more bodily moments. Women may recognize themselves in Lena Dunham's body—in its shape, its movements, its triumphs and humiliations—more so than in more conventional television bodies; and her characters' conflicted and frank relationships with their own bodies demonstrate the knotty status of modern, Western womanhood.

To demonstrate this point, I will examine two key episodes of *Girls*—"Vagina Panic" (season 1) and "Role-Play" (season 3)—that draw particular attention to the unromanticized female body. Between candid discussions of menstruation, sex, birth control, masturbation, and even urination, the show refuses to depict the body as a contained, bordered article that exists in appropriate spheres. Many of the conversations on *Girls* take place in areas or in situations that draw particular attention to the body, such as while having sex, taking showers or baths, changing clothes, eating, or even using the toilet.[18] These actions themselves are physically mundane, but they reconfigure our vision of media bodies by reasserting the fluid, awkward, and often messy experience of maintaining a body. Though many of the female bodies on television appear airbrushed, painted, and perfectly groomed at all times, the women of *Girls* participate in the ordinary, unglamorous processes of everyday life.

"Vagina Panic," season 1's second episode, opens with two different, yet similarly embarrassing, sex scenes. We first observe an extended encounter between Adam and Hannah—one in which we cannot tell if Hannah's sexual experience is at all satisfying for her. As Adam physically dominates Hannah by holding down her face and repositioning her legs, Hannah plays along with Adam's verbal fantasy—what she later calls "abusive rhetoric." After he imagines her as a "junkie" with a "Cabbage Patch lunchbox," he tells Hannah she is never allowed to orgasm without his permission. She allows him to ejaculate on her chest, and when he finishes, she claims that she "almost came." It is difficult to tell if Hannah has derived much pleasure from the encounter.

Marnie's sexual encounter is a failure for entirely different reasons. Though she says it "feels good, fine," her face belies boredom as her boyfriend, Charlie, penetrates her in missionary position. Marnie turns her head and closes her eyes, as if to imagine herself elsewhere. When Charlie asks Marnie to look back toward him so they can "look at each other when [they] come," she quickly moves to her hands and knees. "I'm gonna turn around," she says—preparing for doggie style, even though she believes it makes her "look like a piggy bank." This position does not appear to be any better for the frustrated Marnie, who seems to barely tolerate sex with Charlie. Charlie cannot stop exclaiming his satisfaction, but Marnie's face is statically expressionless.

Hannah's and Marnie's sexual encounters demonstrate the potential awkwardness and dissatisfaction that can characterize sex, especially for women.[19] Neither scene pretends that sex is a one-dimensional act resulting in mutual gratification for both partners.[20] Charlie assumes that both he and

Marnie will climax, while Adam does not seem to care whether Hannah climaxes at all. Though both men seem content with what is happening, neither Hannah nor Marnie is able to fully engage. When Marnie and Hannah later turn to each other to discuss their sexual dissatisfaction, neither can properly articulate what they want from their partners. [21]

In another scene, Hannah—worrying that Adam may have given her an STD—sits on her bed Googling half-formed phrases like "Diseases that come from no condom for one second" and "Stuff that gets up around the sides of condoms." We may laugh as we reflect that we, too, have searched the Internet for answers to embarrassing sexual questions. Freshly bathed, Hannah wears only a towel. As she leans forward to examine herself for signs of sexually-transmitted infections, we are reminded of the awkwardness of exploring one's own body and not knowing the right way to ask questions about sex. In the next scene, as she is dressing for the day, Hannah calls Marnie on the phone and asks her to make her an appointment for an STD test. Even the act of putting on clothes is demystified as Hannah pulls her skirt up and down to make sure her shirt is properly tucked in. When she asks Marnie her question about "the stuff that gets up around the sides of condoms," we can presume that Google has not adequately answered her query.

Over frozen yogurt, Jessa, Hannah, and Shoshanna discuss a fictional book entitled *Listen, Ladies! A Tough-Love Approach to the Tough Game of Love.* As Jessa takes issue with the book's black-and-white argument that "sex from behind is degrading—point-blank," she points out that sometimes during sex she wants to "focus on something else." We cannot help but remember that earlier in the episode, Marnie has asked Charlie to have sex this way—perhaps so she doesn't have to look at his face. When Jessa points out the book's author "doesn't care what [she] wants[s]," she becomes irate and points out that she only has sex on her terms and that she resents "all the supposed-tos." Hannah presumes Jessa's outburst is related to her nervousness about the abortion she is about to undergo, but Jessa denies being anxious or afraid. She reminds Hannah that she wants to be a mother one day and insists upon her competence for the task.

Hannah's confusion regarding sex, its consequences, and the boundaries of normal behavior appear to bleed into her entire life as she ruins an interview by making a massively inappropriate rape joke. Likewise, all of the characters seem confused regarding how to handle Jessa's upcoming abortion, but they plan to meet her at the abortion clinic for emotional backup. Hannah tries to be supportive of Jessa's emotional state without assuming that an abortion is a big deal; Marnie, who considers abortion "the most traumatic thing that can ever happen to a woman,"[22] takes the opportunity to fret over her own fertility; Shoshanna brings candy to the abortion clinic; and Jessa refuses to show up, preferring instead to patronize a bar. As Hannah,

Marnie, and Shoshanna sit at the clinic waiting for Jessa to arrive for her appointment, they discuss Hannah's medical intake questionnaire, and Marnie makes mention of Hannah's irrational, lifelong fear of AIDS. "I don't have an obsessive fear of AIDS," retorts Hannah. "I have obsessive fear of HIV that turns into AIDS. I'm not a fool."[23] Their conversation turns even more ridiculous when it appears that their primary source for scientific information regarding HIV is the broadway play *Rent.* Hannah asks, for the third time, about "the stuff that gets up around the sides of condoms" before being called back for her appointment.

Meanwhile, avoiding her abortion appointment, Jessa is fooling around in the bathroom with a stranger she has just met in the bar. She tells him to put his hands down her pants; and when he pulls out his hand, his fingers are covered with blood. She briefly acknowledges the blood and continues kissing him. Jessa's fearlessness of sex is immediately contrasted by Shoshanna's inexperience, when in the next scene Shoshanna admits to Marnie that she is still a virgin. Marnie tries to convince Shoshanna that sex is "overrated," but her embarrassment for Shoshanna is blatant.

The final scene of the episode begins with close-ups of medical collection vials, a paper-lined medical tray with instruments, a mechanical scale, a metal speculum, and stirrups covered by colorful socks. Hannah wears a pink hospital gown and answers basic medical history questions posed by her female gynecologist. At her first opportunity, she yet again asks the doctor about the "stuff that gets up around the sides of condoms." Before she can answer, the conversation is sidetracked by Hannah's confession of her "*Forrest Gump*-based fear" of AIDS. As Hannah lies back, feet in stirrups and legs wide apart for her pelvic exam, she rambles on to justify or explain her bizarre obsession with AIDS—postulating that perhaps contracting AIDS would make all of her actual problems seem trivial in comparison. "That is an incredibly silly thing to say," says her doctor. "You do not want AIDS." And when she provides concrete statistics to Hannah regarding women who actually *do* contract and die of AIDS, Hannah asks, "So you're saying that if Adam gave me AIDS that I'm definitely going to die of it?" This, of course, is not the doctor's point at all. In the final shot, we see Hannah and the doctor from above as the examination proceeds. When Hannah looks upward and says, "Ow," the doctor asks, "Is that painful?" Hannah replies, "Yeah, but only in the way it's supposed to be."[24] She never gets an answer to her "stuff that gets up around the sides of condoms" question.

Many women can sympathize with Hannah's discomfort in the last scene as they glimpse the familiar gynecological tools, yet such narrative scenes are hardly ubiquitous in media. Female anatomy is regularly configured as an object of conquest—what Luce Irigaray has named the location of men's "exchanges, transactions, transports [. . .] explorations, consummations, exploitations."[25] As Hannah and her narrative are recentered in a gynecological office, the vagina becomes a subject for study rather than occupation. She comes to the doctor with anxieties and fears about the state of her own body; and yet, that Hannah's question remains unanswered bears witness to a set of modern sexual mores that expects women to become sexually active without always preparing them for the experience. Though television tends to represent sex as a relationship commodity—either we are "getting some" or we aren't—"Vagina Panic" effectively demonstrates how sex, especially for women, is a complex exchange that can carry particular consequences (such as pregnancy and disease) and defy socially constructed expectations. Though a book like *Listen, Ladies!* might come in handy to a young woman navigating the tricky world of modern sexuality, the body is too unruly and elaborate an entity for such black-and-white rules to apply.

By season 3, Hannah and Adam's relationship has evolved emotionally and sexually, but the episode "Role-Play" demonstrates that Hannah is still searching for sexual selfhood. After a set of events that lead her to believe Adam is losing interest in her, she tells Elijah that Adam treats her "like an ottoman with a vagina." In an attempt to spice up a sexual routine that has become rote, she dons a blonde wig and pretends to be a wealthy investor's wife when she approaches Adam in a bar. He does not immediately want to play along, and Hannah's role-play is more ridiculous than alluring; but the humor is enough to entertain them both. When they arrive back to Marnie's apartment, which Hannah has arranged to use for the night, Hannah's game assigns Adam to the role of aggressor. When he tells her to take off her clothes, she reveals a strappy, bondage-type costume that looks to Adam like a Christmas tree. Hannah pretends to be humiliated as she crawls, half-naked, onto the bed, where she tries to eat a whole strawberry but winds up spitting it out. Somewhat seriously, Adam tells her, "From now on, the rule is: you can't just have part. You have to take the whole thing, or nothing."[26]

When the narrative returns to Adam and Hannah, they are having sex on Marnie's bed when Hannah tries to change the trajectory of her role-play. She tells Adam that rather than a wealthy, bored wife, she is now a cheer-leader named Kim. Adam abruptly sits up, rips off his condom, and tells Hannah that she "can't change roles in the middle of everything—it doesn't make any fucking narrative sense." An argument ensues as Hannah explains that she was simply trying to "have sex the way that [they] used to"— reminding us of the odd fantasies Adam verbalized during the first season's episodes. "You used to have all these ideas about me being like a little street slut, or like an orphan with a disease or [. . .] a woman with a baby's body or something [. . .] I was just doing your ideas. I was just doing sex the way you wanted to." Adam explains that none of his role-playing was concocted, and that he thought their games were "coming to [them] in the moment." When Hannah admits that none of those games really suited her, it becomes clear that Hannah and Adam have been on different sexual planes for a very long time. "You were outside yourself. You were outside your body, watching everything," Adam tells her. She replies, "So? What does it matter? If you're getting what you want, what do you care if I'm, like, in my body? You can't be, like, the body police."[27]

We wonder if Hannah has been role-playing all along—if she has been unable to see the difference in Adam's approach to sex amid their growing relationship. Likewise, Adam seems blindsided to learn that Hannah's sexual experiences have not been as "in the moment" as his have been. Resenting that Hannah still perceives him as "some angry fuckin' sociopath who wants to meet older women in bars and intimidate them," he tells Hannah that he will be living with Ray for a while. Hannah's plan to bring them closer instead reveals how wide the gap between them has always been.

As the "body police," Adam recognizes that Hannah may be more of an observer and analyzer than a participant in their sexual relationship—but perhaps Hannah is the one policing herself. Such spectatoring can be considered a form of disembodiment, preventing Hannah from fully engaging with Adam and perhaps even herself; and by asking Adam why he cares so much if he is "getting what he wants," Hannah indicates how she may see herself as a sexual object rather than subject. Hannah's earlier comment to Elijah about being perceived as "an ottoman with a vagina" suddenly seems like a third-party observation, an image of her own invention—much like Marnie's comment that doggie-style sex makes her "*look* like a piggy bank" rather than "*feel* like a piggy bank."[28] Though both Hannah and Marnie experience sexual satisfaction at intervals throughout the series, these two moments testify to the ease with which women monitor themselves as outsiders. Like many women, the sexual learning curve is steep for Marnie and Hannah.

Girls is rife with examples of bodily dysfunction, satisfaction, confusion, awkwardness, and exploration—most of which are treated with humor and nuance. The subjects of *Girls* progress emotionally and physically, stumbling through a world of which they know very little. The processes are not always pleasant to watch, because growing into one's body and one's self is not a graceful activity, but the realness of the characters' pratfalls is refreshing and bold, if not painfully relatable. In short, the bodies of *Girls* present an alternate set of rules that defy those set in place by the body police. Dunham controls her own image, and it looks nothing like what we are used to seeing on-screen.

In a chapter of her recent memoir/advice book, Dunham describes how her own mother's collection of nude selfies demonstrated the power of a body in control of its own representation: "She sensed that by documenting her own body, she was preserving her history. Beautifully. Nakedly. Imperfectly. Her private experiment made way for my public one."[29] And what are the results of Dunham's experiment? Richard Brody's early analysis of *Girls* assesses this junction between reality, beauty, and the body rules:

One of the great merits of Dunham's art is to reveal as beautiful the sort of female body that is seldom depicted in movies, though lovers in real life know it to be beautiful. Slightly overweight, slightly out of proportion, with a slight jowl, Dunham does not have the body of a conventional actress—because she is not, after all, an actress. She's a talker, and she gives the impression of doing on-screen something close to what she does in life. [30]

Many components of Dunham's reality certainly do not hit the moving target of "average," but her version of reality comes closest to universal at its most stripped down. *Girls* provides new representations of beauty and experience, provoking growing pains and moments of association in viewers who are willing to examine their responses to what they have seen. If, as Bordo suggests, we have "learned all too well the dominant cultural standards of *how* to perceive,"[31] we can reconfigure those perception settings by acknowledging the difference between a mass-produced construction and a piece of the beautiful real.

NOTES

1. Perez Hilton, "Howard Stern Doesn't Like *Girls* & Calls Lena Dunham 'Fat'!," *PerezHilton.com*, January 8, 2013, accessed June 1, 2014, http://perezhilton.com/2013-01-08-howard-stern-calls-girls-creator-lena-dunham-fat-camera-hog#.U7BthCjMWzc.

2. "Howard Stern Show Lena Denham Interview 01 16 13," (YouTube, February 25, 2014), accessed June 1, 2014, https://www.youtube.com/watch?v=9CsfmELDVaI.

3. Tim Molloy, "Judd Apatow and Lena Dunham Get Mad at Me for Asking Why She's Naked so Much on 'Girls,'" *TheWrap.com*, January 9, 2014, accessed June 1, 2014, http://www.thewrap.com/judd-apatow-lena-dunham-get-mad-asking-shes-naked-much-girls/.

4. Katie McDonough, "TV critic mad because the nudity on 'Girls' doesn't titillate him," *Salon.com*, January 10, 2014, accessed June 1, 2014, http://www.salon.com/2014/01/10/tv_critic_mad_because_the_nudity_on_girls_doesnt_titillate_him/.

5. Susan Bordo, *Unbearable Weight: Feminism, Western Cuture, and the Body* (Berkeley: University of California Press, 2003), 57.

6. Richard Harvey Brown, "Introduction: Theorizing the Body/Self in Global Capitalism," in *The Politics of Selfhood: Bodies and Identities in Global Capitalism* (Minneapolis: University of Minneapolis Press, 2003), ix.

7. Bordo, *Unbearable Weight*, 5.

8. Ibid.

9. Janice Delaney, Mary Jane Lupton, and Emily Toth, *The Curse: A Cultural History of Menstruation* (New York: E. P. Dutton & Co., 1976), 7.

10. Bordo, *Unbearable Weight*, 57.

11. See *Girls*, season 1, episode 3, "All Adventurous Women Do," directed by Lena Dunham, aired April 29, 2012, on HBO, DVD (HBO Entertainment, 2012), disc 1.

12. See *Girls*, season 2, episode 5, "One Man's Trash," directed by Richard Shepard, aired February 10, 2013, on HBO, DVD (HBO Entertainment, 2013), disc 1.

13. David Haglund and Daniel Engber, "Girls on HBO, 'One Man's Trash,' Episode 5 of Season 2, Reviewed by Guys." *Slate.com*, February 10, 2013, accessed May 15, 2014, http://www.slate.com/articles/arts/tv_club/features/2013/girls_season_2/week_5/girls_on_hbo_one_man_s_trash_episode_5_of_season_2_reviewed_by_guys.html.

14. Ibid.

15. "Professor Stacy L. Smith discusses status of women in media on International Women's Day," Sarah Erickson, *Annenberg News Radio*, aired March 9, 2011, accessed May 15, 2014, http://www.annenbergradio.org/segments/women_in_the_media#showmebed.

16. *Girls*, season 1, episode 1, "Pilot," directed by Lena Dunham, aired April 15, 2012, on HBO, DVD (HBO Entertainment, 2012), disc 1.

17. Bordo, *Unbearable Weight*, 224.

18. Ibid. In the audio commentary to "Pilot," Dunham acknowledges the frequency of these scenes, saying (while laughing): "We have a lot of scenes in this show that take place in bathrooms, with one person in the shower, one person on the toilet. We like to have a fight during what should usually be a private, bodily moment."

19. Social science, as well as popular culture, has named this the *orgasm gap*—the data suggesting that heterosexual women orgasm less often than heterosexual men during intercourse. It is important to note that the "orgasmic imperative" (the assumption that orgasm is the natural culmination of sex) has pathologized many women whose sexual experiences do not always result in orgasm, but that sexual satisfaction need not depend upon this imperative. For a discussion of the sociocultural construction of the orgasm, see Hannah Frith, "Labouring on orgasms: embodiment, efficiency, entitlement, and obligations in heterosex."

20. In *Not That Kind of Girl*, Dunham expresses disdain for typical media representations of sex, writing: "Everything I saw as a child, from *90210* to *The Bridges of Madison County*, had led me to believe that sex was a cringey, warmly lit event where two smooth-skinned, gooey-eyed losers achieved mutual orgasm by breathing on each other's faces [. . .] Besides being gross, the images of sex can also be destructive. Between porn and studio romantic comedies, we get the message loud and clear that we are doing it all wrong. Our bedsheets aren't right. Our moves aren't right. Our bodies aren't right" (103).

21. *Girls*, season 1, episode 2, "Vagina Panic," directed by Lena Dunham, aired April 22, 2012, on HBO, DVD (HBO Entertainment, 2012), disc 1.

22. Ibid.

23. Ibid.

24. Ibid.

25. Luce Irigaray, *This Sex Which Is Not One*, Trans. Catherine Porter and Carolyn Burke (Ithaca, NY: Cornell University Press, 1985), 212.

26. *Girls*, season 3, episode 10, "Role-Play," directed by Jesse Peretz, aired March 9, 2014, on HBO.

27. Ibid.

28. *Girls*, season 1, episode 2, "Vagina Panic," directed by Lena Dunham, aired April 22, 2012, on HBO, DVD (HBO Entertainment, 2012), disc 1.

29. Lena Dunham, *Not That Kind of Girl*. (New York: Random House, 2014), 105.

30. Richard Brody, "'Girls' Talk," *New Yorker*, April 5, 2012, accessed May 15, 2014, http://www.newyorker.com/online/blogs/movies/2012/04/girls-lena-dunham.html.

31. Bordo, *Unbearable Weight*, 57.

BIBLIOGRAPHY

Bordo, Susan. *Unbearable Weight: Feminism, Western Culture, and the Body*. Rev. ed. Berkeley: University of California Press, 2003.

Brody, Richard. "'Girls' Talk." *New Yorker*. Last modified April 5, 2012. Accessed May 15, 2014. http://www.newyorker.com/online/blogs/movies/2012/04/girls-lena-dunham.html.

Brown, Richard Harvey. "Introduction: Theorizing the Body/Self in Global Capitalism." In *The Politics of Selfhood: Bodies and Identities in Global Capitalism*, vii–xxi. Minneapolis: University of Minnesota Press, 2003.

Delaney, Janice, Mary Jane Lupton, and Emily Toth. *The Curse: A Cultural History of Menstruation*. New York: E. P. Dutton & Co., 1976.

Dunham, Lena. *Not That Kind of Girl: A Young Woman Tells You What She's "Learned."* New York: Random House, 2014.

Frith, Hannah. "Labouring on orgasms: embodiment, efficiency, entitlement and obligations in heterosex." *Culture, Health & Sexuality* 15, no. 4 (2013): 494–510.

Girls, season 1, episode 1. "Pilot." Directed by Lena Dunham. Aired April 15, 2012, on HBO. DVD. HBO Entertainment, 2012, disc 1.

Girls, season 1, episode 2. "Vagina Panic." Directed by Lena Dunham. Aired April 22, 2012, on HBO. DVD. HBO Entertainment, 2012, disc 1.

Girls, season 1, episode 3. "All Adventurous Women Do." Directed by Lena Dunham. Aired April 29, 2012, on HBO. DVD. HBO Entertainment, 2012, disc 1.

Girls, season 2, episode 5. "One Man's Trash." Directed by Richard Shepard. Aired February 10, 2013, on HBO. DVD. HBO Entertainment, 2013, disc 1.

Girls, season 3, episode 8. "Role-Play." Directed by Jesse Peretz. Aired March 9, 2014, on HBO.

Haglund, David, and Daniel Engber. "Girls on HBO, 'One Man's Trash,' Episode 5 of Season 2, Reviewed by Guys." Slate.com. Last modified February 10, 2013. Accessed May 15, 2014. http://www.slate.com/articles/arts/tv_club/features/2013/girls_season_2/week_5/girls_on_hbo_one_man_s_trash_episode_5_of_season_2_reviewed_by_guys.html.

Hilton, Perez, "Howard Stern Doesn't Like *Girls* & Calls Lena Dunham 'Fat'!" *PerezHilton.com*. Last modified January 8, 2013. Accessed June 1, 2014. http://perezhilton.com/2013-01-08-howard-stern-calls-girls-creator-lena-dunham-fat-camera-hog#.U7BthCjMWzc.

"Howard Stern Show Lena Denham Interview 01 16 13." YouTube, February 25, 2014. Accessed June 1, 2014. https://www.youtube.com/watch?v=9CsfmELDVaI.

Irigaray, Luce. In *This Sex Which Is Not One*. Trans. Catherine Porter and Carolyn Burke. Ithaca, NY: Cornell University Press, 1985.

McDonough, Katie. "TV critic mad because the nudity on 'Girls' doesn't titillate him." Last modified January 10, 2014. Accessed June 1, 2014. http://www.salon.com/2014/01/10/tv_critic_mad_because_the_nudity_on_girls_doesnt_titillate_him/.

Molloy, Tim. "Judd Apatow and Lena Dunham Get Mad at Me for Asking Why She's Naked so Much on 'Girls.'" *TheWrap.com*. Last modified January 9, 2014. Accessed June 1, 2014. http://www.thewrap.com/judd-apatow-lena-dunham-get-mad-asking-shes-naked-much-girls/.

Chapter Three

Owning Her Abjection: Lena Dunham's Feminist Politics of Embodiment

Maria San Filippo

My response is, get used to it because I am going to live to be 100, and I am
going to show my thighs every day till I die.
—Lena Dunham[1]

From her 2007 YouTube short *The Fountain* featuring her bikini-clad and
brushing her teeth in a public fountain, to her post-collegiate sloth and squalid "sex in a pipe in the street" in first feature *Tiny Furniture* (2010), to the
2012 Emmy Awards opening skit "revealing" her sitting naked on a toilet
scarfing cake, to her frequent on-screen nudity and cringe-inducing sex
scenes as alter-ego Hannah Horvath on HBO's *Girls*, to her 2014 memoir's
Not That Kind of Girl redefining of the term "tell-all," Lena Dunham has
devoted the past several years to making her flabby torso and her personal
humiliations (sexual and otherwise) into feminist political performance. By
insistently commanding, rather than passively inviting, our gaze to confront
images of "imperfect" female bodies—most regularly her own—Dunham
accomplishes precisely the opposite of conventional uses of female nudity to
conceal and deny women's humanity. In vivid opposition to HBO's otherwise sensationalizing of idealized female nudity in shows like *The Sopranos*
(David Chase, 1999–2007) and *Game of Thrones* (David Benioff and D. B.
Weiss, 2011–present), Dunham displays yet de-fetishizes naked bodies in
such a way that, Phillip Maciak proposes, "might be HBO's gesture at auto-
critique."[2] In so doing, Dunham makes visible body types that are rarely

screened and positions them in a way that accentuates women's embodied subjectivity, rather than the sexual objectivity to which women are traditionally confined in cultural representation, both artistic and commercial.

Beyond recontouring the gaze and its desired object from the normative scope policed by mainstream cinema and pornography, Dunham pushes further to explore and affirm women's bodies and desires for their most "unruly" and "unladylike" characteristics, elsewhere on screen rendered abject, if not effaced completely.[3] My analysis reads Dunham's body politics through the lens of Julia Kristeva's theory of abjection as a heteropatriarchal tool for coercing female bodies into regulated social subjects, alienating women from their bodies and one another.[4] "And yet," Kristeva notes, "from its place of banishment, the abject does not cease challenging its master."[5] Thus Kristeva proposes a strategy of seizing abjection from the patriarchal arsenal, re-appropriating it for feminist activism. If shame is the coerced response to revealing that which gendered hegemonies dictate must remain hidden, then to apply Kristeva's tactic of "owning" one's abjection is to defy that coercion and to transform self-disgust into self-acknowledgment. Furthermore, through viewer engagement with such images, writes Liza Johnson, "[S]hame can be understood as a type of enabling knowledge by which to see and feel desires and attachments, even weird ones, with a kind of singularity that demands neither identification nor repulsion, that functions, perhaps, more like empathy."[6] Driven to explore and find inspiration in what is typically deemed shamefully abject, Dunham inverts mainstream cinema's "male gaze" and pornography's "frenzy of the visible" to reveal and overcome dehumanizing forces of female passivity and abjection.[7] Over the three seasons and counting of *Girls*, Dunham has established a popular cultural precedent for physical and sexual exhibitionism, revealing bodies and performing acts relegated to the private sphere (from bathrooming to binging to sex), brought into the public and politicized towards explicitly feminist aims.

Dunham's sassy and savvy manipulations of body politics within the visual realm provoke extreme responses: from the proclamations of her Emmy-winning eminence and fan adoration, to gender-policing by haters ranging from anonymous Internet trolls to influential shock-jock Howard Stern, to the withering allegations that her characters and perspective are entitled, self-absorbed, and non-diverse.[8] A blogger for feminist website *xo-Jane* surmises that the vitriolic response to Dunham's bodily self-representation stems from the perceived entitlement of Dunham/Hannah for not having to work particularly hard to get dates or sex despite her "blobby" body which she doesn't even care to change, as if "she is inflicting her body on us, as one might a weapon or a terrible disease."[9] What these rebukes and the collective responses, both supportive and denigrating, to Dunham's performative embodiment ultimately establish is its political potency as a strategy of what Ross Singer calls "*spectacular self-subjugation*—an activist tactic by which the body is given up temporarily to an exploitative system as a means of staging carnivalesque resistance against that system before a mainstream audience."[10] However intentionally "spectacular" Dunham's staging of her body performance may be—the term sits uncomfortably with what I'm characterizing as her de-fetishized, naturalistic self-representation—the outsized reverberations of *Girls* discourse possess carnivalesque proportions that have *post facto* conveyed upon Dunham's body the force of, if not spectacle, symbolism. "We are left, then," Brett Lunceford observes, "with the body as body and the body as symbol, but the two are interrelated" in their cultural context, and thus mutually conducive to what Lunceford terms "naked politics."[11] Dunham's often revealed, smallish breasts convey the same political force as women who publicly brandish theirs in fights for "lactivism," breast cancer awareness, sexual equality, and LGBTQ rights, while her defiant flaunting of her not-thin body (along with that of her contemporaries Mindy Kaling and Rebel Wilson) has already proven its indelible import for popular culture.

Also voluble are the rebukes coming from what would seem to be Dunham's own allies: postfeminist Millennials who allege that her on-screen alter-ego Hannah is regressively fixated on what Serena Daalmans calls "non-fulfilling, awkward, degrading, and unprotected sex with [Hannah's on-again, off-again boyfriend] Adam [Adam Driver] and her passive aggressive self-consciousness about her body."[12] Against Daalmans's and others' criticisms I suggest there is a need to reposition our approach to Dunham's work by understanding her representations of sex and nudity as constituting a feminist critique, one that controversially and perhaps counter-intuitively uses supposedly negative and disempowering images of female (self-)degradation as means to indicate the viewers' complicity in judging both women *and* women's representations according to pious and unequal criteria. While criticized for ostensibly reinforcing masochistic behavior and sexualized depictions of women, Dunham is, I argue, committed to filming feminist consciousness and women's subjectivity as not reducible to but importantly determined by sexuality. Through physically and sexually explicit imagery that is naturalistic and subject-forming, Dunham represents feminist embodied subjectivity as self-determining, intimacy-oriented, women-loving, body-positive, pro-sex, and—to repurpose an advertising slogan—contoured for her pleasure.

Dunham's early short films, made while she was an undergraduate at Oberlin College, preview the themes of bodily abjection and sexual exhibition to come.[13] In *Pressure* (2006), Dunham's character listens eagerly as two female friends discuss orgasms before interjecting to describe a childhood habit of jiggling her finger in her nose in order to experience the subsequent relief of sneezing. Her friends, looking disdainful, desert her in a remote section of the library. After a furtive look around, she repeats her cherished ritual and, after a satisfying sneeze, the screen goes to black. Dunham's next short, *Hooker on Campus* (2007), has her sporting risqué costumes and venturing up to strangers to ask coquettishly, "Want to have a good time?" The scene's incongruity—Dunham's plump frame in fishnets and bustier, hair teased and eyes heavily made up, confronting politely bemused passers-by on a placid Midwestern campus—recalls the work of artist-provocateur Laurel Nakadate, but rather than humiliating her unwitting co-conspirators Dunham shoulders the humiliation herself. Most prophetic of all is Dunham's subsequent short *The Fountain* (2007), which went viral with 1.5 million hits on YouTube, in which she undresses down to her bikini, stomach bulge prominent, in a burbling campus fountain, then performs her toilette (teeth brushing, hair washing) in a manner devoid of Anita Ekberg-style frolicking. A campus security guard appears and awkwardly requests she vacate the fountain and her camera operator to stop filming: "They don't allow it in other fountains on campus," the guard reports. Dunham concedes, but not without noting the fountain's male statuary: "No one's telling him not to be naked in public." Following their abbreviated shoot, Dunham debriefs with her boyfriend/cameraman, debating her penchant for being naked in public. Questioning the false dichotomy, she asks, "If there are ten people is it public or private?" His ultimate diagnosis, "You want to be naked in front of people who don't really want to see you naked," concludes the film.

In devoting herself so rigorously to scrutinizing the ways that images construct and control women's sense of themselves and their desires, Dunham joins in a tradition of female artists using nudity and graphic sexuality to articulate a feminist politics of embodiment. "A lot of my parents' friends were performance artists, so I think I just understood that the body could be a tool in that exploration," Dunham has explained.[14] Writing in *Salon*, Saroya Roberts traces this tradition to 1970s feminist artists such as Carolee Schneemann while disparaging Dunham's motives as being "not as lofty" as these earlier artists.[15] To the contrary, I would connect Dunham to a more radical vein of body art performed by women artists such as Eleanor Antin, Cindy Sherman, Annie Sprinkle, and Orlan, who flaunt their "grotesque" bodies—whether merely average-sized (in the case of Antin and Sprinkle) or cosmetically and surgically manipulated (in the case of Sherman and Orlan)—in resistance to cultural beauty norms and expectations of femininity.[16] No doubt necessary at the time to their attracting such rapt attention within art world circles, Schneemann or Marina Abramović were noticeably slender and conventionally beautiful; their conformity to beauty norms limits and even undermines their work's impact, especially when viewed in a contemporary context. Furthermore, whereas these women performed their "body work" in the rarefied domain of art-world institutions and collectives, Dunham's milieu is that of a contemporary Internet-enabled popular cultural landscape—ranging from cable television and Indiewood, to YouTube vids and Twitter, to nightly network talk-show appearances and podcast interviews—in which she is a conspicuous interloper. As the feminist-branded *Hello Giggles* blog co-founded by actress Zooey Deschanel notes, "Dunham's body is what women see in dressing rooms, in locker rooms, and in the mirror. But seeing it in a space typically reserved for stick-thin starlets seems somehow avant-garde."[17]

Not that stick-thin starlets are omitted altogether from *Girls*; another criticism leveled at Dunham had her ostensibly softening the brunt of her naturalistic appearance by casting three conventionally beautiful women as Hannah's closest friends—Marnie (Allison Williams), Jessa (Jemima Kirke), and Shoshanna (Zosia Mamet). Yet although we have seen each of the three in states of undress and/or having sex, *Girls* denies us unproblematic enjoyment of conventional feminine beauty as spectacular *to-be-looked-at-ness*. This troubling of visual pleasure is deployed most acutely during these female characters' respective sex scenes, and precisely because such encounters consistently prove to be sources either of self-abasing mortification or self-defeating manipulation for increasingly sympathetic characters.[18] Moreover, the more graphic the sex scene, the less intimate and fulfilling it is suggested to be for these women; consider, for example, the contrast between, in episode 2.3 ("Bad Friend"), an overhead shot of a spread-eagled Marnie pinned below a bare-assed, thrusting Booth Jonathan, the unctuous artist whose power games she submits to, and the sequence filmed in close-up and *sans* nudity of Marnie's long-time boyfriend Charlie (Christopher Abbott) bringing her to climax with oral sex during their reunion in episode 2.10 ("Together").

Nakedness between the female characters exhibits a similar rationale: the greater the intimacy between the women, the more naked they get. Hannah's casual nakedness around her girlfriends—even when it goes unreturned—strikes me as another way in which Dunham's representation of bodies seem feminist, both for the way it detaches female nudity from women's heterosexualization, connoting naturalism and intimacy between women instead. Jessa shares Hannah's bohemian comfort with her body, and the two poignantly share an intimate moment when a dejected Jessa joins Hannah in the bath in episode 2.4 ("It's a Shame about Ray"), but Jessa also resolutely rejects postfeminism's appeal to subjugate herself sexually when summing up her search for a post-sobriety job: "Anything that doesn't require me to profit off my sexuality." We have already seen physically modest Marnie do precisely that—willingly submit to a cocktail waitress position at a posh gentlemen's club—even as she protests, keeping her towel on while chatting with a naked Hannah in their bathroom in the series' opening sequence, "I only show my boobs to people I sleep with." Re-aligning female nudity with women's heterosexualization here (notably she uses the phrase "sleeps with" to clarify that emotional intimacy is not necessary), Marnie emerges as the series' embodiment of internalized gender conformity and self-discipline. In direct opposition to Hannah's disruptive nudity, Marnie acquiesces to the cultural dictum that a woman should be both desirable and ladylike, which "requires that the woman keep exposure to a minimum while managing exposure to appear desirable."[19] Yet Dunham's approach to writing this character remains compassionate, forging an understanding that Marnie's judgmental nature, as Ray blatantly and self-reflexively informs her in episode 3.5 ("Only Child"), "comes from a very deep, dank, dark, toxic well of insecurity, [which] allows you to be a sympathetic figure." Rather than simply villainize the less evolved version of the modern feminist woman, one so hindered by gendered constrictions that she tells Ray, "If I liked you I wouldn't be eating pizza in front of you," instead we are encouraged towards an empathetic perspective attuned to the experience of self-denial to which so many women continue to submit in ways big and small.

The response to Dunham's body performance is telling for the way it demonstrates, as Lunceford notes, that "taboos on nakedness do more than reign in sexuality; controls on nakedness function as controls on the body itself—how one can appropriately use one's own body."[20] In perhaps the most infamous voicing of criticism against *Girls* yet, *The Wrap*'s Tim Molloy directed the following objection at Dunham at a 2014 Television Critics Association panel:

> I don't get the purpose of all of the nudity on the show. By you particularly. I feel like I'm walking into a trap where you go, "Nobody complains about the nudity on Game of Thrones ," but I get why they are doing it. They are doing it to be salacious and, you know, titillate people. And your character is often naked just at random times for no reason.[21]

What Molloy's remark reveals, apart from his overlooking of the (arguably more understandable and valid) purpose of using nudity that I describe above, is his chief grievance: Dunham's choice to perform the majority of the female nudity herself. Apart from the instance in which Jessa bares a single breast in an attempt to distract Thomas-John from bringing her to meet his parents in "It's a Shame about Ray," the female nudity on display in *Girls* is dominated by "imperfect" female bodies, insistently and consistently presented as if to affirm their beauty and right to visibility and pleasure. The only breasts besides Hannah's we see in season 1 are those of her middle-aged mother Loreen (Becky Ann Baker), during an intimate and tragicomic shower with husband Tad (Peter Scolari) that directly contrasts with the (self-)duplicity depicted in association with the idealized female bodies of Hannah's friends. Connected to this use of female nudity to convey sexual and emotional honesty, the only woman's pubic area glimpsed apart from Hannah's is that of Adam's intensely neurotic sister Caroline, played by the often naked and proudly hirsute performer Gaby Hoffmann, in a startling moment of self-hurting that also exemplifies *Girls*'s use of female nudity to reveal women's actual embodiment and emotional nakedness.

Still more criticism came Dunham's way with regard to her ostensibly reversing the gaze, fetishizing the well-built and frequently shirtless Adam as object of her (and our) desiring gaze. While full frontal male nudity remains as elusive here as it has throughout film and television history (porn excepted), with the women's chiseled conquests seen only bare-chested and bare-assed, the notable exception occurs in episode 1.6 ("The Return"), when Hannah's father Tad slips during an anniversary tryst with wife Loreen in the aforementioned shower scene. When Hannah arrives back home, she—and we the viewers—confront Tad slumped fully flaccid on the bathroom tile. Though clearly Dunham's choice was dependent on actor Scolari's willingness to be filmed fully nude, that Dunham chooses this character and scene in which to unveil the penis initially seems to conform to what Peter Lehman has documented as the deeply polarized dichotomy structuring screen representations of the penis: "At one pole, we have the powerful, awesome spectacle of phallic masculinity, and at the other its vulnerable, pitiable, and frequently comic collapse."[22] Though, given its representational rarity and father-daughter discomfort, this penis shot may provoke a surprised gasp or laugh of commiseration, ultimately it departs from indulging the symptomatic anxiety Lehman diagnoses. Tad is not the butt of a penis-size joke, or any joke; while middle aged and of short stature, he appears appealingly fit and had just been proving his heteromasculine virility, and he is not an ostracized or excessively pathetic character but a relatable, sympathetic one.[23] Tad's penis is, in a word, anti-spectacular—or, to borrow Lehman's formulation, non-melodramatic; its representation in "The Return" neither inflates its subject's patriarchal power nor robs him of his heteromasculinity. Choosing to use naturalism rather than melodrama or comedy in representing the penis, Dunham eradicates its phallic symbolism. Such a strategy is more effective than leaving the penis veiled, where it retains the mystique of the unrepresented, yet this scene's singularity across three seasons of *Girls* necessarily limits its impact.[24]

In what strikes me as an unlikely coincidence, the only scene in which we glimpse Hannah fully and frontally naked also involves a mortifying incident while showering—a fainting spell brought on by her overzealous use of handsome doctor Joshua's (Patrick Wilson) luxurious steam shower. As with Tad's showering snafu, and echoed by the unconventional female nude scenes with Loreen and Caroline, Hannah's nudity here and elsewhere operates in registers naturalistic and/or tragicomic, with both functioning to defetishize even the sexualized body. Many of Hannah's (semi-)nude scenes take place during and after sex with Adam, or position her naturalistically in mundane moments (changing clothes, in the bath). But a good many others

function as instances of Hannah flaunting a body that onlookers (both diegetic and non-diegetic), influenced by our culture's exacting standards of attractiveness and social decorum, are primed to criticize. Hannah's body becomes
still more "unruly" in refusing to conform to expectations of how women
should look and act: like Dunham herself, she is frequently chided for not
wearing pants; Ray mistakes her hole-filled underwear for crotch-less pan-
ties; and few female performers have been filmed eating so often and with
such gusto.

   Yet how characters and spectators respond to Hannah ultimately reflects
more about the viewer than the viewed. In episode 3.7 ("Beach House"),
when Marnie dismisses Hannah's poolside reenactment of *Spring Breakers*
(Harmony Korine, 2012), complete with Day-Glo string bikini, with a curt
"That's disgusting," to agree is to align ourselves with the show's most
judgmental character, however motivated by insecurity Marnie may be. Al-
ternatively, when Jessa coos affectionately over Hannah's "teensy" breasts
(echoing her character Charlotte's telling Dunham's Aura in *Tiny Furniture*,
"You've got the greatest little tits—like a 1960s porn star"), we are prompted
to agree with the positive assessment made by this free-thinking bohemian.
Indeed, Jessa becomes the counterbalance to Marnie's criticism, affirming
Hannah in her abjection with compliments that might appear left-handed ("I
love you—You're so fucking gross lying on the bathroom floor") but are
reinforced by Jessa's own guileless behavior: showing no embarrassment
when a guy she's making out with finds his hand coated with menstrual
blood; casually lobbing a "snot rocket" in Hannah's direction as they share a
bath; and repeatedly appearing in conversation, unbothered, while on the
toilet. Likewise, the sheer confidence with which Dunham-as-Hannah bran-
dishes her backside (to assess a splinter acquired from rolling around pant-
less), her love handles (commandeering, Dr. Phil-style, a brother-sister intervention between Adam and Caroline while wearing an ill-fitting midriff
shirt), and most of all her breasts (donning a nipple-baring mesh top during a
cocaine-fueled night out, playing topless Ping-Pong), constitute an effect that
is paradoxically one of both absurdist incongruity and banal naturalism. Precisely because we are so unaccustomed to seeing bodies like Hannah's
flaunted within visual culture, her image mobilizes the effects of camp and
the carnivalesque to de-familiarize our cultural notions of beauty and gender
performance. Simultaneously, that Hannah looks—as countless critics point
out—so much like an average, ordinary young woman, works against her
imputation, by Marnie and certain viewers, as an abject object.[25]

> No one could ever hate me as much as I hate myself, so any mean thing
> someone's gonna think of to say about me, I've already said to me, about me,
> probably in the last half hour. (Hannah to Marnie, Episode 1.9 ["Leave Me
> Alone"])

While Dunham's "haters" not so subtly suggest that Hannah, inhabiting a fictional world conceived for verisimilitude, is characterized with an unrealistic surplus of confidence in her physicality, she does voice occasional and altogether human self-criticism—yet still frustrating cultural expectations towards suppression of her selfhood. The series' opening sequence is exceptionally illustrative in this regard: Hannah, sitting naked in a tub while savoring a cupcake, refers to Marnie, perched alongside and wrapped in a towel, as a "Victoria's Secret angel" and herself as "a fat baby angel." But nonetheless it's Hannah—and Dunham—who flaunts her nakedness and refuses to stifle her appetite in accordance with a discourse that insists on heavier women staying covered up, expressing discontent with their larger form, and actively abstaining in an effort to "improve" themselves. Hannah, then, suffers merely a moderate amount of self-doubt rather than the self-hate prescribed unto the abject object, and she largely rejects the doctrine of docile bodies that regulates gender performance and body image through exacting modes of submission and self-denial.[26]

Girls gives voice to the tortuous process by which women learn to be their own harshest critics both through the aforementioned empathizing with Marnie, but also through the struggle endured by even that seemingly more secure "unruly woman" Hannah—and by Dunham herself. In an acknowledgment of actual user comments received in the wake of *The Fountain*'s posting on YouTube, *Tiny Furniture* features a sequence in which Charlotte reads several aloud.[27] "You can't possibly take these seriously?" she asks, but Aura admits, "I do sometimes," echoing Dunham's own admission that, "Sometimes I think, 'Boys were mean to me in high school, so I can take whatever.' Of course that doesn't mean you can handle five thousand commenters saying you're fat, but it does prepare you for feeling like a weirdo."[28] Like Aura, Dunham's *Girls* alter ego Hannah also acknowledges the inevitable sting that social shaming—and its internalization—carries. In the series pilot, when Adam questions her plentiful tattoos, Hannah recounts her motivation as a teenager, "Truthfully, I gained a bunch of weight very quickly and I felt very out of control of my own body and it was this riot grrrl idea, like 'I'm taking control of my own shape.'" When he presses her about whether she has tried losing weight, she shoots back defensively, "No, I have not tried a lot to lose weight because I decided that I was going to have some other concerns in my life!" This self-reflexive tactic of articulating, through Hannah, Dunham's own endeavor to remain imperviously self-affirming in the wake of public personal desecration mirrors that of Hannah's struggle throughout the series to keep her professional integrity intact while facing temptations around money and other self-interests. Dunham's own efforts to create an authentic, purposeful "voice of a generation" frequently exceed the diegetic frame to engage with her critics and even to feed a feminist coalition of change—an exemplary instance being episode 2.5 ("One Man's Trash"), in which Hannah spends two dreamy, sex-filled days in a well-appointed brownstone with the aforementioned, exceedingly handsome doctor, Joshua. Told that she's beautiful, Hannah is surprised; "Don't you think you are?" asks Joshua, to which she replies with a tentative "Um . . . yeah, it just isn't always the feedback I've been given." Cue the deluge of cuttingly indignant responses (not all by anonymous trolls) that took Dunham to task for what they alleged was an unrealistically self-flattering premise; a discussion between two *Slate* staff writers, for example, asked "Why are these people having sex, when they are so clearly mismatched—in style, in looks, in manners, in age, in everything?"[29] In retaliation, actor Patrick Wilson's real life wife Dagmara Dominczyk issued a damning Tweet: "Funny, his wife is a size 10, muffin top & all, & he does her just fine."[30]

Yet another woman artist to whom Dunham seems indebted is French memoirist and filmmaker Catherine Breillat, who shares with Dunham a devotion to representing female abjection as well as to critically referencing pornography, using both as routes to examining women's sexual subjectivities. Also connecting Breillat and Dunham is the particular course this sexual experience en route to subjectivity takes; for both their characters, the path of self-knowledge and self-acceptance is arrived at through mindful, exploratory acts of sexual self-degradation. These socially shameful acts made subject-forming in Dunham's hands is accomplished in terms of diegetic representation that reveals the "real"—the awkward, the messy, the humiliating—of bodies and sex, praised by Dunham's fans as the constitution of her distinctive voice. Or, as Hannah's editor berates her after a short-lived attempt in episode 2.9 ("On All Fours") at writing in a less self-effacing register, "Did your hymen grow back? Where's the sexual failure? Where's the pudgy face slick with semen and sadness? More Anaïs Nin, less Jane Austen." Hannah heeds his words and finds the inspiration to finish her memoir, with stories drawn from her own, however abject, sexual experiences, recounting the "hand-job kidney stone story" but rejecting a heterosexual porn fantasy of her "choking on long balls" that a new editor suggests would distinguish her as being edgier than Mindy Kaling.

Regarding Breillat's frequent incorporation of pornographic elements (casting Italian hardcore performer Rocco Siffredi in her films, filming sex scenes to appear un-simulated, including "money shots" and "beaver shots"), Kristyn Gorton posits, "[T]he allusions to the pornographic allow [us to] reconsider and re-appropriate these images in terms of female desire."[31] An aim of Dunham's work as well, it is one that she lists among her widely Tweeted list of three reasons why she is not comfortable with the *Hustler* parody *This Ain't Girls XXX*: "Because a big reason I engage in (simulated) onscreen sex is to counteract a skewed idea of that act created by the proliferation of porn."[32] As with Breillat, it is not the existence of porn that Dunham condemns but the exploitative nature of so much of it alongside its domination of our sexual imaginary that she criticizes; their mutual aim is to revise rather than reject outright pornography. "Guys my age watch *so* much pornography. There's no way that you, young Jewish man from Chappaqua, taught this to yourself," Dunham declares.[33] And, as Elaine Blair recognizes, Dunham uses pornographic convention to counter, as well, Hollywood sex scenes' lack of interest

> in even hinting at the ways that people actually reach orgasm, [an omission] that is disheartening above all for female viewers . . . A dose of porn, judiciously applied by an extremely intelligent director, can save cinematic sex.[34]

Here too, then, Dunham mobilizes body performance to construct naturalistic representations of sex that enable and empower female subjectivities, though again pointing provocatively at self-degradation as the route to self-knowledge. As Dunham explains it, sex scenes in *Girls* are

> not just in there for the audience to have a titillating break to see, you know, the side of somebody's breast, they're in there because I think it's sometimes when we get the most information about our characters. And so they're always pushing the plot forward, if not in a concrete way, in sort of a more spiritual way.[35]

Though the type of bodies and acts on display are exceedingly different from that of its HBO contemporaries *Game of Thrones* and *Boardwalk Empire* (Terence Winter, 2010–2014), and given how they are designed and function, *Girls*'s sex scenes do belong among those associated with HBO's popularizing of "sexposition"—the term Myles McNutt coined to describe cable television's "purposeful use of sex and nudity in conjunction with a specific piece (or pieces) of information."[36] The chief and ultimate distinction, however, is that in *Girls* that "information" and the sex scenes through which it is conveyed are directly aimed at critiquing heteropatriarchal representations of sex and of women.

Initially the on-screen voice in *Girls* for the feminist potential of porn is Jessa, who like *Sex and the City*'s Samantha (Kim Cattrall), with whom she is often compared, functions as a model for the sexually liberated woman Hannah aspires to be (even if the consequences of that behavior—a pregnancy scare, STDs—tend to be treated with the same light touch *SATC* applied). In episode 1.2 ("Vagina Panic"), when Shoshanna reads from a female-penned *The Rules*-style manual proclaiming that "sex from behind is degrading," Jessa angrily rejects the dictum:

> What if I want to feel like I have udders? This woman doesn't care about what I want . . . I'm offended by all the "supposed to's." I don't like women telling other women what to do or how to do it or when to do it. Every time I have sex it's my choice.

So long as that choice is made, Jessa embraces sexual submission by understanding it as pleasurable performance rather than an oppressive position. During a fevered make-out in a bar bathroom in "Vagina Panic," Jessa's latest conquest tentatively asks "Is that okay?" to which she responds, "Don't ask me that again ever." Granted Jessa's view of sex as experience for experience's sake can be as self-destructive as it is self-affirming; it is she who urges Hannah to turn her boss's semi-harassing behavior in episode 1.4 ("Hannah's Diary") to her advantage: "Fuck him for the story, Hannah!" And it is she who dispels the shame of STDs with her mantra regarding having the HPV virus: "All adventurous women do." But Jessa also extends an apologia for heterosexual pornography in a way that seems to comment on Dunham's own aforementioned denunciations; exclaiming over the plentiful pubic hair in a vintage copy of *Penthouse*, in episode 2.7 ("Video Games"), Jessa muses about nude modeling, "In a way it's the most noble thing you could do, helping a boy find his sexuality and become a man." "The most noble except for being a doctor or a firefighter," Hannah responds. "Who says she's not a doctor?" returns Jessa archly, calling into question our cultural presumptions about women who commodify their sexuality. Having gleaned from Jessa (however shaky) nascent foundation for reconciling feminism with desire, Hannah proceeds further into an intimate relationship with Adam that foregrounds the thorny question of sexual self-degradation, a lynchpin in contemporary feminist discourse and perhaps Dunham's most controversial issue yet explored.

From her short feature *Creative Nonfiction* (2009), in which her character endures a sexless relationship with a male classmate using her for her bed, to the similar encounters Aura suffers with apartment crasher Jed (Alex Karpovsky) and "in a pipe in the street" with her jerk co-worker Keith (David Call) in *Tiny Furniture*, Dunham regularly positions her alter-egos on the receiving end of sexual humiliation. In contrast to her friends' self-destructive relationships, most prominently the sadomasochistic one Marnie endures with Booth—who locks her in a torture chamber disguised as "art" and condescendingly offers payment for her services—Hannah initially (if naïvely) frames her interactions with Adam as personal experiences in service to her becoming a sexually mature woman and professional writer as much as a girlfriend. Emily Nussbaum traces Dunham's work to a tradition reaching from Mary McCarthy to Mary Gaitskill, "stories about smart, strange girls diving into experience, often through bad sex with their worst critics."[37] And as Dunham herself explains, "My goal is to have a sexual verisimilitude that has heretofore not been seen on television. I did it because I felt that the depictions of sex I had seen on television weren't totally fair to young women trying to wrap their brains around this stuff. I didn't do it to be provocative. I did it to be educational."[38] "I do explore," Hannah assures Elijah about her sex life in episode 1.3 ("All Adventurous Women Do"). "Right now, I'm seeing this guy, and sometimes I let him hit me on the side of my body." There is self-delusion in her statement, but it vies with self-agency as Hannah goes about sorting out which are Adam's desires and which are hers. It is clear from their season 1 casual encounters that Adam directs the dialogue, and does so with lines straight out of mainstream porn. "You're a dirty little whore and I'm going to send you home to your parents covered in come," he tells her in "Vagina Panic." She plays along, but upon jokingly referencing their role-play the next morning is met with a blank stare; perhaps Adam is too uncomfortable with his "dirty talk" to acknowledge it in the light of day, or perhaps he simply feels no need to palliate his fantasy life through ironic dismissal. Though *Rolling Stone* claims that "Hannah clearly gets off on being degraded . . . and [Adam's] into *doing* the degrading," it is not at all clear that she actually orgasms during these sessions.[39] But nor are her female friends' admonishments necessarily fact: upon hearing Hannah's report of their "Vagina Panic" role-play, Marnie chides, "Hannah, Adam is not allowed to do that to you; he's not your boyfriend," while a female co-worker, upon seeing in "Hannah's Diary" the dick pic intended for someone else, tells her "You need to have a little self-respect"—responses that are themselves a form of shaming no less disciplinary than Shoshanna reprimanding Jessa about following the rules set out for "the ladies."

Hannah finally voices to Adam, in "Hannah's Diary," that she wants to be with someone "who wants to hang out all the time, and thinks I'm the best person in the world, and wants to have sex with only me." Over the first season, their relationship gradually transforms into a more equilateral if still problematic sexual and emotional coupling; the pair lack the emotional honesty that is required for their dominant–submissive roles to be pleasurable and connective rather than hurtful and distancing. Estranged throughout season 2, each independently explores the meanings of and their personal motivations for sexual (self-)degradation, coming to understand its volatility and potential for inducing shame when engaged in unsafe contexts. "One Man's Trash" reveals Hannah's experience of finding her sexual openness welcomed only to have her emotional openness shamed, as she moves from telling a receptive Joshua "I want you to make me come," to her post-coital confession to an increasingly distant Joshua that "Once I asked someone to punch me in the chest then come on that spot. That idea came from my brain. What makes me think I deserve that?" Hannah's demonstration of trust and need at unburdening herself is neither welcomed nor reciprocated; the intimacy she is clamoring for provokes Joshua to close off. "You basically forced me to tell you all of my feelings, and you're not acting glad, and you didn't tell me anything about you," Hannah protests, but her urging to learn about "his baggage" provokes only shaming silence.

> A phenomenon that Hannah experienced—and Hannah experienced it because I experienced it—was the sense that if you were a girl who didn't have an ideal body, what you had to offer was your willingness to please, your openness to adventure and your desire to do it all . . . "I'm a fat girl, just do it—I'm down for anything. I'm not like those skinny girls. I can't say no." . . . You don't have to, obviously, be chubby to feel this, you just have to feel an essential sense that you yourself are not enough.[40]

Capable of a greater infliction of power as both the sexual dominant and the man in a patriarchal culture, Adam's own explorations with degradation apart from Hannah have far more disturbing ramifications. His next partner, a quintessential "nice Jewish girl" named Natalia (Shiri Appleby), initially rejects Adam's attempts at degradation; "I can like your cock and not be a dirty whore," she informs him. In a later encounter, in "On All Fours," having grown more trusting and emotionally attached, she hesitantly follows his orders to crawl on all fours across his squalid apartment and submits to his ejaculating on her breasts, but tells him afterward, visibly pained, "I don't think I liked that." It is important to note that Natalia's perspective and character are treated respectfully, making her a reminder of the importance of consent between partners as well as the validity of a postfeminist stance against sexual self-degradation in a culture branded by "pornification" and what Ariel Levy memorably named "female chauvinist pigs."[41] Yet Natalia, like Adam, mistakenly conflates sexual self-degradation with emotional injury, understandably rebuking him in episode 3.1 ("Females Only") for having treated her callously but attributing this to their sexual dynamic when she turns to warn Hannah, "He's going to fuck you like he's never met you and doesn't love his own mother." While she is correct in seeing Adam's degradation of her sexually and emotionally as the result of his lack of empathy for her and lack of investment in their relationship, it is not sexual (self-)degradation but its misuse under nonconsensual, uncommitted circumstances that is to blame.

Adam's complicity in that misuse and Natalia's biting words hang heavily over Adam and Hannah's reconciliation at the start of season 3, going unaddressed until they erupt in episode 3.10 ("Role-Play"). Hannah, tired of being treated "like an ottoman with a vagina," attempts to enliven a sex life stalled by monogamous routine and Adam's preoccupation with preparing for his first Broadway role. They try enacting a fantasy role-play scenario that Hannah concocts, but Adam interrupts her mid-coitus, upset by her authorial direction. The resulting argument between them in "Role-Play" allows Hannah to voice the ambivalence she (and *Girls* viewers) have felt around the dynamic of degradation that constituted her and Adam's early sexual exchanges, and her confusion as to its dissolution.

> You used to have all these ideas about me being a little street slut or an orphan with a disease or you said I was a woman with a baby's body or something. I was just trying to do it the way we used to, the way that sex always was for us.

Appearing surprised at her outburst, Adam denies any "creepy" connotations to be drawn from ideas "just coming to us in the moment" and reproves her for being "outside your body watching everything." But Hannah insists by saying incredulously "I don't have ideas like that," finally articulating her own lack of desire for sexual self-degradation. With this proclamation, she also forces him into an awareness that it was (and is) exclusively his desires dictating their sexual dynamic, even if she maintained agency throughout. "So what does it matter, if you're getting what you want? What do you care if I'm in my body?" she explodes. "You can't be the body police." Every bit as revelatory is Adam's subsequent confirmation in "Role-Play" that emotional connectedness (or lack thereof) does determine his sexual fantasies, with sexual degradation confined to when "I fucked women I met in bars or whatever . . . And it was like that with us for a while too. But then we fell in love. And then, I just wanted to have sex with you, as us."

It is a complicated scene for the clarification it provides and the confusion that remains, a vivid marker of the human-like complexity that composes *Girls*'s characterizations. I find it a particularly illuminating instance of the distance between Hannah and Adam—rendered thus not by their lack of intimacy at this point in their relationship, but by the burdensome cultural silence—and thus ignorance—around desire, especially as experienced differently by opposingly socialized women and men. It is also revealing of the distance between Hannah and Dunham, as the former has until this outburst remained silent about her desire and subservient to the desires of others. Dunham has done precisely the opposite, refusing to be silenced or to cater to a cultural logic of desire that accepts shame and disavows women's humanity. When Lunceford posits that "To perform nude embodiment is to make explicit the performance of self," he gestures at the individualism that is written on the body, unveiled of certain social signifiers yet also reduced to others—namely gender and race.[42] These clinging significations are what ultimately limit the political power of body performance by Dunham and others, insofar as they shift cultural meanings tied to bodies rather than untying them altogether. Yet ours remains a culture of "bodies that matter," thus we retain an imperative to examine the materiality of sex and sexuality as it defines and confines our social subjectivities.[43] And so it is of utmost, urgent importance that Dunham, in defiantly and mindfully owning her abjection, wields her body as a weapon for change.

NOTES

1. This article is expanded from and inspired by a brief visual essay I published as part of a *Girls* theme week in *In Media Res*, and I am indebted to my co-contributors and our respondents within that forum for their valuable insights. See San Filippo et al., 2013. As I was completing this essay, concurrent with the release of Dunham's memoir *Not That Kind of Girl*, allegations were hurled via social media and blogs charging that certain of the book's passages constituted remorseless admission by Dunham of her inappropriate sexual treatment during childhood of her younger sister. While I feel compelled to dispute these claims of abuse and child molestation, rather than addressing the allegations at length I believe that what's important to emphasize regarding my project is that the behavior under scrutiny took place off screen, apart from the representational realm of media performance and confined to a time when Dunham was a minor. As such, it does not fall within my purview in analyzing Dunham's representational acts of embodiment performed by consenting adults, i.e. both Dunham herself and the contractually-protected performers with whom she works. For a sensitive yet level-headed response to the allegations against Dunham, see Tolentino, 2014.

In one of the more vicious press attacks on Dunham, she was criticized for wearing what appeared to some to be a pant-less outfit to a 2012 industry event. She stated in reply, "If Olivia Wilde had gone to a party in . . . little shorts, she might have been on a 'weird dressed list' or been told her outfit was cute. I don't think a girl with tiny thighs would have received such no-pants attention. I think what it really was . . . 'Why did you all make us look at your thighs?'" Quoted in Hazlett, 2012.

2. Maciak, 2013.

3. I am referencing Kathleen Rowe's notion of the unruly woman as a subversive figure within patriarchal culture. See Rowe, 1996.

4. See Kristeva, 1982.

5. Ibid., 2.

6. Johnson (2004), 1382–83.

7. I refer here to two fundamental feminist critiques of classical Hollywood film and heterosexual male pornography, respectively: Mulvey, 1975 and Williams, 1999.

8. The scope of this essay does not allow me to include discussion of the significant commentary on racial and class privilege in Dunham's work, though my co-contributors address these topics in this collection. On a January 2013 broadcast of his satellite radio show, Howard Stern said of Dunham, "It's [*sic*] a little fat girl who kinda looks like Jonah Hill and she keeps taking her clothes off and it kind of feels like rape . . . I don't want to see that." Ironically, Dunham also faced reprisals for appearing *too* attractive; when Jezebel offered $10,000 for untouched photographs of Dunham's fashion shoot for *Vogue* (and, upon receiving, published them), commentators decried her alleged hypocrisy in assenting to airbrushing.

9. Lesly, 2013, "Blobby" was the adjective notoriously applied by female critic Linda Stasi in a 2013 *New York Post* article.

10. Singer quoted in Lunceford (2012), 6.

11. Lunceford (2012), 143.

12. Daalmaans (2013), 360.

13. The short films Dunham made as a student that are referenced herein are included as special features on the Criterion Collection DVD of *Tiny Furniture*.

14. Quoted in Hattenstone, 2014.

15. Roberts, 2013.

16. I am thinking in particular of Antin's work *Carving: A Traditional Sculpture* (1972), 148 black-and-white photographs documenting her loss of ten pounds over thirty-seven days; Sherman's "society portraits" from 2008 of herself in the guises of aging matriarchs; Sprinkle's

"Public Cervix Announcement" performance, in which she invites audience members to view her cervix with speculum and flashlight; and Orlan's theatricalized documenting of her multiple plastic surgeries throughout the 1990s.

17. Konstantinovsky, 2012.

18. I am thinking of Marnie's debasement by Booth Jonathan (Jorma Taccone), in season 2 and her self-described disrespect "for the emotional property of other women" in season 3; Shoshanna's desperate efforts to first lose her virginity then embrace her sexual freedom following her breakup with Ray (Alex Karpovsky), all while staying in accordance with her *The Rules*-style "we're the ladies" dictate; and Jessa's toying with marriage, first that of the couple who employs her as their nanny then that of her own to Thomas-John (Chris O'Dowd), as a diversion from taking responsibility for her life.

19. Lunceford, 135.

20. Ibid., 8.

21. Quoted in Rosenberg, 2014.

22. Lehman (2001), 26.

23. See ibid. Tad's heteromasculinity is impugned on occasion, though always by characters whose remarks are designated as judgmental and superficial; for example, Hannah's catty ex, Elijah (Andrew Rannells), takes Tad's single earring as evidence of his closeted homosexuality.

24. It is intriguing that Dunham's father, Carroll Dunham, is a painter known for his cartoonishly exaggerated images of penises—a representational strategy opposite that of his daughter's, but I would argue offering a similar demystification of the phallus.

25. The *Onion* has parodied Dunham's penchant for self-abjection with an article titled "Next Episode of 'Girls' to Feature Lena Dunham Shitting Herself during Gyno Exam While Eating a Burrito," which faux-quotes a television critic's rapturous review ("These are real girls with real bodies doing things that real girls do"). See Anon., 2013.

26. I refer here to Michel Foucault's concept of self-discipline as an internalized mode of social regulation, applying the concept specifically to efforts to dismantle what postfeminism frequently shores up: women's physical and sexual self-subjugation through consumerist practices of diet, exercise, fashion, cosmetics, and surgery. See Foucault, trans. Sheridan, 1978; Foucault, trans. Hurley, 1978.

27. Examples included "Look, whales ahead!" "What a blubber factory!" and "No, her stomach isn't huge, it's just that her boobs are really small—it's an optical illusion."

28. Quoted in McCammon, 2012.

29. Hagland and Engber, 2013.

30. @DagDom17, Twitter (February 12, 2013).

31. Gorton, 121.

32. Also listed: "Because *Girls* is, at its core, a feminist action while Hustler is a company that markets and monetizes a male's idea of female sexuality," and "Because it grosses me out." @lenadunham, Twitter, May 24, 2013. The parody's writer-director replied to Dunham; see Breslaw, 2013.

33. Quoted in Bruni, 2012.

34. Blair, 2012.

35. Lena Dunham interviewed by Terry Gross, *Fresh Air*, WHYY/NPR (September 29, 2014): http://www.npr.org/templates/transcript/transcript.php?storyId=352276798.

36. See McNutt, 2012.

37. Nussbaum, 2013.

38. Rensin, 2013.

39. Hiatt, 2013.

40. Lena Dunham interviewed by Terry Gross, *Fresh Air*, WHYY/NPR (September 29, 2014): http://www.npr.org/templates/transcript/transcript.php?storyId=352276798.

41. See Levy, 2005.

42. Lunceford, 142–143.

43. I am referencing, of course, Judith Butler's canonical text *Bodies That Matter*.

BIBLIOGRAPHY

Anon., "Next Episode of 'Girls' to Feature Lena Dunham Shitting Herself during Gyno Exam While Eating a Burrito," The *Onion* (March 14, 2013). Accessed July 3, 2014: http://www. theonion.com/articles/next-episode-of-girls-to-feature-lena-dunham-shitt,31661/.

Blair, Elaine. "The Loves of Lena Dunham," The *New York Review of Books* (June 7, 2012): http://www.nybooks.com/articles/archives/2012/jun/07/loves-lena-dunham/.

Breslaw, Anna. "Director of *Girls* Porn Slams Lena Dunham for Being Too Conservative." *Jezebel* (June 1, 2013): http://jezebel.com/director-of-girls-porn-slams-lena-dunham-for-being-too-510837480.

Bruni, Frank. "The Bleaker Sex." The *New York Times* (April 1, 2012): http://www.nytimes.com/2012/04/01/opinion/sunday/bruni-the-bleaker-sex.html?pagewanted=all.

Butler, Judith. *Bodies That Matter: On the Discursive Limits of "Sex."* London: Routledge, 1993.

Daalmans, Serena. "'I'm Busy Trying to Become Who I Am': Self-Entitlement and the City in HBO's *Girls.*" *Feminist Media Studies* 13.2 (2013): 359–62.

Dunham, Lena. *Not That Kind of Girl: A Young Woman Tells You What She's "Learned."* New York: Random House, 2014.

Foucault, Michel. *Discipline and Punish: The Birth of the Prison*. Trans. Alan Sheridan. New York: Pantheon, 1978.

———. *The History of Sexuality, Vol. 1: An Introduction*. Trans. Robert Hurley. New York: Random House, 1978.

Gorton, Kristyn. "'The Point of View of Shame': Re-viewing female desire in Catherine Breillat's *Romance* (1999) and *Anatomy of Hell* (2004)." *Studies in European Cinema* 4.2 (2007): 111–24.

Hagland, David and Daniel Engber. "Guys on *Girls*, Season 2." *Slate* (February 10, 2013): http://www.slate.com/articles/arts/tv_club/features/2013/girls_season_2/week_5/girls_on_ hbo_one_man_s_trash_episode_5_of_season_2_reviewed_by_guys.html.

Hattenstone, Simon. "Lena Dunham: 'People called me fat and hideous, and I lived.'" The *Guardian* (January 10, 2014): http://www.theguardian.com/culture/2014/jan/11/lena-dunham-called-fat-hideous-and-i-lived.

Hazlett, Courtney. "Lena Dunham Explains Her Thighs—And the 'No-Pants' Look." *Today.com* (October 9, 2012). http://www.today.com/entertainment/lena-dunham-explains-her-thighs-no-pants-look-1C6358990?franchiseSlug=todayentertainmentmain.

Hiatt, Brian. "Girl on Top." *Rolling Stone* Issue 1177 (February 28, 2013): http://www. rollingstone.com/movies/news/lena-dunham-girl-on-top-20130228.

Johnson, Liza. "Perverse Angle: Feminist Film, Queer Film, Shame." *Signs*, 30.1. *Beyond the Gaze: Recent Approaches to Film Feminisms*. Spec. issue ed. Kathleen McHugh and Vivian Sobchack (Autumn 2004). 1361–84.

Konstantinovsky, Michelle. "Why Lena Dunham's Body Matters (And Why It's Ridiculous That It Does)." *Hello Giggles* (April 26, 2012): http://hellogiggles.com/why-lena-dunhams-body-matters-and-why-its-ridiculous-that-it-does/#read.

Kristeva, Julia. *Powers of Horror: An Essay on Abjection*. Trans. Leon S. Roudiez. New York: Columbia University Press, 1982.

Lehman, Peter. "Crying over the Melodramatic Penis: Melodrama and Male Nudity in Films of the 90s." In *Masculinity: Bodies, Movies, Culture*. Ed. Lehman (New York: Routledge, 2001), 25–41.

Lesly. "The Audacity of Lena Dunham, and Her Admirable Commitment to Making Us Look at Her Naked." *xoJane* (January 9, 2013): http://www.xojane.com/issues/lena-dunham-naked-nude.

Levy, Ariel. *Female Chauvinist Pigs: Women and the Rise of Raunch Culture*. New York: Free Press, 2005.

Lunceford, Brett. *Naked Politics: Nudity, Political Action, and the Rhetoric of the Body*. Lanham, MD: Lexington, 2012.

Maciak, Phillip. "Slapstick 'Sexposition': *Girls* vs. the Body Politics of HBO." *HBO's Girls and the White Box* theme week. *In Media Res*. (January 9, 2013): http://mediacommons. futureofthebook.org/imr/2013/01/09/slapstick-sexposition-girls-vs-body-politics-hbo.

McCammon, Ross. "Lena Dunham Is Building an Empire." *Esquire* (November 13, 2012): http://www.esquire.com/features/americans-2012/lena-dunham-interview-1212?link=rel& dom=buzzfeed&src=syn&mag=esq

McNutt, Myles. "*Game of Thrones*: 'The Night Lands' and Sexposition." *Cultural Learnings* (April 8, 2012): http://cultural-learnings.com/2012/04/08/game-of-thrones-the-night-lands-and-sexposition/.

Mulvey, Laura. "Visual Pleasure and Narrative Cinema." *Screen* 16.3 (Autumn 1975): 6–18.

Nussbaum, Emily. "Hannah Barbaric." The *New Yorker* (February 11 and 18, 2013): http://www.newyorker.com/magazine/2013/02/11/hannah-barbaric.

Rensin, David. "20Q Lena Dunham." *Playboy* (March 14, 2013): http://www.playboy.com/playground/view/20q-lena-dunham.

Roberts, Saroya. "Naked If I Want to: Lena Dunham's Body Politic." *Salon* (February 9, 2013): http://www.salon.com/2013/02/09/naked_if_i_want_to_lena_dunhams_body_politic/.

Rosenberg, Alyssa. "5 Productive Ways to Ask Lena Dunham about the Nudity on 'Girls.'" *Think Progress* (January 10, 2014): http://thinkprogress.org/alyssa/2014/01/10/3148721/lena-dunham-girls-nudity/.

Rowe, Kathleen. *The Unruly Woman: Gender and the Genres of Laughter*. Austin: University of Texas Press, 1996.

San Filippo, Maria et al. *HBO's* Girls *and the White Box* theme week. *In Media Res*. http://mediacommons.futureofthebook.org/imr/theme-week/2013/02/hbos-girls-white-box-january-7-january-11-2013.

Stasi, Linda. "New Girl on Top." *New York Post* (January 24, 2013): http://nypost.com/2013/01/04/new-girl-on-top/.

Tolentino, Jia. "The Right to a Sexual Narrative: On the Lena Dunham Abuse Claims." *Jezebel* (November 4, 2014): http://jezebel.com/the-right-to-a-sexual-narrative-on-the-lena-dunham-abu-1654187731.

Williams, Linda. *Hard Core: Power, Pleasure, and the 'Frenzy of the Visible.'* Expanded ed. Berkeley, University of California Press, 1999.

Chapter Four

Girls' Issues: The Feminist Politics of *Girls*'s Celebration of the 'Trivial'

Yael Levy

Girls, a Lena Dunham-created dramedy that focuses on four twenty-some-thing women, has been characterized, by both critics and viewers, as a text that centers on "trivial" issues.[1] Congruently, the work of *Girls*'s protagonist, Hannah Horvath, an aspiring writer who composes essays based on her own life, has also been labeled trivial, as reflected in the dismissal of some of her peers. "I just didn't feel like anything happened in it," Hannah's early sec-ond-season boyfriend, Sandy, tells her after reading one of her essays. De-spite the fact that in that essay, according to Hannah, "a girl's whole perspec-tive on who she was and her sexuality changed," to Sandy the text nonethe-less "felt like just waiting in line and all the nonsense that goes through your brain when you're trying to kill time."[2]

The fact that the discourse regarding textual triviality is both diegetic and hypodiegetic indicates that not only does *Girls* focus on issues that are not culturally perceived as worthy of representation, but also that Dunham's dramedy is aware of its labeling as trivial and that its representation of the "trivial" may consequently work as key to understanding the construction of the show's *weltanschauung*. This chapter examines *Girls*'s purported triviali-ties, both diegetically, through the story lines unfolded in the series' epi-sodes, and hypodiegetically, through the stories that Hannah writes. In exam-ining these trivialities, I will argue that the series' representation of the "trivial" is a form of feminist resistance, seeing as issues that are considered trivial are in fact trivialized often due to their correlation with that which is considered feminine. The show's insistence to represent said issues is, I will suggest, an act of reclaiming that which has been underrepresented for its correlation with women's culture. I therefore intend to demonstrate that *Girls* offers a "feminist-inspired reworking of what counts as legitimate public discussion,"[3] in its recentralization of marginalized and trivialized stories that pertain to the lives of women.

The marking of the trivial in *Girls* is explicitly set in the first season's ninth episode, "Leave Me Alone,"[4] in which death and intimacy signify the most serious of themes and the most inconsequential of themes, respectively. In the episode, Hannah is invited to present her writing in a public reading. She decides to read an essay about a guy she had liked in college whom she found out was a hoarder. "I slept in his dorm room on top of a pile of collapsed Chinese food boxes like a semester's worth," she tells Ray, a friend and the manager of a café where she works. "I don't know if that sounds really trivial to you," she utters, adding, "it's definitely supposed to be funny; it's not supposed to be super serious, but it's also supposed to take on bigger issues, like fear of intimacy—" at which point Ray interrupts, insisting: "What in the world could be more trivial than intimacy?"[5]

Ray namely stresses that it is exactly the theme with which Hannah attempts to defend her story line that is triviality apotheosized, as he distinguishes it from "real" issues, such as "cultural criticism. How about years of neglect and abuse? How about acid rain? How about the plight of the giant panda bear? How about racial profiling? How about urban sprawl? How about divorce? How about death? How about death? Death is the most fucking real. You should write about death. That's what you should write about. Explore that. Death."[6]

Even more so than "cultural criticism" and various environmental concerns, that is, what Ray perceives to be the ultimate "real" subject matter is death. That juxtaposition, between intimacy—here trivialized—and death—here elevated, draws a clear line between themes that are worthy of exploration and those that are not. For Hannah, however, intimacy is a major issue, as she points out, implicitly endorsing the notion that relationships and friendships encompass profundities interesting enough to explore. Ray's criticism is nevertheless so disorienting for her, and, coupled with others' criticism, eventually leads her to present a different piece at the reading—an essay that fittingly focuses on death.

The division between "worthy" and "unworthy" themes thus overcomes Hannah's initial creative drive and she ostensibly abandons the "trivial" subject matter of intimacy in favor of the "real" subject matter of death. Still, Hannah's death-related story in "Leave Me Alone" does not delineate an existential study of the human condition vis-à-vis mortality. It rather unfolds the specificities of the protagonist's experience when a boy she had met in a chat room died, and the brief reading that is presented in the episode (only the first few sentences of the essay are represented on screen) is not at all devoid of "trivial" details: "I met Igor online in a chat room for fans of an obscure punk band my vegan friend Marina liked. Igor's screen name was 'pyro000,' which belied a level of articulation unusual for an Internet boyfriend. So he became my Internet boyfriend for six blissful months, until his friend IM'd me to say that he had died. Died."[7] Though Hannah reiterates, perhaps for dramatic effect, the fact that her boyfriend has died, the majority of the exposition features seemingly mundane details, far removed from the "real" seriousness that a theme such as death seems to require. Most of the excerpt consists of mapping the strain of emotional attachments that led the narrator to Igor, focusing on her friend Marina—including Marina's diet and her musical preferences—in much greater detail than on the circumstances of Igor's death.[8]

Even when addressing the serious issue of death, that is, Hannah does so as supplement to that which is considered trivial, rather than as the nucleus of the text, thereby calling attention to the so-called trivial, in this case popular culture and intricacies of friendships and relationships. Maša Grdešić notes that the "Leave Me Alone" story line regarding Hannah's reading posits as its theme the triviality of Hannah's essays as well as the triviality of the show itself, but also refers to the status of women's (popular) culture in general. Women's popular culture has been marginalized and criticized as aesthetically less valuable, trivial, and sentimental from the perspective of "high" culture and "masculine" popular culture, and also as apolitical from the standpoint of feminist criticism.[9]

Bearing on Charlotte Brunsdon,[10] Grdešić addresses the fact that the perception of an issue such as intimacy as trivial (opposite the issue of death) is reflected in the criticism both against *Girls* in particular and against artifacts of women's culture in general,[11] corresponding with the classification of both Hannah's and Dunham's texts as focusing on the trivial.[12]

A similar notion arises in *A Room of One's Own*, in which Virginia Woolf notes that women's stories are culturally tagged as trivial:

> Speaking crudely, football and sport are "important"; the worship of fashion, the buying of clothes "trivial". And these values are inevitably transferred from life to fiction. This is an important book, the critic assumes, because it deals with war. This is an insignificant book because it deals with the feelings of women in a drawing-room. A scene in a battle-field is more important than a scene in a shop—everywhere and much more subtly the difference of value persists.[13]

Drawing on Woolf's highlighting of the perception of women's narratives as trivial, Judy Little notes that in the writing of Barbara Pym, "the large event or the narrative material (deaths, marriages) that could provide a novel with a more conventional structure, a big, mythic discourse, and perhaps a more recognizable moral significance, are sidestepped."[14] Pym, that is, as Little points out, bypasses "large events" that might reflect "a more recognizable moral significance," in favor of the commonplace, the trivial that "does not glow."[15] Seeing as "the trivial, by definition, attempts to signify something that is insignificant,"[16] Little argues that the "ideology of the trivial is that it has no significant ideology, belongs to no master narrative, no great codes of quest or romance, and no *sermo patrius*."[17]

The representation of the trivial thus opens up the possibility to envisage an escape from the ideology of the master narrative, and in keeping with the classification of artifacts of women's culture as trivial, one could say that representation of that which is considered trivial in fact offers an escape from patriarchal order—namely from the master narrative that exclude women. In other words, by nontraditionally placing the "trivial" in the foreground of the narrative, a text refuses to perpetuate textual conventions that vilipend women's stories. Correspondingly, *Girls*'s resolve to represent that which is considered trivial and insist on stories that deal "with the feelings of women"[18] is a form of feminist resistance, in its "bringing to the fore some of the major issues of feminist media and cultural studies."[19] More so than that, though, the way in which *Girls* represents the "trivial" becomes an apparatus of feminist politics in and of itself, as the series does not merely sidestep the "large events," as Little asserts that the work of Pym does. *Girls* does depict traditionally "important" or "real" themes, but it does so in a way that in fact uses the "important" and the "real" as vehicles to explore the feelings of women, rather than as subject matters that are explored on their own merits.

As can be seen in the episode "Leave Me Alone," death (which is "the most fucking real"[20]) is actually used—both diegetically and hypodiegetically—as a device through which various forms of intimacy ("what in the world could be more trivial than intimacy?"[21]) are explored. The "real," that is, is used as means to the "trivial," and not for its own sake. That mechanism, of using death (representative of the "real") as a vehicle that carries the exploration of intimacy (representative of the "trivial") is further employed in *Girls*'s third season's fourth episode, "Dead Inside."[22] Most of the story lines in the aptly titled episode are in one way or another related to death—both via the story arc surrounding the passing of David Pressler-Goings, who was the editor of Hannah's e-book, and via the realization of Jessa, Hannah's friend, that a friend she was told had died is in fact alive.

In a way, it seems that "Dead Inside" is a reboot of Hannah's essay excerpt in "Leave Me Alone," as it applies the same instrumentalization of death from theme to vehicle and uses death as a literary device through which to explore intimacies. After finding out that her editor has died, Hannah tells the news of his death to her friend Jessa, in a manner that echoes her narration of Igor's death. "It's just so insane," she tells Jessa about David: "we had a meeting, and then he had to reschedule the meeting, because he was dead [. . .] and that's why he couldn't come."[23] The reiteration of the mere fact of someone's death rather than a focus on the meanings of it, as in the case of the telling of both David's and Igor's deaths, seems to transfigure the reiterated fact into a rhetorical device, the main significance of which is to generate emphasis. In both cases, that is, Hannah seems to instrumentalize death into a rhetorical device—to promote the classification of the text in which death is represented as valuable—rather than examine the theme of death as the subject of the story. She does not sidestep death; she steps right into it, but then harnesses its powers in furtherance of other, more "trivial" stories.

Correspondingly, David's death becomes a device through which the episode looks into Hannah's relationship with her boyfriend Adam and how each of them perceives their relationship's function in his or her life. It also serves to reveal Hannah's passion for her work, and the potential clash between her commitment to her writing and her investment in her relationship. Moreover, David's death operates as a catalyst for the episode's second death-related story line, driving Jessa to examine her bond with a friend whom she thought had died, which in turn catapults her to examine herself and her attachments, after realizing she was told her friend had died so as to keep her and her toxicity away.

That instrumentalization of death, from theme to device, is epitomized in one of the scenes in "Dead Inside," a sequence that actually situates the occurrence in the realm of death—a cemetery—but nonetheless enacts a scene rife with "trivialities." Grappling with the effects David's death has on her relationships, Hannah runs into Caroline, Adam's sister, who invites her and her downstairs neighbor Laird to her "afternoon constitutional," in the course of which the three arrive, ostensibly randomly, at a local cemetery. In the cemetery, they run around, play catch with a bottle in which Laird's dead turtle lies, climb on tombstones, and do cartwheels along the cemetery lanes. The scene thus literally uses the place of death to carry a narrative of frivolity.

After frolicking, Hannah, Caroline, and Laird rest among the graves, and Caroline tells a story about her and Adam's cousin, who died of muscular dystrophy when she was twelve years old—a story she then confesses to have made up. The made-up, albeit highly intricate story about the fake cousin Margaret, amid gravestones and flowerbeds, is again not staged for the sake of debating the decay of the body or the fear of mortality, but rather for the sake of studying the value of honesty in relationships and the signification of sensitivity, as the story is not only concocted by Caroline to test Hannah's response, but is also later retold by Hannah, as she recounts it to Adam, this time as the bearer of the lie. Here, again, death serves as vehicle for the study of the trivialized "feelings of women."[24]

Hence, as Hannah's unfolding of the story of Igor's death is in fact a tale of intimacy that instrumentalizes death, so is her experience of David's death in fact employed to delve into the minutiae of intimacies. Both "Leave Me Alone" and "Dead Inside" thus resist expectations of what a serious portrayal of human perception of mortality should be, as the characters indulge in the fake, the marginalized, and the improper, rather than express reverence or awe in the face of death.[25] The instrumentalization mechanism in fact reverses narrative conventions that use the "trivial" as garnish to more "substantial" literary explorations, by using "real" subject matter as curtain raiser before the "trivialities" take center stage.

Death is only one example of an "important" theme used in *Girls* as an instrument for the foregrounding of "trivial" stories of women's feelings, and was used here as a model due to the text's classification of death as the most "real" of themes.[26] *Girls* instrumentalizes various themes that are culturally championed en route celebrating themes that are culturally trivialized. Jessa's attempt to deal with her drug abuse in a rehab center is not represented as a tale of battling addiction, but rather as an allegory of the complexities of women's friendships.[27] Social hierarchies in Hannah's workplace are not explored as paradigms of struggle for authority, but rather work to generate talk of sexual harassment vis-à-vis her conduct with her boss and sexual power dynamics vis-à-vis her relationship with Adam.[28] Adam's physical injury is not unfolded as an account on the vulnerability of the body, but rather serves as catalyst for exploring the aches of his and Hannah's break-up.[29] Echoing Ray's first season classification of "real" issues, then, *Girls* represents instances of potential cultural criticism, but uses them as vehicles to explore women's issues.

The reversal utilized by *Girls* thus offers feminist resistance to the marginalization of stories about women and their feelings. That resistance works to expose the fact that the category of triviality is a gendered construct and exposes its formulation as such. By using traditionally "important" themes as instruments for destabilizing a "symbolic order that polices and reinforces gender hierarchy and identity,"[30] *Girls* in fact calls into question normalized social constructs, their gender-based classification, and "the criteria that [. . .] determine the artistic and social merit of creative expressions."[31] I thus argue that *Girls*'s cultural and feminist significance stems from, among other things, its resistance to the dismissal of that which is considered feminine, and its foregrounding of marginalized and trivialized issues in women's lives, insisting that the "feelings of women"[32] matter.

NOTES

1. See Anna Holmes's "The Age of Girlfriends," *The New Yorker*, July 6, 2012, accessed October, 23, http://www.newyorker.com/books/page-turner/the-age-of-girlfriends; and Neil Drumming's "'Girls' grow up: Lena Dunham wrestles with reality," *Salon*, January 9, 2014, accessed October 23, 2014, http://www.salon.com/2014/01/09/girls_grow_up_lena_dunham_wrestles_with_reality.

2. *Girls*, "I Get Ideas" (2:2), HBO, January 20, 2013.

3. Malcolm Gamson, *Freaks Talk Back: Tabloid Talk Shows and Sexual Nonconformity* (Chicago: University of Chicago Press, 1998), 6.

4. HBO, June 10, 2012.

5. *Girls*, "Leave Me Alone" (1:9).

6. Ibid.

7. Ibid.

8. In Dunham's book, a chapter titled "Igor: Or, My Internet Boyfriend Died and So Can Yours," tells a similar story, of meeting Igor in a chat room, and later hearing he passed away. Though the book's version of the narrative is a much extended one, compared to the excerpt presented in the fictionalized televisual reading, Igor similarly appears at a later stage in the story, rather than in its beginning (despite him being the subject of the chapter), following a detailed account of how Dunham's school, and later parents, purchased computers, and a description of female friends sharing chatroom experiences. Lena Dunham, *Not That Kind of Girl* (New York: Random House, 2014), 24–32.

9. Maša Grdešić, "'I'm Not the Ladies!': Metatextual Commentary in *Girls*," *Feminist Media Studies* 13, no. 2 (2013): 357.

10. Brunsdon notes that "high culture" has been repudiating "mass culture," dismissing artifacts of "women's culture," such as soap opera and romance, as "trash." *The Feminist, the Housewife, and the Soap Opera* (Oxford: Oxford University Press, 2000), 24.

11. Both Brunsdon and Grdešić assert not only that masculine high culture has been dismissing women's popular culture, but also that feminist criticism has been denouncing products of women's popular culture as "apolitical" (Grdešić, 357) or "trash," (Brunsdon, 24). As I intend to demonstrate, however, the popular culture text *Girls* promotes its own brand of feminist politics.

12. In her book, Dunham explicitly states her admiration for women's insistence on telling their trivialized stories, noting "There is nothing gutsier to me than a person announcing that their story is one that deserves to be told, especially if that person is a woman. As hard as we have worked and as far as we have come, there are still so many forces conspiring to tell women that our concerns are petty, our opinions aren't needed, that we lack the gravitas necessary for our stories to matter. That personal writing by women is no more than an exercise in vanity and that we should appreciate this new world for women, sit down, and shut up." Dunham, *Not That Kind of Girl*, xvi.

13. Virginia Woolf, *A Room of One's Own* (London: Penguin Books, 2000 [1928]), 74.

14. Judy Little, *The Experimental Self: Dialogic Subjectivity in Woolf, Pym, and Brooke-Rose* (Carbondale: Southern Illinois UP, 1996), 86.

15. Ibid, 85.

16. Ibid, 76.

17. Ibid, 76.

18. Woolf, 74.

19. Grdešić, 358.

20. *Girls*, "Leave Me Alone" (1:9).

21. Ibid.

22. *Girls*, "Dead Inside" (3:4), HBO, January 26, 2014.

23. Ibid.

24. Woolf, 74.

25. A representative example of media criticism regarding the women's conduct when faced with death in "Dead Inside" can be seen in Aly Semigran's "*Girls*: 'Dead Inside,' the Most Appropriately Titled Episode Yet" in *Televeisionwithoutpity*, January 27, 2014, accessed June 30, 2014, http://www.televisionwithoutpity.com/telefile/girls-file/2014/01/girls-dead-inside-the-most-appropriately-titled-episode-yet.

26. *Girls*, "Leave Me Alone" (1:9).

27. *Girls*, "Truth or Dare" (3.2), HBO, January 12, 2014.

28. *Girls*, "Hannah's Diary" (1.4), HBO, May 6, 2012.

29. *Girls*, "It's About Time" (2.1), HBO, January 13, 2013.

30. Drucilla Cornell, in Pheng Cheah et al., "The Future of Sexual Difference: An Interview with Judith Butler and Drucilla Cornell," *Diacritics* 28, no. 1 (Irigaray and the Political Future of Sexual Difference, Spring 1998): 24.

31. Lana F. Rakow, "Feminist Approaches to Popular Culture: Giving Patriarchy Its Due," *Feminist Critiques of Popular Culture: A Special Issue of the Journal Communication* 9, no. 1 (1986): 32.

32. Woolf, *A Room of One's Own*, 74.

BIBLIOGRAPHY

Brunsdon, Charlotte. *The Feminist, the Housewife, and the Soap Opera*. Oxford: Oxford University Press, 2000.

Cheah, Pheng, Elizabeth Grosz, Judith Butler, and Drucilla Cornell. "The Future of Sexual Difference: An Interview with Judith Butler and Drucilla Cornell." *Diacritics* 28, no. 1 (Irigaray and the Political Future of Sexual Difference, Spring 1998): 19–42.

Dunham, Lena. *Not That Kind of Girl*. New York: Random House, 2014.

Gamson, Joshua. *Freaks Talk Back: Tabloid Talk Shows and Sexual Nonconformity*. Chicago: University of Chicago Press, 1998.

Grdešić, Maša. "'I'm Not the Ladies!': Metatextual Commentary in *Girls*." *Feminist Media Studies* 13, no. 2, (2013): 355–58.

Little, Judy. *The Experimental Self: Dialogic Subjectivity in Woolf, Pym, and Brooke-Rose*. Carbondale: Southern Illinois UP, 1996.

Rakow, Lana F. "Feminist Approaches to Popular Culture: Giving Patriarchy Its Due." *Feminist Critiques of Popular Culture: A Special Issue of the Journal Communication* 9, no. 1 (1986): 19–42.

Woolf, Virginia. *A Room of One's Own*. London: Penguin Books, 2000 (1928).

Chapter Five

Falling from Pedestals: Dunham's Cracked *Girls* and Boys

Marc Edward Shaw

If you are reading this book, then you probably already know that actor James Franco does not identify with HBO's *Girls* ("A Dude's Take on Girls," *Huffington Post*, 2012).[1] Even though I feel differently than Franco, I could not hold that against him recently as I watched his commercial—"The Fall"—for the new Verizon/Motorola Droid Turbo phone.[2] Have you seen it? It's funny, sexy, and effective, *but* it's also a one-minute, popular culture reminder of the omnipresent power of hegemonic, corporate masculinities in our late capitalist age.

Franco—looking perfectly suave in a white shirt, tie, and suit—attends a New York City rooftop party one evening with a beautiful date. But conflict has arisen: his date's red scarf flies away and is now, as the commercial begins, perched on a gargoyle at the end of the roof. Like any good date, Franco must go after that red scarf (is that symbolism, or is sometimes a red scarf just a scarf?). "No worries," he coolly takes control, "I've got this." He inches along the ledge, reaching for the scarf, while his date protests that it's not worth it. We see his black shoe slip from the ledge and he falls, the red scarf flying away in the night wind. Oh no, James Franco is going to die! But, no, wait . . . now he's falling backwards, and there is a shift in mood—the tension is all gone. Franco is in slow motion, swimming in the air, while now a catchy song playing in the background reminds us "I've got all the time in the world."[3] Quicker than you can say "Motorola-Droid-Turbo-with-unlimited-Verizon-plan" Franco has whipped out his phone, and time has slowed down! He's like a superhero now (probably Spiderman, but Harry Osborn may disagree) in total control of the elements around him. Franco's fall in slow motion is a place we all want to be: 100 percent relaxed, 100 percent in control, opening different apps: to navigate past another gargoyle statue, to find a Chinese restaurant below, to text his date a date update, and to communicate with the Chinese-speaking restaurant employee. All is well, as Franco lands in his suit, charges his phone with turbo speed in the restaurant, greets his date who he texted, and, finally, with a coy smile, hands her the red scarf. It's on. Adventure, chivalry, sex, technology, super powers— it's a one-minute blockbuster, ladies and gentlemen.

Franco is *The Man*—a hyper-masculine, idealized construction appropriated by corporations to sell us stuff: the Sexiest Man Alive with a sales pitch.[4] Like the scarf in the wind, the masculine ideal he peddles flies away from our (the consumers) grasp, seemingly obtainable, but always out of reach. In "The Fall" that ideal is young, wealthy, handsome, urban, tech-savvy, white, straight, and famous. One or two of those listed descriptors might change, but marketers rarely stray far from their formula. Judith Kegan Gardiner reminds us what is at stake when we spotlight Franco's gendered position or identify aspects of gender in the *Girls*'s male characters: "When masculinity is the object of feminist study, the customary specular relationship of subject and object between a male gaze and female body is reversed."[5] That work is incomplete if we only focus on alternative masculinities in *Girls* (non-heteronormative, non-white, etc.); as much as possible we want to grab the opportunity to reveal dominant positions that often remain unnoticed. Sally Robinson emphasizes this when she advocates that an approach like that, focusing only on non-dominant masculinities

> [l]eaves dominant masculinity free of scrutiny and [therefore] still defining the field of the masculine. It is for this reason scholars interested in deconstructing *dominant* masculinity—straight, white, middle-class masculinity—have recently begun to argue that by making hegemonic masculinity visible we begin to erode its power. The logic of this position is that while over the past three decades scholars have focused attention on women, femininity, and female sexuality, little attention has been paid to men, masculinity, and male sexuality as constructs and contingent historical fictions. This freedom from scrutiny has enabled the white, middle-class, masculine norm to remain invisible, natural, and thus unchallenged.[6]

To emphasize that Franco is not just a default normal guy in the commercial but a construction too defies the dominant social reality. He is not merely "a dude" as he names himself in his *Girls* essay title.

Like most commercials, "The Fall" encourages us to want. Corporations try to guide our body practices (what we do with our selves) toward their idea of prescriptive happiness. They show us ways of doing things, insinuate how to be more masculine, feminine, likeable. We want that urban chic lifestyle (location, clothes, products, events). We want the looks. We want the phone (its case has Kevlar fibers!). We want the woman, Franco, or both. We want to embody the idealized (masculine) cool to which none of us measures up. Yes, we know this sixty-second, phone-pushing movie is a big joke (no one can fall that many stories and live); we admire its creativity, but the punchline still stings a bit. Our gender identities are "closely tied to the economic circumstances in which they are formed and re-formed. [. . .] [But, at the end of it all,] what strain is placed on men and women as workers, consumers, breadwinners," roommates, and partners?[7] "How does gender adjust to economic influences or financial troubles? And more generally, how does the workplace reconfigure gender identity? How does late capitalism regulate sexuality or market specific gender possibilities?"[8] Harry Brod reminds us that "gender is a relationship of power and hierarchy between individuals and not the property of single individuals."[9] So how do masculinities and femininities relate in *Girls*?

One reason to celebrate *Girls*'s existence on our TV screens is that it becomes a weekly questioning of hegemonic gender practices. It is *Girls*, but it could be titled *Girls . . . ?* with a big question mark included in the title. Or *Girls and Boys?* Or *Women and Men?* The series' written/enacted masculinities and femininities are questioning, changing, and forever wondering what is possible in the fluid present. With *Girls*, are you not slightly tempted to belt out Britney Spears's pop ode to liminality: "I'm not a girl, not yet a woman / All I need is time / [. . .] While I'm in between"?[10] In the pilot's first scene, Hannah's parents cut her off financially, thrusting her into the realities of a capitalist New York City in the early twenty-first century. She grows from girlhood to womanhood in that moment, *perhaps*, but the entire series is Hannah learning about the different possibilities of her selves. She steals money meant for the hotel maid; she dominates Adam into giving her cab money and pizza (lording over him to his delight). This is how she grows up.

These girls *inside* Hannah are possibilities of identity that the series cannot avoid exploring: her career, relationships, loves, hopes, ways of talking, eating, dressing—being, becoming. The same can be said for every character in *Girls*, both male and female. To identify gender in this manner is a reaffirming feminist act consistent with Dunham's stated feminist aims: to make her audience aware of the doings and undoings within the genderscape. It adds to *Girls* that the characters are mostly in their twenties; none of them has anything figured out fully yet—they are "in between" as far as their journey to adulthood. But, that does not mean that only twenty somethings have evolving identities: several older characters (Jeff, Ray, Laird) transform before our eyes. We see that gender formation is always a becoming. Like a television series that has unlimited season renewals, our becoming a man or a woman can be forever changing.

An appropriate theoretical touchstone for *Girls*, *The Men and the Boys* by R. W. Connell, reminds us that "in western popular culture, the media represents the most honoured or desired [the hegemonic]."[11] But, as Connell continues, "masculinities don't sit side-by-side, they relate."[12] They create a network of relations of hierarchy: "some subordinated, others dominant." But "properly handled, the theorized life history," and we might say fictional character history here too for our purposes, "can be a powerful tool for the study of social structures and their dynamics as they impinge on personal life and are reconstituted by personal action."[13] Harry Brod adds that "Literary studies cannot be expected to give the whole 'truth' about manhood in relation to a particular social, economic, racial-ethnic environment, [. . .] but they can offer valuable insights into areas for further, potentially corroborating research by [social scientists]."[14] There are truths to be unmined in the dominant and the subordinate, the strong and the weak, and the array of positionings in between.

Dunham recognizes human imperfection, and unlike a corporation's calculated campaign, she lets her characters flail and fail and fall without any safety app to stop injuries. And not just for kicks and giggles: she's writing them thus to see the possibilities of who they are. George Bernard Shaw (1856–1950), whose play *Major Barbara* (1905) is Adam's Broadway debut in season 3, allowed his female characters to become like real human beings with checkered pasts and presents. Some of the most coveted roles for female actors even today are Shavian creations. In fact, like his character, Adam Driver's (Adam) Broadway debut was in a George Bernard Shaw play, *Mrs. Warren's Profession* (Roundabout Theatre, 2010), with the venerable Cherry Jones and Sally Hawkins as the two generations of Warren women. Mrs. Warren's profession is a high-priced escort/madam, and her daughter Kitty, on finding out this truth, cuts herself off completely from her mother because she no longer wants to be funded by that livelihood. It can be an electrifying play with an ending that feels like Ibsen's Nora in *A Doll's House* (1879) letting go of her past and her family—"the door slam heard 'round the world." In the *New York Times*, theater critic Ben Brantley introduces and then quotes Shaw in making this point and reminds us of realism as a powerful dramatic tradition and of the protofeminist ideas that pushed boundaries over a century ago in Europe:

> [I]t is the self-assertive, protofeminist, sexually predatory Woman, who earns her capital W, who is most responsible for wrenching Shaw's plays off the speaker's podium. *"No male writer born in the 19th century outside Norway and Sweden did more to knock Woman off her pedestal and plant her on the solid earth than I,"* said Shaw, with a respectful nod to Ibsen and Strindberg. That solid earth, however, is usually on a mountaintop. Shaw regarded the sexual vitality of women—nature's vehicles, after all, for passing on the life force—with a mix of adoration and terror that made them monumental. Like

his own Henry Higgins with Eliza Doolittle, Shaw couldn't quite control his female characters once he set them on their paths to glory. Played by the right performers, they vibrate, radiate and crush the mere men in their paths. [15]

Dunham lets girls and boys fall off their pedestals. When Adam texts a photograph of his penis to Hannah, and quickly follows that by saying it was not meant for her, he falls off a pedestal. It's a complicated, potentially ugly, gasp-inducing moment: he is either honest, and a privates-forwarding play-boy, or dishonest and playing head games with Hannah. This must be the final straw for Adam, we think. How can Hannah stand for this? Marnie, with Charlie nearby, sees the photo and calls Adam a "noted psychopath," encouraging Hannah to ignore him. Of course Hannah will! But, no, Hannah takes off her shirt and starts sending a naked selfie back. Hannah's fall might be further, her humiliation greater, or not: it all might be a spot of digital fun. Like Shaw, I feel adoration and terror.

There is this moment as Franco falls, about twenty seconds into the commercial. Franco rotates in the air, and in the background we see a couple who are staring out of their apartment window. The man's got a beard, a bit disheveled, not dressed too fancy; the woman looks comfortable, like she is home for the night. They look not finely quaffed, not models, normal. But to say they are *normal* is loaded with issues of class and race and shows a definite privileged position: they are white, (upper) middle class, with enough money to live in a decent apartment in New York City. Still, they were not invited to the party on the roof. Like us, these spectators marvel at James Franco defying science with his phone. In those ways, in that they are *not*-Franco in this moment, they are us. Whoever you are reading this. The couple watches Franco, perfection-in-motion, pass by from their dinner table, interrupting their argument about the rent or weekend plans. The window is their frame; the television screen is our frame. But we're all suddenly boxed in to the same realization of our falling short of that dominant corporate ideal. Adam, Hannah, Ray, us, we are not starring as superhumans in a Droid commercial. (I can only imagine Adam and Hannah using the Droid Turbo to film role-playing exploits, something unsuitable even for HBO.

The Man and A Dude

Perhaps it is not a big surprise, then, that James Franco does not identify with *Girls,* or that he calls the men on the program: "the biggest bunch of losers I've ever seen." [16] In the *Huffington Post* article, "A Dude's Take on *Girls*," Franco reverts to the stereotypical schoolyard bully role who positions himself as superior to the rest of his class. He may title himself the benign "dude," but he calls the others names: "drip" (Charlie), "wussy hipsters" (anyone Jessa dates), "struggling male idiots" (general insult), and "the shirtless dude who talks funny" (Adam). It is saddening that Franco can no longer see the truth or appeal in Dunham's "drips" and "idiots," especially since he got his first acting break in Judd Apatow's *Freaks and Geeks* series. Apatow, of course, is a producer on *Girls*, and bolstered Dunham's career after seeing her film *Tiny Furniture* (2010). Apatow came under scrutiny for focusing too much on male-heavy, laddish projects like *Anchorman*, *40 Year Old Virgin*, *Knocked Up* and *Superbad*; but with *Bridesmaids*, *Girls* and *Trainwreck* (film written by Amy Schumer [2015]), we can see Apatow as evolving somewhat.[17] James Franco should listen to John Cameron Mitchell (who plays Hannah's literary manager, David Pressler-Goings), creator of the title character in the musical *Hedwig and the Angry Inch*, who sings on "Midnight Radio" that all the "misfits and losers" and "strange rock and rollers" are "doing alright," "so hold on to each other / you gotta hold on tonight."[18] There's a cachet in outsider status too, but Franco must not see the possibilities.

To his absolute credit, Franco has played an impressive array of characters that cover a wide range of masculinities in films from *James Dean* to *Spiderman* to *Pineapple Express* to *Milk* and *Howl*. But this time he cannot identify with Dunham/Apatow's losers, and links them to a limiting binary—a males-versus-females, HBO series conspiracy theory in which all unlikable characters are revenge for stereotypes of seasons gone by:

> I know this sorry representation of men is fair payback for the endless parade of airheaded women on the West Coast male counterpart to *Girls*, *Entourage*, which in turn was fair payback for the cast of male dorks on *Sex in the City*. (They seemed like dorks to me, at least, on the occasions when my ex-girlfriend tuned in while I happened to be around.)[19]

Franco is wrong because Dunham's representations of men are not "sorry." At times their actions may be sorry or shameful or disgusting or sweet. They fall off their pedestals. Adam becomes enraged at a passing car that almost hits Hannah and him at a crosswalk. In that moment, Adam seems dangerous, on edge, temperamental. Later that night, he asks forgiveness by plastering dozens of posters that read "SORRY" on a Williamsburg wall. The apologies are for the driver he confronted, but also the "sorry representation," to recycle Franco's phrase, is for Hannah. Masculinity or femininity is not a solid, unchanging construction like a "drip" or a "dork." Yes, we all label each other—the title of the episode with Adam's postering is "Weirdoes Need Girlfriends Too"—but Dunham and cast knock weirdoes off their weirdo pedestals by giving them pathos and respect and humanity. "An individual does not guard one definitive gender position: from moment to moment, forces re-dictate, replace, and reimagine its reconstructing."[20] And that's the reality that Dunham and her fellow creators (actors, writers, casting agents) have created—one in which characters are human, dorks and all. In the pilot we hear Hannah talk a few times about Gustave Flaubert, the great novelist of literary realism. Flaubert keeps us intrigued via the depth of detail he gives us. Although perhaps Dunham is guiding me towards this compliment by mentioning Flaubert in her first episode (much like calling herself "a voice of her generation"), it fits to an extent. Her words and gaze capture the details and complexity of her subjects.

We are not here to judge whether Adam, Charlie, or Hannah's dad is the biggest winner or loser we have ever seen. Instead, in what ways do Dunham's creations, possible masculinities and femininities, interrelate and react in key moments? And what specific gendered choices do the actors-as-creators add to the series? Franco gives Dunham the benefit of the doubt that her female characters have just as many "flaws as the guys."[21] But, in his essay's final lines, he cannot resist imagining bifurcated camps, with Dunham and her *Girls* creative team hell-bent on making women victorious (and/or seek revenge for *Entourage*): "[T]he twist is twofold: we get to hear the girls' insider conversations, so we side with them against the men."[22] I can only speak from my own personal reaction to the series, but I never once sided with any group in *Girls*. Yes, at first we wonder about Adam and his motives, but we are also left scratching our heads at how Hannah, Marnie, and Jessa act. I yell "nooo" at Hannah for texting Adam back or showing up at his doorstep more than I side with her *against* Adam. How can we fully take Marnie's "side" when she treats Charlie so poorly in the initial episodes? It is more likely that we see them both in need of a fresh start, perhaps, and not in competitive terms as Franco infers. We want what is best and good for them, and our empathy is not finite or based on a duel.

An analysis benefits from a more nuanced approach to moments and ideas in the program. Sally Robinson asserts that

> To study masculinity, and to study it in relation to systems of power, requires that we develop a more nuanced and sophisticated conceptualization of complicity and resistance. How to think of complicity and resistance together—not from the position of women, but from the position of men? At what moments, with what effects, do men actively resist performing the dominant fictions of masculinity, and does this resistance necessarily mean that men opt out of male empowerment?[23]

There are moments in *Girls* where we can unpack the nuance, complicity, and resistance that Robinson describes. Franco ends his essay with suspicion because he does not want to see the nuance in *Girls*: "Lena is the ultimate creator, so no matter what she puts the girls through, she is always in control." Is Franco afraid of having a young woman in control? He continues: "Her name is always at the end, where it says 'Created by.' They say living well is the best revenge, but sometimes writing well is even better." I could be wrong, but he comes off as jealous. After all, as Franco puts it, "A young woman who does it all on a show that is on everyone's lips—that sounds pretty great to me." Yes, it does. So let's have, in Robinson's words, a more nuanced "conceptualization of complicity and resistance" of noting the "dominant fictions of masculinity," by looking at *Girls* in depth. Dunham's show contains awareness about gender, noticeably in the third episode when her former boyfriend, Elijah, comes out as gay. If you'll recall, Hannah tries to keep a brave face, but she takes it personally as she asks him if he was attracted to men when they were together. Elijah eventually admits that he was attracted to a certain "handsomeness" in Hannah that made it work. This exchange captures the idea of female masculinities, and masculinities as a construction—detaching gendering (handsome masculine) from the sex (Hannah's vagina is a frequent topic of discussion considering all the STD talk in this episode). "Female masculinity actually affords us a glimpse of how masculinity is constructed *as masculinity*," says Judith Halberstam in her groundbreaking work.[24] "[T]he shapes and forms of modern masculinity are best showcased within female masculinity," and we see this as Hannah's "[m]asculinity does not need to be committed" or "linked to maleness."[25] Furthermore, after a crescendoing back-and-forth about STDs, their past, and Hannah's lack of gaydar, she brings up his new "fruity little voice" and his scarf, and his tone and mannerisms—all enacted aspects of gender. Elijah declares he is his "authentic self," which adds to the humor and complexity. Later in the season, the seventh episode is especially worth exploring in terms of gender, focusing on the masculinities/feminities and the relationships that shift over time, where crackcidents will always happen.

"The Kind of Man That You Are": Redefining Masculinities in Bushwick

At the end of "Welcome to Bushwick: aka The Crackcident" (episode 1.7), Marnie confronts Adam, telling him to get away from Hannah. Marnie's rescue is ill-timed and uninformed, threatening to press charges against Adam because of his "sick instincts" and announcing that she wants everyone to know "about the kind of man that you are!" This moment is jarring because Adam and Hannah are having perhaps their most intimate, nuanced, and heartfelt conversation of the show's run so far, about alcoholism, sex addiction, and their relationship expectations. The pair are off the pedestal, hearts open. Then Marnie arrives, reducing Adam the man, in all that complexity, to criminal, pervert, or abuser. She cannot see the forest, only one imagined crooked tree.

Marnie has had experience so far with this sort of reduction of men to a single masculine status. Pathetic Charlie gets branded, by her, to the part of "creepy uncle" whenever he touches her (episode 1.1). Charlie's trajectory in the whole first season is as the anti-Adam. There's a definite Adam/Charlie chiastic binary that develops. While a whole plot strand exists around Adam's penis, Charlie is branded a "vagina" in Hannah's diary. Charlie marvels at the photo of Adam's penis, at its size and saying he could club baby seals with it. Of course this is an exaggerated signifier of *The Man* status, but cleverly, how do things evolve? Charlie moves up the traditional masculinities ladder as he has success with his app. He's got an app worthy of James Franco's phone. He's rich and Marnie wants that signifier. By Jessa's wedding, however, Adam gets too close too fast—he's moved by the love there—and Hannah insinuates that she does not want Adam to be the Charlie to her Marnie.

Before we see Marnie in Bushwick, we have also seen her deal with the pompous artist Booth Jonathan when he corners Marnie against the Highline security fence, reminding her that he is the ultimate artistic creation, and perhaps she cannot handle this much man: "The first time I fuck you, I might scare you a little. Because I'm a man, and I know how to do things" (episode 1.3). Because Dunham casts Lonely Island comedian Jorma Taccone as Booth Jonathan, we cannot take his promises without a smile or half a laugh—thus resisting the dominant form of masculinities that the character embodies/exudes/performs. Booth's self-promotion to *The Man* status—essentially putting himself at the top of any heap when it comes to masculine dominance, with all that sexual knowledge—is indeed comedy gold, and puts a pin in the overinflated MAN. From the beginning Booth's character is over the top. When they first meet, he cockily tells Marnie to "try and give less of a shit" when she tells him she's a fan of his artwork. In her mind at that time, he is everything Charlie her boyfriend is not. So while we might laugh at the portrayal, Marnie is fully aroused sexually, and after their Highline encounter she masturbates to, what we can imagine, are mental portraits of the artist as *The Man*. Dunham does not let the story end there however; the climactic punchline is coming. When the two eventually consummate their relationship in the second season, the results are underwhelming. His sexual prowess, and the *Kama Sutra*-esque position he enacts, "The Starfish," are played with a wink. And the evil-looking doll he brings into the mix is as funny as it is terrifying (as much as the enclosed tower/closet of televisions in which he locks Marnie). One line that was trimmed from the final cut was Booth telling the doll and/or Marnie "I love you, you're horrible."[26] We too feel adoration and terror (to use Brantley's words describing Shaw and his female characters) along with hilarity, disgust, and pathos at this scene. Taccone-within-Booth-Jonathan satirically resists dominant modes of sexuality and gender.

At the beginning of "Welcome to Bushwick: aka The Crackcident," we are welcomed to a part of Brooklyn that hosts a huge party: chaotic, wild, free—according to Jessa's hyperbole: "every single person is coming" . . .

"all of Brooklyn and two-thirds of Manhattan will be there." In other words, this is their entire world, lots of people, and within that revelry, there will be room for shifts in consciousness. Like any Dionysian affair, when mind-altering substances and revelry converge, we will see the characters change. Dionysus is the god of fertility, ecstasy, wine, and theatrical performance (catharsis and epiphany), and in the mythological tradition, he is "twice born" of woman and man, Semele and Zeus, feminine and masculine. As in Euripides's work about Dionysus, *The Bacchae*, the *Girls* revelers leave their usual confines to further discover who they are (but not to a rural location like when the Bacchants leave Thebes to revel and honor Dionysus in their worship). "Welcome to Bushwick" is an invitation to rites of passage in a new place, an altered state from regular being, a chance to pass from child-hood to adulthood for a night or forever. When our characters enter into the Dionysian state, anything goes: transformation, insight, fall from grace. In *The Bacchae*, the revelers perform miracles in Dionysus's name: milk and wine flow from the hills. In Bushwick, the revelers perform and watch Questionable Goods, drink from a keg, drop wine bottles on strangers, get too high from questionable pipes, practice sobriety, dance, fight, run away. And truths are revealed. Hannah gets a boyfriend. Ray sees Shoshanna with new eyes. Jessa draws the line. This *episode*—a Greek word signifying part of the theatrical narrative—adds to the growing gender map for each of the characters.

"Never Tried It on a Real Man Before": Ray and Shoshanna in Bushwick

The titular portmanteau, "Crackcident," wherein Shoshanna accidentally consumes crack cocaine, is not the only crack on display. Many of those cracks that start to show open up explorations in gender identity—how the characters perceive themselves and the others in relation to their masculinities and femininities. Cracks are at the heart of any dramatic structure: how does the character behave under pressure? Will our heroes show weakness, compassion, ignorance? How will their identities shift when the given circumstances change? The crackcident is no coincidental raising of the stakes by Dunham: she wants to get the party started.

We see a crack in Ray's exterior because of his caring for Shoshanna. At the beginning of the episode he is his brash dominant masculine self, yelling at audiences on the microphone from the stage during Questionable Goods's act: "Whoever brought a fucking baby, you don't bring a baby to a party like this! Use your fucking head!" That's Ray. He even resists taking care of Shoshanna at first. But by the end of the episode he is future boyfriend material. Ray forgives Shoshanna for her violent, drug-fueled acts against his private parts. He sees her as quirky and loveable. Zosia Mamet's embodiment of Shoshanna is off-kilter, intense, and naïve all at once; it is a great counterbalance to Alex Karpovsky's Ray: paternal, funny, sweet, awkward, assholish behavior. Gender is always in relation to someone else, and they change together here and in the rest of the season.

The uptight, virginal, cracked-out Shoshanna, under the influence of what she thought was pot, sprints around skirtless, showing off too much of her derriere (a punny crack usually reserved for plumber jokes). But her Bushwick behavior is a real transformation from how we have perceived her in episodes up until now. She has been the one reading the dating books on the rigid standards of how to act, how to get a date, how to keep that boy. Paralyzed by sex, Shoshanna hides in the closet watching Jessa and her ex, intrigued/appalled like Euripides's Pentheus spying on perceived deviance. She wants to leave her girlhood behind but the only one who will almost have sex with her is a friend from a children's summer camp, Matt Kornstein. Does she still see the boy she knew in her mind? When he refuses to have sex with her because she is a virgin, does he still see the girl he knew? Shoshanna's most full contact with the adult-male world is kickboxing self-defense class: she fears potential violence, but also practices it by kicking mattress-covered men.

That's why her crack trip is transformational to her identity. Yes, the wisecrack is there: we crack up at her hyperactive talking and intense antics, but the crack cocaine causes her to bond with Ray in ways she never would normally. Her future, first, real, adult boyfriend acts as Shoshanna's "crack spirit guide" and tries to lead his charge to safety. But for his mostly charitable efforts, he receives a crack between the legs from his new friend. She gets him right in the manhood:

Ray: My balls are throbbing.

Shoshanna: I took this model mugging course and you beat up a guy dressed like a giant mattress to learn self-defense.

Ray: I don't have a mattress okay? And you're ridiculously strong, like inexplicably mutant strong.

Shoshanna: I've really never tried it on a real man before.

Ray: It's an honor to be your first.

Shoshanna: I think it was probably the crack.

Ray: It might have been the crack.

She recognizes Ray as a "real man," and the "never tried it" and "It's an honor to be your first" are saucy foreshadowing to losing her virginity later in the season. We are left questioning how Shoshanna would relate to Ray if she were not high. He's older, unmotivated, not as conventionally attractive. Only last semester, Shoshanna admits, she took a sports therapy class to meet jocks. Ray is the opposite of the jock stereotype we imagine. It's the first step to a new intimacy with a new adult man. Ray's softer than we have seen him in the past. He's not creepy or rapey. She offers to use her sports massage training to massage Ray's groin "in a, like, non-sexual way." There's a wonderful acting moment where Alex Karpovsky plays the slight subtext of Ray not believing his good fortune in this moment. He looks into Shoshanna's eyes to make sure she is as sincere and naïve as she seems. To him, there's no way a groin massage cannot be sexual. This is the start of their trajectory and journey together in which both grow up and mature as adults, Ray taking on more responsibility (moving from "homeless" to general manager of the coffee shop), and Shoshanna passing through so many firsts (sex, love, cheating, . . .).

"I'm that guy": Jeff, Jessa, and Part-Life Crises

If we are going to pass judgment at all, "The Crackcident" reveals widening cracks in Jeff's (Jessa's boss) relationship with his family; Jeff might blame it on Jessa, calling her a "tease"—but by the Bushwick episode's end, Jessa has transformed because of Jeff: "I can't. I can't do this kind of thing anymore," she says. Jessa has more life experience than the other three young ladies, and no longer wants to be objectified at this point in her life (reinforced when she does not want a job in a club/lounge like Marnie gets). Call it a quarter-life reevaluation for Jessa; but for Jeff this is his midlife crisis— the rejection, to some degree, of the traditional male roles of husband, father, breadwinner, and authority figure in the home. Was there a time he fully embraced those roles? Or has he always been a man-boy with his wife, Katherine, pulling the financial weight? The casting choice of James LeGros fits well, with his greying goatee and ponytail, still trying to look cool—he is "that guy" he fears he is. And we are also haunted by memories of other parts LeGros has played in *Point Break* and *Ally McBeal*. He is a tired, fading version of his former selves. Jessa's initial text, giving false hope in lettered form, is a common comic conceit perfected by Shakespeare for one, as in *Twelfth Night* when Malvolio gets his hopes up enough to act impulsively too (cross-gartered yellow stockings, not a bottle of wine to a warehouse).

Dunham lets Jeff be "that guy" despite his own voiced concerns that he might be judged as such. "This is insane. I can't believe I texted you to hang out. Oh, my God. I'm *that guy*. I'm the guy that brings a bottle of wine to a party like this." Jessa picks up on the reference to age: "Well, maybe let's put a pin in your midlife crisis right now and go dance." But maybe there is no crisis. He is horny for Jessa and alone when he sends her the text, "What are you up to?" because Katherine is out of town. Looking back, from the first scene when Jessa and Jeff meet in his home where she babysits his two girls, we observe the subtext of Jeff's desire for Jessa—an effect she has on most heterosexual men. Then we watch Jeff play the cool boss type (Jessa, the sexy nanny type) by offering to smoke pot with her in their first encounter. There's always the uncomfortable question in our minds, what would his wife think of this? And, does unemployed Jeff not have a job because of bad fortune or deep apathy? Although he worries about being reduced to a specific gender stereotype, he never lets that anxiety motivate change or stop his transgressive actions.

This is also a positive "crack" in the solidified routines for Jessa. Maybe in the past this would be normal to have a fling with him. In *The Bacchae*, Pentheus gets his head ripped off by his own mother for spying on the wine-fueled revelries; in Bushwick, Jeff is beat up because Jessa drops the wine bottle on some "crusty punks." When they go to the emergency room, Jeff tries some tired lines on Jessa which she rejects, and Jeff is upset. There is a wonderful acting moment when (Jeff) James LeGros sobs that he's sick and Jessa (Jemima Kirke) looks off into the distance like she would rather be cleaning her bathroom or anything else. Jeff/LeGros looks up with a great desperation and intensity like his whole life hinges on her decision. Jessa deflects his desperation (and sexual invitation) and reduces Jeff to an essential gendering that we are never too sure of from the start: "I liked you better when you were being *the good guy*." Dunham creates a believable character in Jeff, who is fallen from his pedestal, and by showing us his likable daughters and wife Katherine too, our empathies lie with the entire family as a unit. We hope that the daughters don't get dragged down too: it's good drama for the titular *Girls*-becoming-Women to fall from their pedestals in the Shaw tradition, but the actual young girls deserve their childhood. Katherine thanks Jessa for letting her see cracks in her marriage that she's been ignoring, and admits that she's having strange dreams involving all her own family and violent/scatological acts toward Jessa. In the dreams, Jeff is breastfed by Katherine's mother—perhaps Freudian overkill here, but it puts an exclamation mark on Jeff's permanent boyhood. Richard Linklater could still make a movie (in less than twelve years) about Jeff's Peter Pan syndrome.

"Like the original man": The Fall of Adam . . . and Hannah

There's also a crack in Adam's shell as he falls off the pedestal: we discover his alcohol addiction and that he attends Alcoholics Anonymous. Up until now he has been defined as Hannah's crush and sex partner, but in this episode, his mysterious exterior cracks open to new clarity and complexity.

The effect is that by the end of the episode we see Hannah and Adam differently. Their sense of each other evolves together as they become boyfriend and girlfriend—the "genesis" of their newfound life together builds to an Edenic state, watching home movies and cuddling at the beginning of the next episode—love blossoming. By season 1's end, the pairing and thoughts of cohabitating are too intense for Hannah. The closest she can get to official coupling permanency is eating Jessa's wedding cake on her own private (Coney) Island. But, back in Bushwick, Dunham cleverly points us to Adam as the first man: "He does sort of look like the original man" says Jessa. But he also has the crowd of women with him like a Dionysius figure surrounded by Bacchants—and here Adam seems fun and harmless in the glow of black light and a group of wrestling lesbians. Hannah has never seen Adam "with a shirt on" (naked like biblical Adam) or "outside his house," but by removing Adam/Hannah from that natural habitat, they see each other as more than sex toys. Hannah is afraid. But after a hide and seek that lasts half the episode, Hannah and Adam will have their first conversation. Hannah thinks they are going to break up, so she says the cliché "you seem great" that echoes Marnie/Charlie post-break-up ten minutes earlier.

Working through that cliché, the two actors find the most delightful sequence of acting in the entire series. As Hannah accepts defeat, Adam grabs the situation by the elbow (Hannah's), swaying her back and forth like a hipster swing dancer. He spins her around twice, and then holds her body closer to his a bit. It's not sexual like we have seen them before, but it is enough proximity to say without words that she should not leave. It's not sappy though because it is too improvisational and awkward, and the dance music is too upbeat and peppy. The important thing is that Adam takes control of the situation through his movements, and once he knows Hannah is staying to dance with him, he lets his freaky, (anti-)mating dance-moves begin (*not* freaky-deaky like "get your freak on;" freakish in that Adam's moves could be in a show). He burrows around Hannah like a harmless badger. He picks her up and spins her around as she beams with delight. How could anyone pull this scene off but Adam Driver? No other actor could; not Oscar-nominee James Franco or superstar Shia LaBeouf. Could actual icon Daniel Day Lewis? I'm not being facetious. In that scene, Driver simultaneously plays awkward, intense, confident, funny, loving, and vulnerable. It is the best unexpected dance magic I have seen caught on screen since the end of Claire Denis's *Beau Travail* when Denis Lavant simultaneously drops your jaw with his moves and gives deep insight into the character and narrative. Yes, Adam might be leading Hannah in a twenty-second dance that changes their fallen lives forever. It might just be the twenty-second dance of a generation.

NOTES

1. James Franco, "A Dude's Take on *Girls*," *The Huffington Post* (May 30, 2012), accessed November 20, 2014: http://www.huffingtonpost.com/james-franco/girls-hbo-lena-dunham_b_1556078.html.
2. Verizon Wireless, "Droid Turbo, 'The Fall' with James Franco [one-minute version]," *YouTube.com* (October 30, 2014), accessed November 8, 2014.
3. Afie Jurvanen (Bahamas). "All the Time" Bahamas is Afie (album), Brushfire Records, 2014.
4. *Salon.com* named Franco its sexiest man alive, as did *Glamour* (U.K.) magazine. *People* has given Franco an honorable mention.
5. Judith Kegan Gardiner, "Introduction," in *Masculinity Studies and Feminist Theory*, ed. Judith Kegan Gardiner (New York: Columbia UP, 2002), 9.
6. Sally Robinson, "Pedagogy of the Opaque: Teaching Masculinity Studies," in *Masculinity Studies and Feminist Theory*, ed. Judith Kegan Gardiner (New York: Columbia UP, 2002), 147.
7. Marc E. Shaw and Elwood Watson, "Introduction," *Performing American Masculinities: The 21st-Century Man in Popular Culture* (Bloomington: Indiana UP, 2011), 2–3.
8. Ibid., 3.
9. Harry Brod, qtd in Sally Robinson, "Pedagogy of the Opaque: Teaching Masculinity Studies," in *Masculinity Studies and Feminist Theory*, ed. Judith Kegan Gardiner (New York: Columbia UP, 2002), 151.
10. Max Martin, Rami, and Dido, "I'm Not a Girl, Not Yet a Woman," *Britney* (album), Jive Records, 2001.
11. R. W. Connell, *The Men and The Boys*, (Berkeley: UC Press, 2001) 10.
12. Ibid., 10.
13. Ibid., 70.
14. Harry Brod, *The Making of Masculinities* (Boston: Allen & Unwin, 1987), 291.
15. Ben Brantley, "Celebrating Shaw, a Serious Optimist," *New York Times*, September 16, 2005, accessed November 10, 2014: http://www.nytimes.com/2005/09/16/theater/newsandfeatures/16shaw.html?pagewanted=all&_r=0. Italics mine.
16. Ibid.
17. Amy Schumer's Comedy Central roast of Charlie Sheen and friends is an act of ruthless evisceration.
18. Stephen Trask, "Midnight Radio," *Hedwig and the Angry Inch: Original Cast Recording*, Atlantic Records/WEA, 1999.
19. Ibid., Franco.
20. Ibid., Shaw and Watson, 1.
21. Ibid, Franco.
22. Ibid.
23. Ibid., Robinson, 152.
24. Judith Halberstam, *Female Masculinity*, (Durham, NC: Duke UP, 1998), 1.
25. Judith Halberstam, *Female Masculinity*, (Durham, NC: Duke UP, 1998), 1, 14.
26. Michelle Ruiz, "The Booth is Back: Jorma Taccone on Returning to *Girls* . . . " *Cosmopolitan* (Jan 27 2013), accessed November 15, 2014: http://www.cosmopolitan.com/entertainment/celebs/news/a4163/jorma-taccone-girls-interview/.

BIBLIOGRAPHY

Brantley, Ben. "Celebrating Shaw, a Serious Optimist." *New York Times*. September 16, 2005. Accessed November 10, 2014. http://www.nytimes.com/2005/09/16/theater/newsandfeatures/16shaw.html?pagewanted=all&_r=0. Italics mine.
Brod, Harry. *The Making of Masculinities*. Boston: Allen & Unwin, 1987.
Connell, R. W. *The Men and The Boys*. Berkeley: UC Press, 2001.

Franco, James. "A Dude's Take on *Girls*." *The Huffington Post* (May 30, 2012). Accessed
    November 20, 2014. http://www.huffingtonpost.com/james-franco/girls-hbo-lena-dunham_
    b_1556078.html.
Gardiner, Judith Kegan. Introduction to *Masculinity Studies and Feminist Theory*. Ed. Judith
    Kegan Gardiner. New York: Columbia UP, 2002.
Girls. TV series. Lena Dunham, creator. HBO. Various episodes cited textually. 2012–2014.
Halberstam, Judith. *Female Masculinity*. Durham, NC: Duke UP, 1998.
Martin, Max, Rami, and Dido. "I'm Not a Girl, Not Yet a Woman." *Britney* (album). Jive
    Records, 2001.
Robinson, Sally. "Pedagogy of the Opaque: Teaching Masculinity Studies." In *Masculinity
    Studies and Feminist Theory*. Ed. Judith Kegan Gardiner. New York: Columbia UP, 2002.
Ruiz, Michelle. "The Booth is Back: Jorma Taccone on Returning to *Girls* . . ." *Cosmopolitan*
    (Jan 27 2013). Accessed November 15, 2014: http://www.cosmopolitan.com/entertainment/
    celebs/news/a4163/jorma-taccone-girls-interview/.
Shaw, Marc E. and Elwood Watson. Introduction to *Performing American Masculinities: The
    21st-Century Man in Popular Culture*. Bloomington: Indiana UP, 2011.
Trask, Stephen. "Midnight Radio." *Hedwig and the Angry Inch: Original Cast Recording*.
    Atlantic Records/WEA, 1999.
Verizon Wireless. "Droid Turbo. 'The Fall' with James Franco [one-minute version]." *You-
    Tube.com* (October 30, 2014). Accessed November 8, 2014.

Chapter Six

Capitalizing on Post-Hipster Cool: The Music That Makes *Girls*

Hank Willenbrink

Spotify[1] user Jillian Nichols has cataloged songs from HBO's *Girls* into one playlist. Nichols's collection features 171 songs (eleven hours of music) and is followed by over fifty-five thousand Spotify listeners as of November 2014. Browsing through this list is an exercise in eclectic listening. Take, for example, the song selection from season 1 episode 7, "Welcome to Bushwick AKA The Crackcident." Here the song choices for a large warehouse party in the Bushwick neighborhood of Brooklyn flips from Latino club superstar Pitbull to Wu-Tang Clan member Ghostface Killah and then to Atlanta-based punk band Black Lips. Such a mixture of styles and artists is a hallmark of the show *Girls* is as comfortable using 1990s one-hit wonders as it is tween pop stars and independent artists.

With no specific, predetermined style or affiliation, music supervisor Manish Raval[2] describes his process as first attempting to find new tracks before resorting to more traditional selection techniques: "We're into finding crazy things, stuff that's really out there. You can't slack off and you can't just listen to what's pitched to us. We have to find great stuff [show creator Lena Dunham] hasn't heard—I feel like there's a responsibility there—and if at the end of the process we need a song, we do it the traditional way."[3] Furthermore, Raval asserts that choosing music for *Girls* isn't only about discovering and popularizing new artists, it also has to live up to the show's fan base: "If we post a link to a song on YouTube, I would see fifteen pages of comments related to the song's use on *Girls*. It has captivated [an audi-ence] in a completely different way [than other shows]."[4] The music on *Girls* has generated a life of its own. In their recaps of the series, for example, *The Guardian* blog features a "Stereo Watch" section for comments solely on the music used in each episode.[5] Thus, as Raval insinuates, the music on the show is evaluated not only as song selections to aid in the episode's storytelling, but also as a tastemaker designed to lead its watchers to new music.

Two watershed moments epitomize how the show's musical selections have transcended the program and granted exposure to a musical artist or track. The first moment occurs in season 1 episode 3, "What Adventurous Women Do," when Hannah's laptop elicits an impromptu dance party to the sounds of Robyn's "Dancing on My Own." The second, and perhaps more impactful moment, comes in season 2 when Swedish duo Icona Pop's "I Love It" provides the soundtrack (and sing-along) for Hannah and Elijah's coke-fueled dance. Chosen after Rihanna turned down the show's request to license her hit "Talk that Talk," *Girls* launched Icona Pop into American musical consciousness. As the website *Pop Dust* puts it, the allure of Icona Pop's track is in its ability to make you think you were a part of the party:

> Not only does "I Love It" sound great—it always does, assuming it's not a super-depressing and rainy Monday morning (and even then it usually powers through)—but in the scene, Hannah and Elijah sing along (inaudibly) to every word, thus proving what an important part of their lives the song already is. (In all likelihood, as two hip-ish Brooklyn twenty-somethings, it probably would be in real life.) So if you're watching at home, and don't already know the song, you feel left out of the loop and left out of the moment, and you just might want to hit up iTunes as soon as possible after to be able to join the party yourself.[6]

Though the song was originally released in 2012 and made an appearance in both *Rolling Stone* and *Pitchfork*'s year-end "best of" lists, it wasn't until after the song appeared on *Girls* in 2013 that it entered the *Billboard* Hot 100. Getting the track, as *Pop Dust* suggests, isn't only about listening to great music. To download Icona Pop offers access into the world of *Girls*.

Through musical selection, *Girls* offers its audiences the ability to join the milieu of Hannah, Adam, and the cast of twenty somethings Brooklyn denizens. The show occupies a unique position as tastemaker *for* and perpetuator *of* this cultural moment, which Dunham refers to as "that rarefied white hipster thing."[7] "Hipster" is a complicated and conflicted term, in part because the cultural experience of the group is difficult to pinpoint and often self-denying. Furthermore, the term's almost ubiquitous contemporary usage obfuscates its identification of a specific group. In this essay, I engage with the music in *Girls*, reading it as an embodiment of a conundrum at the heart of hipster culture and illustrate how the show, ultimately, is a part of a post-hipster moment. While hipster culture asserted independence and individuality, this claim was ultimately tied to a consumerist ideology where the accruing of social standing is determined by what Sarah Thornton terms "subcultural capital." In the post-hipster cool of *Girls*, subcultural capital is freely exchanged through consumerist means, which expands the reach of hipster culture through media. Building off the work of Pierre Bourdieu and his term "cultural capital," Thornton describes subcultural capital in relation to cultural capital:

> Subcultural capital confers status on its owner in the eyes of the relevant beholder. [. . .] Subcultural capital can be *objectified* or *embodied*. Just as books and paintings display cultural capital in the family home, so subcultural capital is objectified in the form of fashionable haircuts and well-assembled record collections [. . .]. Just as cultural capital is personified in "good" manners and urbane conversation, so subcultural capital is embodied in the form of being "in the know," using (but not over-using) current slang and looking as if you were born to perform the latest dance styles. Both cultural and subcultural capital put a premium on the "second nature" of their knowledges. Nothing depletes capital more than the sight of someone trying too hard.[8]

Subcultural capital keeps members of a subculture relevant to both their peers and the culture at large. Whereas in prior formations, subcultural capital was largely encoded within a particular group "in the know," hipsterdom's relationship to consumerist approaches and dissemination through shows like *Girls* has created a post-hipster cultural/consumerist group whereby allegiance to cultural objects provides social standing.[9]

Taste is one of the dominant forms for establishing socio-cultural standing for hipsters. It does not matter so much what one does in hipster culture as much as what one adopts. Raval's previous quotation about "finding crazy things" reflects paranoia at the heart of hipster culture—once the masses recognize a cultural commodity, its subcultural capital is negated. Remaining a relevant agent in hipster culture means staying constantly ahead of one's peers in subcultural capital. However, this capital is often disseminated and consumed through the consumer carousel of contemporary capitalism. In the post-hipster moment, however, consumption enables both the spread of and tension over subcultural capital. Those who adopt first and fit within a cultural structure, like the version of hipsterism perpetuated on *Girls*, are rewarded with social standing, which is in turn perpetuated through media. *Girls*'s music enables a reading *into* and *of* contemporary post-hipsterdom as a social arena marked by the conflict over and spread of subcultural capital.

To understand how *Girls* perpetuates, demonstrates, and capitalizes on hipster culture, it's necessary to underscore how television enables the spread of musical culture through track licensing. David Wagner, writing for *The Atlantic*'s The Wire blog, states: "*Girls* might just be the next *Grey's Anatomy* or *Dawson's Creek*—the kind of TV show that plays kingmaker to just-under-the-radar musicians and sends their record sales abuzz."[10] Since the truncation of the recording industry in the early 2000s, musical artists and record labels have hunted for ways to get songs heard despite limited options. Bethany Klein cites electronic musician Moby (after his album *Play* was widely licensed to movies, television, and advertisements in 2000) as one of the first musicians to capitalize on a shifting of dynamics that wedded the destinies of musicians to advertisements and other licensing opportunities. In "'The New Radio': Music Licensing as a Response to Industry Woe," Klein writes:

> As transformations in the US radio and music industries have resulted in narrower opportunities for a narrowing range of artists, the advertising industry gladly stepped in to offer musicians and labels large amounts of money and potential widespread exposure. The sum of all of these shifts and changes created a distinct environment for the production of music culture, and cast relationships between popular music and advertising in a new light, with advertisers playing hero to the damsel-in-distress of the struggling artist. [11]

Thus, television shows like *Girls* become a launch pad for artists like Robyn and Icona Pop.[12] Greater exposure benefits both the artist and its particular launch pad, whether it is an advertisement, TV show, or film. In so doing, the musical artist draws an implicit connection between her work and the medium airing it and perpetuates the airing vehicle. *Cornell Daily Sun* columnist Kaitlyn Tiffany sums it up best: "Lena Dunham, Make Me a Pop Star."[13]

Over the course of three seasons, *Girls* has made pop stars, helped launch albums, and become, as Wagner suggests, one of the premiere shows for music. Thus, as Tiffany's title suggests, *Girls* has transcended and promulgated its particular cultural milieu. Implicit in the show's star-making ability is that it has, in many senses, given up the hipster pretense of independence. Rather, *Girls* exemplifies a post-hipster paradigm, which draws from hipsterdom's ideas while simultaneously giving up its pretext for existence outside of mainstream culture.[14] In the next section, I highlight discourse about hipsters to frame my analysis of *Girls* by positioning the show within the contemporary post-hipster moment. Following this, I embark on a reading of the music in *Girls* and how it defines hipster culture. Finally, I offer a counterpoint to the music used in *Girls* by analyzing how characters that make music are treated in *Girls*.

Death of the Cool?

By 2007, the idea of hipsters as a legitimate subculture was under heavy fire. Satirical barbs like the YouTube video "Hipster Olympics," where a gaggle of apathetic, craft beer drinking trust fund kids don't really care enough to finish a race, and *Look at this Fucking Hipster*, a *People of Wal-Mart* styled website featuring youthful hedonism and fashion eccentricities openly mocked hipster culture. In the eyes of cultural critics and the blogosphere, hipsters were judged to be not only pretenders but narcissistic and un-hip. *Time Out New York* writer Christian Lorentzen penned an even more damning critique in "Why the Hipster Must Die: A Modest Proposal" where he compared hipsters to the diseased. "Hungry for more, and sick with the anxiety of influence, they feed as well from the trough of the uncool," Lorentzen states "turning white trash chic, and gouging the husks of long-expired subcultures—vaudeville, burlesque, cowboys and pirates."[15] A similarly alarmist article, "Hipster: The Dead End of Western Civilization," by *Adbusters* writer Douglas Haddow followed Lorentzen's in 2008. Haddow declares hipsters the end of civilization and their group as "suicidal." He states: "While previous youth movements have challenged the dysfunction and decadence of their elders, today we have the 'hipster'—a youth subculture that mirrors the doomed shallowness of mainstream society."[16] For Lorentzen and Haddow, the group's inauthenticity and relation to mainstream culture are the most damning elements. As Haddow argues:

> "the hipster is a consumer group—using their capital to purchase empty authenticity and rebellion. But the moment a trend, band, sound, style or feeling gains too much exposure, it is suddenly looked upon with disdain. Hipsters cannot afford to maintain any cultural loyalties or affiliations for fear they will lose relevance."[17]

The inauthenticity of the hipster seemed to extend from cultural materials to identity.

In 2009, Mark Greif and colleagues at the New School began a sociological investigation into hipster culture which would ultimately result in the book *What Was the Hipster?: A Sociological Investigation*.[18] Greif describes finding someone who called themselves a hipster next to impossible: "No one, it seemed, thought of himself as a hipster, and when someone called you a hipster, the term was an insult. Paradoxically, those who used the insult were themselves often said to resemble hipsters—they wore the skinny jeans and big eyeglasses, gathered in tiny enclaves in big cities, and looked down on mainstream fashions and 'tourists.'"[19] Greif, too, notes the importance of taste, which he calls the hipsters "primary currency."[20] Utilizing Bourdieu, Greif sees taste as not only currency but social capital:

> Taste is not stable and peaceful, but a means of strategy and competition. Those superior in wealth use it to pretend they are superior in spirit. Groups closer in social class who yet draw their status from different sources use taste and its attainments to disdain one another and get a leg up. These conflicts for social dominance through culture are exactly what drive the dynamics within communities whose members are regarded as hipsters.[21]

Thus, a certain group of hipsters look down on another group which in turn looks down and devalues another group. Taste provides the ultimate (sub–)cultural capital. "All hipsters play at being the inventors or first adopters of novelties: pride comes from knowing, and deciding, what's cool in advance of the rest of the world," Greif states. "Yet the habits of hatred and accusation are endemic to hipsters because they feel the weakness of everyone's position—including their own."[22] In such a fraught social atmosphere, the only means of surviving and social relevance is in a constant jockeying for the cultural capital of "cool." As Rob Horning, executive editor of *The New Inquiry* explains: "The problem with hipsters seems to me to be the way in which they reduce the particularity of anything you might be curious about or invested in into the same dreary common denominator of how 'cool' it is perceived to be. Everything becomes just another signifier of personal identity."[23] Hipsters partake in consumer culture to pull from other culture(s) and sustain social standing. Such an emphasis on the "cool" flattens the signification of cultural material appropriating it into identity, thereby negating a cultural product's intrinsic features at the service of social status and identity creation.

This blatantly consumerist stance positions hipsters as the antithesis of the independent scenes of the 1990s and early 2000s out of which the contemporary version of hipsters emerged. Kaya Oakes analyzes the crisis year of 2007 when things went mainstream: "in an age of 'branding,' whatever slivers of indie culture people claimed for their own were rapidly becoming not much more than labels and tags."[24] Appropriating from indie culture to create a brand identity, Oakes states, relates directly to the ascendency of hipsters. "This mainstreaming of indie culture, which encouraged increasing availability to larger and larger audience—enabling its co-opting by advertisers and filmmakers, promoting a narrowing down to the clichéd image of a hipster in skinny jeans and big glasses," Oakes writes, is still happening.[25] Hipsterism is, in short, a commercialized version of independent culture prepackaged, reductionist, and branded to be sold back to youths hungry for "rebellion."

Rather than being an outgrowth of indie culture, hipsters were created from labels and tags taken and rebranded by mainstream culture. As Greif contends in *What Was the Hipster?*, the hipster can be understood as a reaction to the co-opting of independent cultures: "the contemporary hipster seems to emerge out of a thwarted tradition of youth subcultures, subcultures which had tried to remain independent of consumer culture, alternative to it, and had been integrated, humiliated and destroyed."[26] From this thwarted tradition, hipsters see themselves, Greif argues, as both a member of a rebellious subculture and a part of mainstream consumer culture opening, in his words, a "poisonous conduit between [a rebel subculture and the dominant class]."[27] By contrast, late 1990s and early 2000s indie culture's primary mode of creation was DIY, do-it-yourself. Oakes states that "indie is not just about DIY, though DIY remains its central tenant." Furthermore, DIY enables "self-actualization via creativity, and it is about empowerment" of both self and community.[28] The generation of a hipster brand is the exact opposite of DIY. Though it took from indie culture to establish itself, hipsterdom is, by and large a marketed scheme; however, instead of building one's self, hipsters focus on self-construction through other materials. Individuality and independence remain two of the dominant ideas overrunning most other trends within hipster culture. Thus, self-identification as a hipster would seemingly negate participation within the culture, since to be a part of something leaves one open for media co-option and squashes perceived self-expression, which is the ultimate key to social standing. With such caché placed on individuality and social stance in hipster culture, there's little room left for community empowerment or self-actualization.

For Greif, the "hipster moment" has passed. He positions this time as roughly 1999 to 2003. The post-2004 hipster is one who has spawned from popular culture visions of hipness as the 1999–2003 hipster cannibalized its subcultural brethren. *Girls*'s role as a tastemaker, therefore, can be seen as part-and-parcel of the post-2004 trend. The use of music in *Girls* underscores this consumer-driven hip stance. As *Pop Dust* highlights, the musical choices of the show provide audience members a way to live vicariously through the tracks used. In return Wagner and Tiffany illustrate how the show creates its own pop stars through track licensing. Subcultural goods are refashioned in *Girls*, and as I will illustrate later in the essay, often these goods are more highly prioritized than the cultural creations that the show dramatizes.

Perhaps because of its ability to take from and reuse other subcultural goods, hipsterdom has proven to be remarkably resilient. One of the reasons that hipsters seem here to stay, at least in some form or fashion, is because the paradigm has shifted. In *Neo-Bohemia: Art and Commerce in the Postindustrial City*, Richard Lloyd analyzes the bohemias of the twenty-first century through culture and the relation to the cities that house them, in particular the Wicker Park neighborhood of Chicago. Lloyd's analysis follows economic trends as well, and he argues that: "contemporary participants in the Wicker Park scene insist upon their opposition to an imagined mainstream. [. . .] Yet this image of the mainstream is anachronistic, as the old promises of career and social security under the terms of the Fordist corporation and the welfare state have increasingly evaporated."[29] The proliferation of communication and contemporary form of capitalism, Lloyd asserts, is uniquely suited to take advantage of potential creativity in these "neo-bohemias." Thus, the conformist mainstream, which previous subcultures have marked as the opposition, is no longer in operation. Contemporary capitalism, Lloyd asserts, doesn't co-opt so much as it takes advantage of taste. In this way, there seems to be no true demarcation between contemporary capitalism and hipster culture as both seek to capitalize on subcultural capital, one in the name of profit, the other in the name of social standing. Lloyd writes:

> Knowing how to dress, how to evince the appropriate demeanor, how to talk knowledgably about various non-mainstream cultural offerings—these skills are honed in the local milieu, and are attributes that can be conceived of as subcultural capital, though only in specific contexts. What makes competence into capital is the opportunity to leverage it for social rewards. Under the right circumstances, subcultural capital can confer privileges of status and money. [30]

Lloyd's analysis reinforces Greif's claims that the hipster version of hip-ness has persevered through their consumerist position. In a *New York Magazine* article, Greif further articulates that adoption of cultural goods, not genera-tion of materials is what characterized the hipster moment:

> "One could say, exaggerating only slightly, that the hipster moment did not produce artists, but tattoo artists [. . .]. It did not produce photographers, but snapshot and party photographers [. . .]. It did not yield a great literature, but it made good use of fonts. And hipsterism did not make an avant-garde; it made communities of early adopters." [31]

Given, then, the adoptive, consumerist paradigm, the post-hipster, that is the hipster post-2004, exists as many of the characters on *Girls* between the world of independent communities and mainstream culture often blending the two into their own unique cultural-consumer practice. Subcultural capital, once tied to specific context(s), is readily and almost effortlessly disseminat-ed through shows like *Girls*. And, as the next sections will illustrate, the show does not celebrate musical creation as much as it makes use of and promulgates cultural material around it in a consumerist spirit.

Music Makes *Girls*

User courtnac asks: "do you only aim for certain genres for girls [*sic*] or whatever goes?" Manish Raval answers: "Whatever goes."[32] Musical appro-priation by hipsters runs the gambit from indie music to mainstream hits. Though ostensibly an expression of identity, hipster music reveals the extent to which the culture is beholden to mainstream media as much as it is to independent forms of music. In this section, I trace through how musical licensing and the idea of independence has radically changed since the turn of the millennium. One of the responses to this transition has been the rise of irony as a position. As *Girls* illustrates, irony not only functions as a way to buffer individuals from being branded (and socially marked) with having bad taste, it also contributes to the consumerism of hipsters by making all cultural materials available to be used if branded as an ironic choice.

As the term implies, indie music exists outside of the mainstream musical sphere. In general, what this means is that an indie band has not signed a contract with a major record label, that is, the "Big Three": Universal Music Group, Sony Music Group, and Warner Music Group. The instability of the recording industry and truncation of media outlets since 2000, however, has forced a number of formerly independent bands to join up with major labels, who can offer the bands more security and resources than smaller labels like Jagjaguwar. A case in point is The Decemberists, a Portland, Oregon-based band who made their name in the early 2000s with hyper-literate lyrics and a musical style which draws from sources as disparate as sea shanties and progressive rock. Though the group started out on Kill Rock Stars, a label based in Portland, in 2005 they moved to Capitol Records, currently owned by Universal Music Group. The Decemberists were hardly the first indie group to jump to the big time. Bay Area punk group Green Day began as a part of the 924 Gilmore street punk scene (a scene which included the influential Bay Area punk bands Operation Ivy, the Dead Kennedys, and others), released their early records from Berkeley-based Lookout! Records; and made their major label debut *Dookie* through Reprise Records, an offshoot of Warner Music Group. The band's departure form Lookout! engendered ire among their fan base, flames that were fanned when *Dookie* became a breakout hit selling over ten million records in the United States. True to indie's communal aesthetic, the fans felt Green Day had betrayed their community by bringing the aesthetic to the mainstream. Green Day is since persona non grata at punk club 924 Gilmore, where the band cannot even play, after their major label contract.[33] By the time The Decemberists jumped to a major label, the move didn't provoke the sort of vitriol that Green Day had eleven years earlier. I saw The Decemberists front man Colin Meloy in a solo show at the Henry Fonda Theatre in 2006, after the band's label change had been announced. Meloy was touring and offered a homemade record entitled *Colin Meloy Sings Shirley Collins*. In the concert he admitted that there was nothing better to help someone get over the guilt of selling out (The Decemberists record *The Crane Wife* was forthcoming from Capitol records later that same year) than to burn and fold thousands of disc sleeves.

There was little ire focused on Meloy in part due to the open season on licensing begun in the early 2000s. A *New York Times* article from 2001 entitled "For Rock Bands, Selling Out Isn't What It Used to Be," analyzed how the successes of Moby's music licensing and Volkswagen's advertisements from the 1990s featuring cult singer-songwriter Nick Drake drew independent artists toward licensing. More broadly, the article suggests that the advent of music videos changed artists' perspectives on their songs, many of who saw no real difference between advertising and music videos. Both were ways for bands to "brand" themselves. "In the Nick Drake spot, [filmmaker Jonathan] Dayton saw the song more as something the people in the ad might

be listening to, reflecting on the characters, not on the car. 'It's acknowledging the place music has in people's lives,' he says. 'It's not meant as an
endorsement.'"[34] Licensing music, once a form of selling out akin to joining
a major label, became a way for indie artists to create musical experiences
linked to the lives of their fans. In this vein, *Pop Dust*'s call for fans of *Girls*
to download Icona Pop functions in a similar manner, by enabling artists to
create relationships with their songs through *Girls*. Even music supervisor
Raval admits that he couldn't hear the song without thinking of the scene in
which it appears in the episode.[35]

While the use of certain music like Icona Pop seems to emerge from an
indie mindset, other musical choices like LMFAO's "I'm Sexy and I Know
It" and Demi Lovato's "Skyscraper" pull from popular music for storytelling
purposes. The latter is used at a pivotal and seemingly poignant moment for
Marnie, who cries to the song, mourning her breakup with Charlie by looking
at pictures of him and his new girlfriend on Facebook, as Hannah and Adam
have sex in the background. Lovato's saccharine ballad undercuts the emotional weight of the moment. In the commentary on the episode for the
Onion's A.V. Club, Todd VanDerWerff notes: "This week's episode includes Demi Lovato's 'Skyscraper,' which is just the worst."[36] The joke,
presumably, is on Marnie, though not for the musical taste as much as it is for
her emotional despondency and romantic state relative to Hannah, which the
choice of Lovato serves to highlight through irony.

A trademark of hipster taste, irony functions as a method by which hipsters inure themselves against potential emotional turmoil. Such a disposition
and tastes serve to reinforce the popular image of hipsters as disaffected,
buffered youth incapable of authentic interaction and whose relationship to
subcultural capital is perpetually self-critiqued. Kristofor Vogel states: "A
trait that has come to define how hipsters are interpreted is the causal display
of insincere (possibly derogatory) behavior and cultural goods under the
guise of irony. It could be the ways they dress, the music they listen to or the
manner in which they treat others, but before hipsters can mold an identity,
they must perform a self-critique of their tastes."[37] Listening to something
like Demi Lovato during a breakup or Booth Jonathan's tortuous media
onslaught of a "TV coffin" blaring Duncan Shiek's "Barely Breathing"
(which he subjects Marnie to and she loves), are ironic choices that destabi-
lize emotional connection. As Vogel suggests, "[t]he irony of *Girls* lies in the
sincerity of the characters' insincerity."[38] Marnie's experience in Booth's TV
coffin epitomizes Vogel's point—she says she loves what is clearly a tortur-
ous experience. Thornton states that media is a key difference between the
natures of cultural and subcultural capital: "the difference between being *in*
and *out* of fashion, high or low in subcultural capital, correlates in complex
ways with degrees of media coverage, creation, and exposure."[39] To stay up
with fashion and tastes, hipsters must utilize media; however, this usage

negates an independent ethos and aesthetic. Thus, irony functions as a way to neutralize the panoptic gaze of co-option through cultivated apathy, or in Marnie's case bad taste for the sake of emotional connection.

Marnie's relationship to music also illustrates how irony buffers emotional connection to people and cultural material as well. By liking things ironically hipsters are able to pull their taste from diverse sources without social repercussions. Marnie's auto-tuned cover of Edie Brickell and the New Bohemians's "What I Am" from season 3 generates shame because of her relationship with Charlie. Shot with faux-1990s flair, the video is distributed by Charlie, without Marnie being able to erase it from going viral (just as she can't seem to erase Charlie). The video is a continuing source of embarrassment for Marnie, however, Ray's coffee shop patrons watch it gleefully while joyless Marnie looks on. Later in season 3, just before her duet with Desi, he instructs her to perform the opposite of that video. Marnie's antipathy, and Desi's instruction, stem from the sincerity with which she recorded the video/song. Unable to see the ironic predicament that she's put herself into (just as she was unable to see the displeasure at the end of season 2 when she sang Kanye West's "Stronger" to the horror of Charlie's office), Marnie's embarrassment is heightened with every view. The joke here is that Marnie cares too much about herself and her relationship with Charlie, and, even when that is gone, she's unable to look at, pun intended, what she is. Of course, this irony is deepened by Marnie's ambivalence to Charlie at the beginning of season 1, where she wishes that he didn't care as much about her. Marnie's inability to see what she's done as ironic and to engage in self-critique renders her as a shallow and pitiable figure.

Irony defines the relationships of hipsters to each other and independent and mainstream culture. Living under the panoptic eye of advertising, irony enables hipsters to maintain a relationship to independent culture(s) while distancing themselves from the emotional connection to these sources. Likewise, irony opens up a multitude of cultural materials to be used by hipsters. Hannah and Shoshanna sing along to Maroon 5's "One More Night" (a moment which causes Adam to break the car stereo out of rage) without social repercussions because taking an ironic stance toward what is being consumed can negate actual taste. In the music in *Girls* anything goes, while, ironically, for characters making music in *Girls*, music is limited.

Girls Make Music

The closing track (and inspiration for the title) of season 2 episode 2 is "I Get Ideas" by M. Ward.[40] Ward is an accomplished independent guitarist who has won widespread recognition as the counterpart to Zooey Deschanel in the band She & Him. While the episode ends with Ward's track, it begins in a more somber moment as Adam, no longer with Hannah, has sent a series of

YouTube videos of him playing songs that she watches with horror. Though to be fair, that may have had to do with some of Adam's lyrics: "Standing outside not making a sound / Creeping around / You destroyed my heart."[41] At the end of the episode, Adam apologizes for the songs, saying that he shouldn't have sent anything so hostile. The song allows Adam to get away with something he would never say aloud. However, his self-expression reinforces, for Hannah, the image of Adam as psychotic.

The overall negative view of Adam's music by Hannah in this episode is emblematic for most of the characters on the show that make music.[42] To give a sense of how much the show leans toward musical placement rather than character-created tunes, out of the eight best musical moments from season 1 that music website *Stereogum* listed, only two involved character-created music—Charlie reading Hannah's diary and Thomas John's "mash-ups" of music and animal sounds.[43] Despite the show's ability to make musical stars from strategic placement, the characters of *Girls* don't make music that is able to transcend the same way. In fact, much of the music made on the show—from Adam's "hostile" songs, to Marnie's video and Kanye West cover, to bad karaoke at Hannah and Elijah's housewarming, to Ray and Charlie's Questionable Goods—is a punch line or ends in embarrassing emotions likely to be regretted when the music's over.

Questionable Goods shows how music evinces emotional turbulence in *Girls*

Questionable Goods first appears as a two-piece with Charlie on guitar and Ray playing congas. Ray, initially, pushes the band along, giving a rundown of one of the songs they're planning to Charlie "And are you comfortable? Like, does the concept of the song is that clear to you," Ray asks. Charlie retorts: "You're walking behind a girl on the street and she's wearing Keds."[44] The superficial concept juxtaposes with what the band plays next, "Hannah's Diary," which uses our leading lady's penned private thoughts as lyrics. Charlie sings: "What is Marnie thinking, oh? / How does it feel to date a man with a vagina? / Doesn't she want to feel an actual penis?" The bitterness of the moment is lost on Shoshanna: "Is this a love song?" Marnie throws her drink on Hannah before storming out, leaving Jessa to comment "That was awesome!" To which Hannah replies, "I'm going to puke."[45] This song breaks up Marnie and Charlie for the first time, but seems, according to Jessa, to have actual artistic merit (or at the very least elicits an "awesome" fight between friends), as opposed to the song about Ray watching a girl in Keds. Questionable Goods return in episode 7, "Welcome to Bushwick AKA The Crackcident" with more instruments. Despite her reaction the last time the band played, Marnie admits to Charlie that the band sounds great. Charlie's reversal of fortune is personal too: as Marnie is talking to him, his new girlfriend, Audrey, tackles him. Two weeks since their breakup, Charlie hasn't only filled out his band; he's got a new girlfriend as well. In her conversation with Charlie, Marnie tells him, "all I ever wanted for you was to be able to find satisfaction outside of our relationship."[46] When satisfaction arrives, Marnie is indignant.

Alongside the success of Questionable Goods, Charlie appears the most successful career-wise when he develops an app in season 2. Ray, older-but-less-accomplished, is suspicious of Charlie's newfound wealth. The tour through Charlie's office in episode 4 impresses Shoshanna, whereas Ray continues a line of acerbic comments culminating with "[a]re some of the women here prostitutes?"[47] Ray's implication is that Charlie has, to use the lingo of the independent music scene, "sold out." Charlie doesn't bite, telling Ray: "I'm not doing this with you, man."[48] Ray's tension toward Charlie underscores a key element of social standing—the accruing of social standing must appear effortless. Charlie's overnight success contrasts with Ray's hard-won place as a coffee shop manager. He may employ Hannah and Marnie, date Shoshanna, but the fact that he's older (thirty-three, while Hannah turns twenty-five in season 3) gives him a different perspective on life than the other characters. His response to Charlie's success seems childish and stuck in a late-nineties perspective rather than sharing the millennial joy of the others. Marnie and Shoshanna revel in Charlie's success, but Shoshanna takes a dig at Ray's professional apathy by telling Charlie that his office is "stupidly grown-up," implying that Ray's coffee shop is by extension immature.[49] Even so, Ray remains unimpressed and views Charlie's newfound wealth and standing as akin to selling out.

Questionable Goods alienated Marnie twice, yet she decides to use music as a way to get Charlie's attention. During the party, she covers Kanye West's "Stronger," which she (with the persistence of Shoshanna) made with Ray's help. Though the song is a failure in the eyes of the partygoers, Ray included, it's the spark that brings her back into Charlie's life at the end of season 2. Whereas Charlie's music was emotional and charged, Marnie's delivery is all technique, as well as a cover song. After flaming out in front of the guests, Marnie tells Charlie—"I'm on a journey. It's my journey, and I am okay. And please don't pity me"—before they begin kissing.[50] The emotional catharsis of "Hannah's Diary" severed the relationship; however, Charlie's pity for Marnie's performance reunites the couple.

Pity also brings together Jessa and Thomas John. In his initial seduction of Jessa and Marnie, trying too hard makes Thomas John laughable. After the businessman meets them at a bar, he invites them to his place where he plays for them an album of "mash-ups" that he's working on. If Marnie's cover of "Stronger" from season 2 was subtly ironic, Thomas John's songs are a punch line that Jessa wields to make fun of him. In the first song he plays, he mixes Len's 1999-hit "Steal My Sunshine" with the sounds of kids playing in a field. When Jessa tells Marnie what Thomas John is up to, Jessa says that he's mixed Len with "field recordings of children playing," but Thomas John corrects her: "They're children playing in a field."[51] A field recording is when someone records sounds outside of a studio. While Jessa was correct in calling it a field recording, Thomas John shows off his ignorance by correcting her. "Sounds, uh, awesome," Jessa tells Marnie with deadpan sarcasm. Jessa's insincerity will become eminently ironic by the end of that season when she and Thomas John are wed. For the moment, however, his attempts at seduction are over-the-top and ignored by Marnie and Jessa who begin to kiss each other. When Thomas John takes this as a cue to move in, the girls spill wine on his rug, launching Thomas John into an anti-hipster rant directed at the group of people to whom trying too hard is a turn off:

> It kinda ticks me off when I come to Williamsburg after working hard all fucking day in the real world and I see all these stupid little Daddy's girls with their fucking bowler hats. What are you doing wearing a fucking bowler hat, stupid? And then you come over and you flirt and flirt and flirt and kiss and kiss and listen to my amazing tunes, drink my beautiful wine, and then spill it all over my gorgeous rug and laugh about it.[52]

Jessa's response highlights how Thomas John's music, as an extension of his personality has done the opposite of seducing her: "Yeah, well, we're not laughing at your *rug*, trust me. [. . .] We're laughing at your mash-ins." Unable to get the joke, Thomas John shouts back—"It's mash-ups!"[53] The humor of Thomas John's mash-ups is not just their strangeness or his lack of musical ability (he admits that he's playing the tracks from two different iTunes windows on two different computers), but also how out of touch and sincere he is about the music. As shown in his speech, Thomas John's displacement arises from the emotional boundaries put up by the culture of Williamsburg. Everyone, in his mind, wants to enjoy the lifestyle that he has created but without enjoying him. The problems that he articulates here will spell the end for his marriage to Jessa in season 2. Culturally, Thomas John's critique is aimed at perceived hipsters, Jessa and Marnie. The pair remains unaware of what they represent, inured to emotion through their use of irony. They exist outside of the "real" world and are, therefore, unable to get any pleasure from his wine and "amazing tunes," choosing instead to destroy (in this case his rug) and laugh about it.

Thomas John's creations are mockable; however, his treatment for making music is not unique. Even outside of the series itself, one woman of *Girls* received a similar reception to Thomas John. Zosia Mamet (who plays Shoshanna) failed to fund a $32,000 Kickstarter campaign to make a music video with her sister. The Cabin Sisters, their band, takes a series of off-handed barbs from *Gawker* writer Maggie Lange: "As of writing, nine people have donated $456 of the $32,000 goal. So there is a full 98.6 percent left that you can fund, if this band suits your fancy. But why, you might ask, has the Internet failed to leap to fund a *Girls* girl's musical whimsy? Are hipster folk bands with an inept banjo player no longer the latest? Oh, they still are."[54] *Gawker*'s sister site, *Jezebel*, likewise, delighted in the Mamets' failed attempt: "We were really hoping that Zosia Mamet's music video Kickstarter was a deft parody of celebrities who make Kickstarters, given that she talked about wanting to hang out with her sister more while sitting on a pile of wood. In front of a cabin, because David Mamet's daughters call their band the 'Cabin Sisters.' Parody at its best!"[55] Part of *Gawker* and *Jezebel*'s snark derives from who was doing the asking. Daughter of a famed playwright/screenwriter/director, Zosia also appears on *Mad Men*. What was she doing asking for such a grand sum for a music video so that she could "hang out" with her sister? The failure of the project seems like it could have been ripped from one of the show's scripts. When *Girls* can create stars for its licensed artists, why are the artists from the show, on and off screen, so laughable when they try to make music?

At the center of the joke is this: the music makers are characters who try too hard. Adam, Marnie, Thomas John, and Zosia Mamet seem to be victims of their own attempts to express emotions, be heard, or fit in.[56] Like Thomas John, once someone looks as if he or she is trying too hard—to get back together, to make it, or to even "hang out" with her sister—the subcultural capital becomes bankrupt. By contrast, Charlie's success, both with his band and as an app developer, is heightened, because it comes, seemingly, out of the blue. Even in his first gig with Ray, Charlie doesn't seem to be the one working at music. Ray is the one with the "concept" for a song that pales in comparison to the reaction which Charlie receives from incorporating Hannah's diary into a song. Trying too hard undercuts a hipster's social standing: coolness, irony, and distance are necessary counterparts to taste. One of the reasons that music is an unsuccessful venture for some is that the music they make has to fit into the emotional arc of a character or episode. How do we show that Adam is crazy? Have him write some hostile songs! How do we show that Marnie is desperate? Show her wanting to impress someone by singing! In these moments, a character reaches the point of highest stakes by becoming emotionally vulnerable with their social standing on the line by displaying poor taste (unfiltered with irony) or working too hard and without self-critique. Accordingly, it's when Marnie is able to self-critique her performance in the music video, before she and Desi take the stage—Desi in season 3, episode 11—that she reaches her musical pinnacle. Though Elijah decried Marnie's musical performance as "too stiff and too hopeful," he later praises her seeming naturalness on stage with Desi.[57] Marnie, too, feels the connection both musically and personally, but (ironically) Desi rebuffs her and introduces Marnie to his girlfriend.

Conclusion

What works on *Girls* is prepackaged music: downloadable, consumable, transporting us closer to a party where the show's culture is *in*, and in so doing, perpetuating the culture. Listening to Icona Pop gives you the feeling you are partying with AndrewAndrew[58] as part of the show. This is Baudrillard's simulacra, where the fake is realer than the real, merging with contemporary consumer capitalism, media, and celebrity to create a self-perpetuating market where watchers and producers feed off one another. *Girls* has helped create and cultivate a market where musical choices are one method by which the show helps perpetuate itself outside of screens and into its audience's lives. In this way, music used in *Girls* articulates a post-hipster paradigm by openly adopting a consumerist strategy and working to maintain its subcultural capital through musical choices, irony, and emphasis on social stance. *Girls*, so far, has stayed ahead of the curve by creating its own capital. Season 3, for example, features new music from artists Miguel, Beck, Jenny Lewis, and Lily Allen. By reaching out to artists, the show's creators offer an opportunity to work in unison with *Girls*, to the benefit of both sides. What is less clear is how the show will develop characters that make music within each episode. Given Marnie's predilection for musicals and Alison Williams's foray into live television musicals with *Peter Pan*, I'd venture a guess that Dunham has an audition in mind for season 4, which would surely infuriate Elijah. However, given how the show has played into taste and social standing as the primary motivations for the characters, it's difficult to see much changing in the musical or personal fortunes of *Girls*"s characters.

In hipsterdom's drift away from independent culture, its inability to nurture artists has been one of the most alarming trends. While indie tended to focus around scenes, geographically-centered cultivation of art and music, hipster consumption has tended to erode, rather than raise up, other subcultural loci. The result has been a steady disintegration of scenes in favor of a more easily consumed culture. Post-hipster, these geographically-centered areas of cultural creation are overtaken by the marketing of a "subculture." Musicians who don't license their music will go unheard—pushing the independents further away from potential listeners. The post-hipster paradigm that *Girls* evinces offers a range of opportunities for those who license, like Icona Pop and Robyn, yet, this also ties their work to the buyer. As Raval admitted, it is impossible to hear Icona Pop without picturing Hannah and Elijah; and it is just as impossible to imagine *Girls* without its own self-created and branded, iconic pop.

NOTES

1. Spotify is a streaming web music service based in Sweden, which was launched in the United States in 2011. The service hooks into various forms of social media and enables users to stream music licensed to the service from various record companies. Users can "follow" public playlists generated by other users.

2. Raval supervises the music for the show with his partner Tom Wolfe. Raval has also worked on NBC's *Community* and FOX's *The New Girl*. Music decisions are made by committee between Raval, Wolfe, Aperture music library chief Jonathan Leahy, executive producers Judd Apatow and Jenni Konner, and the show's creator and star Lena Dunham.

3. Quoted in Gallo 2013. Phil Gallo, "'Girls' Music Supervisor Manish Raval Talks about Finding 'Cool Music,'" *Hollywood Reporter*, January 14, 2013, http://www.hollywoodreporter.com/news/girls-music-supervisor-manish-raval-412258.

4. Ibid.

5. The *Guardian* isn't the only one to take notice of the show's musical selection. The *Onion*'s A.V. Club regularly references music on the program as well as *Vulture* (vulture.com).

6. Andrew Unterberger, "Is 'Girls' Finally Gonna Make a Hit Out of Icona Pop's 'I Love It'?," *Pop Dust*, January 28, 2013, http://popdust.com/2013/01/28/girls-icona-pop-i-love-it-soundtrack/.

7. Emily Nussbaum, "It's Different for 'Girls,'" *New York Magazine*, March 25, 2012, http://nymag.com/arts/tv/features/girls-lena-dunham-2012-4/.

8. Sarah Thornton, *Club Cultures: Music, Media, and Subcultural Capital* (Cambridge, UK: Polity Press, 1995), 11–12.

9. As I will explore further in the next section, sociologists like Mark Greif contend that the hipster moment is over; however, I argue that the subculture has morphed into a fully fledged and powerful consumer group, which perpetuates a hipster vision through media and post-capitalist structures.

10. David Wagner, "Proof that Lena Dunham Has the Power to Make Hip Songs into Huge Hits Now." *The Wire*, January 15, 2013, http://www.thewire.com/entertainment/2013/01/girls-soundtrack-sales-numbers/61035/.

11. Bethany Klein, "'The New Radio': Music Licensing as a Response to Industry Woe," *Media, Culture & Society* 30, no 4 (2008): 463–64.

12. Recognition through placement on *Girls* extends beyond songs. In a March 19, 2014 article for the *New York Times*, Alex Williams compared the show's ability to draw from its peer circle as akin to Woody Allen's films of the 1970s and 1980s featuring socializing at Elaine's. The demographic and population is different. AndrewAndrew, the DJ duo who spin Icona Pop in *Girls*, have gained celebrity for their placement in the dance club where Hannah and Elijah have their musical freak out. Unsurprisingly, AndrewAndrew are constantly asked to spin Icona Pop (Williams 2014).

13. Kaitlyn Tiffany, "Lena Dunham, Make Me a Pop Star," *The Cornell Daily Sun*, April 15, 2014, http://cornellsun.com/blog/2014/04/15/tiffany-lena-dunham-make-me-a-pop-star/.

14. Kristofor Vogel, in a master's thesis, describes hipsters as a "pop-subculture" (see Vogel 2013). My use of post-hipster in this essay illustrates the problematic nature of identifying hipsters as a subculture when their ties to consumer culture—illustrated in the ability of a show like *Girls* to draw popular recognition—are readily apparent.

15. Christian Lorentzen, "Why the Hipster Must Die: A Modest Proposal to Save New York Cool," *Time Out New York*, May 30, 2007, http://www.timeout.com/newyork/things-to-do/why-the-hipster-must-die.

16. Douglas Haddow, "Hipster: The Dead End of Western Civilization," *Adbusters*, July 29, 2008, https://www.adbusters.org/magazine/79/hipster.html.

17. Ibid.

18. Greif's symposium on the Hipster, which is captured in the book, includes Lorentzen, who wrote "Why the Hipster Must Die: A Modest Proposal"; musician DJ/rupture, pseudonym of Jace Clayton; and theorists like Jennifer Baumgardner.

19. Mark Greif, 2010, "The Hipster in the Mirror," the *New York Times*, November 12, 2010, http://www.nytimes.com/2010/11/14/books/review/Greif-t.html?pagewanted=all&_r= 1&.

20. Ibid.

21. Ibid.

22. Ibid.

23. Rob Horning, "The Death of the Hipster," in *What Was the Hipster? A Sociological Investigation*, eds. Mark Greif, Kathleen Ross, and Dayna Tortorici (Brooklyn: n+1, 2010), 81.

24. Kaya Oakes, *Slanted and Enchanted: The Evolution of Indie Culture* (New York: Holt Paperbacks, 2009), 16.

25. Ibid.

26. Mark Greif, "Positions," in *What Was the Hipster? A Sociological Investigation*, eds. Mark Greif, Kathleen Ross, and Dayna Tortorici (Brooklyn: n+1, 2010), 6.

27. Ibid, 9.

28. Kaya Oakes, *Slanted and Enchanted: The Evolution of Indie Culture* (New York: Holt Paperbacks, 2009), xiii.

29. Richard Douglas Lloyd, *Neo-Bohemia: Art and Commerce in the Postindustrial City* (New York: Routledge, 2010), 243.

30. Ibid, 247.

31. Mark Greif, "What Was the Hipster?" *New York*, October 24, 2010, http://nymag.com/news/features/69129/.

32. HBO. "Q&A with Manish Raval," Accessed October 25, 2014. http://connect.hbo.com/events/girls/q-manish-raval/.

33. Only the band has been banned from playing. Billie Joe Armstrong, lead singer of Green Day, still plays the venue as a member of another band, Pinhead Gunpowder, because this band hasn't signed a major label contract.

34. John Leland, "For Rock Bands, Selling Out Isn't What It Used to Be," the *New York Times*, March 11, 2001, http://www.nytimes.com/2001/03/11/magazine/1SELLOUT.html?src= pm&pagewanted=1.

35. Shannon Carlin, "'Girls' Music Supervisor Manish Raval Reveals What Fans Will Hear on Season Three," *Radio.com*, January 8, 2014, http://radio.com/2014/01/08/interview-girls-music-supervisor-manish-raval-season-3/.

36. Todd VanDerWerff, "*Girls*: 'Weirdos Need Girlfriends, Too,'" the *Onion*, June 3, 2012, http://www.avclub.com/tvclub/girls-weirdos-need-girlfriends-too-75587.

37. Kristofor Vogel, "Perceptions of Subversion: The Formulation of a Pop-Subculture" (master's thesis, University of Texas at Arlington, 2013), 8.

38. Ibid, 17.

39. Sarah Thornton, *Club Cultures: Music, Media, and Subcultural Capital* (Cambridge, UK: Polity Press, 1995), 13–14.

40. Season 2 features three episodes with their titles lifted from song titles. In addition to "I Get Ideas," "It's about Time," and "It's a Shame About Ray" are song titles from The Lemonheads.

41. Jenni Konner, "I Get Ideas," *Girls*, directed by Lena Dunham, HBO, aired January 20, 2013, DVD.

42. This is not the case for musicians who play characters on the show. To date, *Girls* has enjoyed a number of cameos from prominent musicians including Kim Gordon (formerly of Sonic Youth), the aforementioned Jorma Taccone (The Lonely Island), the DJing duo AndrewAndrew, and Ezra Koenig (Vampire Weekend).

43. Corban Goble, "The 8 Best Music Moments of HBO's *Girls*," *Stereogum*, June 18, 2012, http://www.stereogum.com/1067341/the-8-best-music-moments-from-hbos-girls/franchises/listomania/.

44. Lena Dunham, "Hannah's Diary," *Girls,* directed by Richard Shepard, HBO, aired May 6, 2012, DVD.

45. Ibid.

46. Lena Dunham and Judd Apatow, "Welcome to Bushwick AKA the Crackcident," *Girls,* directed by Lena Dunham, HBO, aired May 27, 2012, DVD.

47. Lena Dunham and Jesse Peretz, "It's a Shame About Ray," *Girls*, directed by Lena Dunham, HBO, aired February 2, 2013, DVD.
48. Ibid.
49. Ibid.
50. Ibid.
51. Lena Dunham and Jody Lee Lipes, "Weirdos Need Girlfriends, Too," *Girls*, directed by Jody Lee Lipes, HBO, June 3, 2012. *Girls*, DVD.
52. Ibid.
53. Ibid.
54. Maggie Lange, "Only Nine People Have Given to Zosia Mamet's Hipster Band Kickstarter," *Gawker*, May 29, 2013, http://gawker.com/only-nine-people-have-given-to-zosia-mamets-hipster-ba-510278912.
55. Katie Baker, "Zosia Mamet's $32,000 Folk Music Kickstarter Failed," *Jezebel*, June 10, 2013, http://jezebel.com/zosia-mamets-32-000-folk-music-kickstarter-failed-512321567.
56. Even a *Glamour* interview with Mamet entitled "O-M-G, You Guys. Zosia Mamet Has a Band and Tells Us All About It!" makes use of Shoshanna's lingo in an interview about Zosia's band, conflating the actor and character.
57. Lena Dunham and Paul Simms, "I Saw You," *Girls*, directed by Jesse Peretz, HBO, March 16, 2014.
58. AndrewAndrew is the alias of a New York-based DJ duo, whose first names are both Andrew (they refuse to reveal their last names), noted for their mirrored, enigmatic personas.

BIBLIOGRAPHY

Baker, Katie. 2013. "Zosia Mamet's $32,000 Folk Music Kickstarter Failed." *Jezebel*, June 10, 2013. http://jezebel.com/zosia-mamets-32-000-folk-music-kickstarter-failed-512321567.
Brody, Caitlin. 2013. "O-M-G, You Guys. Zosia Mamet Has a Band and Tells Us All About It!" *Glamour*, July 10, 2013. http://www.glamour.com/entertainment/ blogs/obsessed/2013/07/o-m-g-you-guys-zosia-mamet-has.
Dunham, Lena. "Hannah's Diary." *Girls*. Directed by Richard Shepard. HBO. May 6, 2012. DVD.
Dunham, Lena and Judd Apatow. "Welcome to Bushwick AKA the Crackcident." *Girls*. Directed by Lena Dunham. HBO. May 27, 2012. DVD.
Dunham, Lena and Paul Simms. "I Saw You." *Girls*. Directed by Jesse Peretz. HBO. March 16, 2014.
Dunham, Lena and Dan Sterling. "Weirdos Need Girlfriends, Too." *Girls*. Directed by Jody Lee Lipes. HBO. June 3, 2012. DVD.
Gallo, Phil. 2013. "'Girls' Music Supervisor Manish Raval Talks about Finding 'Cool Music.'" *Hollywood Reporter*, January 14, 2013. http://www.hollywoodreporter.com/news/girls-music-supervisor-manish-raval-412258.
Goble, Corban. "The 8 Best Music Moments of HBO's *Girls*." *Stereogum*, June 18, 2012. http://www.stereogum.com/1067341/the-8-best-music-moments-from-hbos-girls/franchises/listomania/.
Greif, Mark. "The Hipster in the Mirror." *New York Times*, November 12, 2010. http://www.nytimes.com/2010/11/14/books/review/Greif-t.html?pagewanted=all&_r=1&.
———. "Positions." In *What Was the Hipster? A Sociological Investigation*, edited by Mark Greif, Kathleen Ross, and Dayna Tortorici, 4–13. Brooklyn: n+1, 2010.
———. 2010. "What Was the Hipster?" *New York Magazine*, October 24, 2010. http://nymag.com/news/features/69129/.
Haddow, Douglas. "Hipster: The Dead End of Western Civilization." *Adbusters*, July 29, 2008. https://www.adbusters.org/magazine/79/hipster.html.
HBO. "Q&A with Manish Raval." Accessed October 25, 2014. http://connect.hbo.com/events/girls/q-manish-raval/.

Horning, Rob. "The Death of the Hipster." In *What Was the Hipster? A Sociological Investigation*, edited by Mark Greif, Kathleen Ross, and Dayna Tortorici, 78–84. Brooklyn: n+1, 2010.

Klein, Bethany. "'The New Radio': Music Licensing as a Response to Industry Woe." *Media, Culture & Society* 30, no. 4 (2008): 463–78.

Konner, Jenni. "I Get Ideas." *Girls*. Directed by Lena Dunham. HBO. January 20, 2013. DVD.

Lange, Maggie. "Only Nine People Have Given to Zosia Mamet's Hipster Band Kickstarter." *Gawker*, May 29, 2013. http://gawker.com/only-nine-people-have-given-to-zosia-mamets-hipster-ba-510278912.

Leland, John. 2001. "For Rock Bands, Selling Out Isn't What It Used to Be." *New York Times*, March 11. Accessed October 25, 2014. http://www.nytimes.com/2001/03/11/magazine/11SELLOUT.html?src=pm&pagewanted=1.

Lloyd, Richard Douglas. *Neo-Bohemia: Art and Commerce in the Postindustrial City*. New York: Routledge, 2010.

Lorentzen, Christian. "Why the Hipster Must Die: A Modest Proposal to Save New York Cool." *Time Out New York*, May 30, 2007. http://www.timeout.com/ newyork/things-to-do/why-the-hipster-must-die.

Nussbaum, Emily. "It's Different for 'Girls.'" *New York Magazine*, March 25, 2012. http://nymag.com/arts/tv/features/girls-lena-dunham-2012-4/.

Oakes, Kaya. *Slanted and Enchanted: The Evolution of Indie Culture*. New York: Holt Paperbacks, 2009.

Peretz, Jesse. "It's a Shame about Ray." *Girls*. Directed by Lena Dunham. HBO. February 2, 2013. DVD.

Thornton, Sarah. *Club Cultures: Music, Media, and Subcultural Capital*. Cambridge, UK: Polity Press, 1995.

Tiffany, Kaitlyn. "Lena Dunham, Make Me a Pop Star." *The Cornell Daily Sun*, April 15, 2014. http://cornellsun.com/blog/2014/04/15/tiffany-lena-dunham-make-me-a-pop-star/.

Unterberger, Andrew. "Is 'Girls' Finally Gonna Make a Hit Out of Icona Pop's 'I Love It'?" *Pop Dust*, January 28, 2013. http://popdust.com/2013/01/28/girls-icona-pop-i-love-it-soundtrack/.

VanDerWerff, Todd. "*Girls*: 'Weirdos Need Girlfriends, Too.'" *Onion*, June 3, 2012. http://www.avclub.com/tvclub/girls-weirdos-need-girlfriends-too-75587.

Vogel, Kristofor. "Perceptions of Subversion: The Formulation of a Pop-Subculture." Master's Thesis, University of Texas at Arlington, 2013.

Wagner, David. "Proof that Lena Dunham Has the Power to Make Hip Songs into Huge Hits Now." *Wire*, January 15, 2013. http://www.thewire.com/ entertainment/2013/01/girls-soundtrack-sales-numbers/61035/.

Williams, Alex. "Riding the Wave of 'Girls.'" *New York Times*, March 19, 2014. http://www.nytimes.com/2014/03/20/fashion/girls-television-cameos-new-york-city.html?_r=0.

Chapter Seven

Generation X Archetypes in HBO's *Girls*

Tom Pace

Many of us who come from that sometimes-maligned and often-forgotten group of Americans known, for better or for worse, as Generation X, probably remember our heyday of the 1990s. We remember those days not so much because it was some magical, golden era (it was not), but rather we remember those days, in part, because it is the only time the culture at large remembered us. During the early to mid-1990s, popular culture was awash in trying to figure out who we were, often presenting us with films and television shows that purported to reflect who we were, what we were thinking, and what we wanted. These films and shows included such offerings as NBC's *Friends*, Ben Stiller's *Reality Bites*, Richard Linklater's *Slacker* and *Before Sunrise*, Kevin Smith's *Clerks*, and MTV's *Daria*, among many others. As a result, many of these cultural representations wound up presenting Gen-Xers in one or all of the following ways: slackers, whiny, entitled, over-educated, depressed, lazy, alienated, or materialistic. In other words, many Gen-Xers were being portrayed and described in terms very similar to the way the Millennials are being described in HBO's *Girls*.

Girls, a critically-acclaimed comedy written by, directed by, and starring Lena Dunham, and co-produced by Judd Apatow and Jenni Konner, follows four single women in their twenties as they, according to Dunham, make their way "one mistake at a time" in New York City, trying to find work, love, and themselves during the always-complicated post-college years.[1] While *Girls* has maintained high ratings and is a popular HBO offering, responses and reviews to the show have been polarizing. On the one hand, some reviewers have lauded the gritty, realistic portrayal of female friendship and the difficulty these women have finding love and happiness in a post-feminist, post-recession America. In her initial review of *Girls* for the *New York Times*, Alessandra Stanley contrasts the show with its spiritual godmother, *Sex and the City*, noting that "*Sex and the City* served up romantic failure wrapped in the trappings of success. *Girls* offers romantic failure wrapped in the trappings of failure."[2] Dunham, Stanley notes, makes "great comedy out of her own shortcomings. Her sense of humor is sardonic and unsentimental enough to appeal to" a broad audience.

On the other hand, many have criticized *Girls* for presenting characters that lack diversity, are entitled, privileged, whiny, and unlikeable. In his takedown of the show for *BuddyTV.com,* John Kubicek admits that "*Girls* feels less like a commentary on this generation and more like an indictment on it. These characters have been raised believing that they're special and that they can do anything they want. The problem is that none of them seem to want to do anything."[3] But, as Jesse Levine of the *Huffington Post* noted shortly after *Girls* premiered, that is the point. "The first episode of *Girls*," Levine writes, "presents one of the most critical portrayals of middle class, college educated, young, white people I have ever seen. What's revelatory about the show, and perhaps inspired some of the hype, is that by focusing on this narrow segment of our culture, *Girls* shows the hypocrisy shared by many young people."[4] And not just for Dunham's generation, the Millennials. Stanley points out "the baseline joke of *Girls*" resides in its reminder that young people don't change from generation to generation, despite the show's obvious focus on struggles shared by Millennials.[5] "There was a lot of sex in the '60s, but not much sexual revolution," Stanley observes. "For all the talk of equality, liberation and independence, the love lives of these young women are not much more satisfying than those of their grandmothers."[6] Stanley, Levine, and others are correct in their arguments that *Girls* is a critique of millennial culture by Millennials, a searing self-aware examination of educated, upper-middle class, post-college New York City whites. But, while the show focuses primarily on the lives of four female Millennials, I would also suggest that this portrayal draws heavily from images of Generation X youth culture of the 1990s.

This chapter argues that HBO's *Girls* draws from what I like to call Generation X archetypes, patterns of behavior and characteristics of young people that found their way in the popular cultural landscape in the early to mid-1990s, and the show appropriates these characteristics and patterns in their portrayal of Millennials in ways much more complex and compelling than most television shows and films from the 1990s. To do so, I draw from Northrop Frye's theory of archetypal criticism to suggest that multiple images of Generation X culture have turned into various kinds of archetypes in current popular culture. To make this argument, I address three components of the show that draw from and appropriate these Generation X archetypes. One, the portrayal of the cynical, male slacker character who lacks ambition, as represented on *Girls* by Adam. Two, the Generation X archetype of the reliance on friends and the distrust of parents, specifically in the characters of Hannah, Jessa, Marnie, and Adam. Finally, I analyze a specific episode from *Girls*, "One Man's Trash," in which Hannah spends a weekend with the settled-down, adult Gen-Xer Joshua and gets a glimpse at what her life may ultimately become, suggesting a metacommentary that Hannah, like the Gen-Xers before her, will struggle during her post-college years before finally finding happiness. In doing so, this chapter shows these archetypes as narrative foundations that unveil the differences as well as the similarities in the way these two generations have been portrayed in the popular imagination.

Archetypes, of course, are universal themes, images, traits, or characteristics found in philosophies, myths, dreams, religions, and works of art—including popular culture texts. Connected primarily to the work of Carl Jung, archetypes tend to, in the words of Arthur Berger, "exist beyond the realm of the personal unconscious of individuals; they are connected to past history and an alleged collective unconscious found in all people."[7] Jung argues that humans become aware of these images and patterns through dreams or artistic representations, manifesting themselves via symbolic images. Jung defines them this way: "These manifestations are what I call archetypes. They are without known origin; and they reproduce themselves in any time or in any part of the world—even where transmission by direct descent or 'cross fertilization' through migration must be ruled out."[8] For my purpose in this paper I am not suggesting that characteristics of Generation X reflect universal patterns and images found in other cultures' art, philosophy, or religion. Indeed, the notion of archetype, Berger reminds us, is "very controversial, and many people reject it as being both unproven and unprovable. It may be possible to infer a collective unconscious that generates archetypes," Berger writes, "but how does one demonstrate it exists?"[9] Rather, I am suggesting that the patterns, characteristics, and images of Generation X culture act as a *kind* of archetypal frame that subsequent texts, such as *Girls*, draw from (consciously or not), to tell their own stories. Although the manifestation of these Generation X archetypes originated in the late 1980s and early 1990s they do in Jung's words "reproduce themselves" in the work of millennial popular culture, such as *Girls* and as Berger notes, connect "to past history and an alleged collective unconscious" from early 1990s Generation X culture. As such, these characteristics act as cultural touchstones that are almost archetypal in their narrative function on *Girls*.

To help me unpack this understanding of archetype even further, I turn to the work of Northrop Frye, whose work on archetypal literary criticism in the mid-twentieth century serves, among other things, as one of the foundations of popular culture studies. Indeed, his understanding of the role of archetypes in literature and other cultural texts provides a framework to help us see how the various characteristics of Generation X culture, characteristics that emerged in the early 1990s, become archetypal patterns in such later cultural texts as *Girls*. In his influential 1957 book *Anatomy of Criticism*, Frye takes Jung's insights on archetype and develops a comprehensive plan of literary and cultural criticism in which he identifies numerous modes, symbols, myths, and genres that, as David Richter describes, creates a "multidimensional space in which one may locate the position of any work of literature and its relationship to any other."[10] Specifically, Frye identifies such archetypes as the hero, the different seasons and how they correspond to specific genres, the images of demons and gods, as well as numerous other myths found in world culture. In an earlier essay, "The Archetypes of Literature," Frye sums up this whole program of criticism by arguing that archetypal patterns in narratives go beyond pure signification and act as a narrative itself. He writes:

> Patterns of imagery, on the other hand, or fragments of significance, are oracular in origin, and derive from the epiphanic moment, the flash of instantaneous comprehension with no direct reference to time . . . By the time we get them, in the form of proverbs, riddles, commandments, and etiological folk tales, there is already a considerable element of narrative in them. They too are encyclopedic in tendency, building up a total structure of significance, or doctrine, from random and empiric fragments. And just as pure narrative would be an unconscious act, so pure significance would be an incommunicable state of consciousness, for communication begins by constructing narrative.[11]

Here, Frye argues that narratives—literary as well as popular, proverbial as well as folk—rely for their existence on myth and archetype. Much of this development and creation of a narrative, he insists, is an unconscious act on the part of the creator and, as a result, the reliance on previous myths and archetypes is unconscious as well. Later, Frye argues that "the myth *is* the archetype, though it might be convenient to say myth when referring to narrative, and archetype when speaking of significance."[12] In other words, the use of archetypes in narrative is not only an unconscious act on the part of the creator, but those archetypes serve to signify numerous cultural concepts of which both creator and audience are already cognizant. Frye even suggests, as noted by Ian Balfour, that archetypal criticism exists in the popular as well as the literary. Balfour insists that Frye understood that "The archetypal critic looks at literature as a product of civilization and these objects of study are typically primitive and popular, using these two terms in their nonpejorative senses."[13] As such, images and patterns of Generation X culture, which had their "epiphanic" origins quickly and seemingly out of nowhere in the popular culture of the 1990s, ultimately provided narrative grist and archetypal significance for Lena Dunham and her show *Girls*.

While these images and patterns initially materialized in early to mid-1990s popular culture in the context of the larger culture trying to define Generation X, much of the rhetoric and the language used to describe the Millennials echoes that rhetoric from the 1990s used to define Gen-Xers. But, Gen-Xers can be a hard-to-define generation, a generation constantly in the shadow of their Baby Boomer predecessors and, now, their Millennial successors. Many even disagree about what years to use to define when Gen-Xers were born. In his study from the University of Michigan, "Active, Balanced, and Happy: These Young Americans are not Bowling Alone," Jon Miller uses the years 1961–1981 and includes eighty-four million people.[14] In his report for the Harvard Joint Center for Housing Studies, "Defining Generations," George Masnick cites 1965–1984 so that Boomers, Xers, and Millennials "cover equal twenty-year age spans."[15] Masnick also points out that America experienced low birthrates during the 1960s and early 1970s, the core years of Generation X births.[16] Because the core years for Generation X fall during the late 1960s and early 1970s, I follow Elwood Watson's time frame of 1965–1979 in which he observes that "the vast majority of demographers, journalists, cultural critics, economists, and social scientists agree that the mid-1960s to the late 1970s is the most accurate timeframe to describe this group of forty-six million Americans."[17]

In the early 1990s, journalists, economists, politicians, educators, and other public intellectuals began to write earnestly about Generation X in an effort not only to define this generation of young people in their twenties but to identify characteristics that distinguished them from the Boomers. In their 1993 study of Generation X *Thirteenth Gen: Abort, Retry, Ignore, Fail?*, Neil Howe and Bill Strauss collected numerous newspaper columns, studies, and other research on Gen-Xers published between the late 1980s and 1992.[18] The majority of what they found appeared to spell doom for this generation and for America. Their research immediately characterized Gen-Xers as disenfranchised, alienated, materialistic, unwilling to work, ignorant yet overeducated, and narcissistic. Here is a sampling of what Howe and Strauss gathered: They quote then-United States Senator Bill Bradley, who bemoaned young people when he stated, "This news is not only shocking; it is frightening . . . When 95 percent of college students cannot locate Vietnam on a world map, we must sound the alarm."[19] They cite the head of an advertising agency, Penny Erikson, who argues that "Unlike Yuppies, younger people are not driven from within. They need reinforcement. They prefer short-term tasks with observable results."[20] From a 1992 *Washington Post* report on the lack of political awareness among Xers: "It's a far cry from twenty years ago, when the legal voting age was dropped from 21 to 18. Student rallies, speeches, and petitions flooded almost every campus . . . Today, hardly a whimper."[21] And, from a high school teacher in Alexandria, VA, "The clothes and cars I see every morning are a symptom of a rampant materialism that is changing for the worse the relationships between teenagers and their school, their peers, their community, and, most importantly, their families."[22] As such, the stereotype of the Gen-Xer as alienated from parents, overeducated but non-ambitious, disenfranchised, and cynical solidified into a set of cultural archetypes that have affected popular culture ever since.

Interestingly, though, recent studies on Gen-Xers, now in their late thirties and forties, dispel the alienated slacker stereotype developed in the early 1990s. In his 2011 report on Generation X, Miller calls Gen-Xers in their thirties and forties "active, balanced, and happy"[23] Specifically, his study undermines the stereotypes that arose in the 1990s about Xers. Miller's research shows that 86 percent of Generation X "work part-time or full-time; 70 percent spend forty or more hours working and commuting each week; and 40 percent spend fifty or more hours each week working or commuting."[24] Overall, the report shows that "Two-thirds of Generation X young adults are satisfied with their current job."[25] In response to the earlier stereotype that Xers are alienated from parents and from family in general, Miller's report shows that Xer parents "report a high level of involvement with their children and high expectations for their future" and that most Xers "are family oriented."[26] In short, most Generation Xers, according to Miller's study, report strong social relationships, have achieved a satisfying work-life balance, derive satisfaction from becoming involved in community and religious activities, and overall are happy with their lives. Yet, many still hold that earlier slacker image of Generation X very much at the fore of their understanding of Xers and, as a result, it has solidified into a popular archetype, one that winds its way into our understanding of Millennials and their popular culture.

In recent years, Millennials, that group of Americans born between the early 1980s and 2001, have begun to be written about, talked about, and portrayed in various popular culture media. Typically, Millennials are described as over-reliant on and inundated with technology and social media and, as a result, are often viewed as self-focused and self-absorbed. Also, they are often described in terms very different from the way Gen-Xers were described. Most importantly, whereas Xers were seen as alienated from parents and many authority figures, Millennials, Watson observes, "have been smothered with an unconditional amount of love and attention by their parents."[27] However, much of what has been written about Millennials echoes what was written about their Generation X forbearers. They too are being referred to as lazy, entitled, overeducated, and self-indulgent. In a 2013 *Time* magazine cover story, for instance, *Time* writer and Gen-Xer Joel Stein calls them "lazy, entitled, selfish, and shallow" and called them out for their reliance on cell phones, texting, iPhones, and other technological innovations.[28] Interestingly, though, in a 1985 *Newsweek* cover story on what they termed "The Video Generation," editors bemoaned a new generation for its self-indulgent focus on video cameras, suggesting that this generational rhetoric does not change much over the decades; if in the 1980s it was the over-dependence on video cameras, thirty years later, it's the over-dependence on iPhones, texting, and social media.[29] In short, while significant generational differences exist between Generation X and the Millennials, much of the language and rhetoric used to describe them revolves around similar themes of entitlement, lack of work ethic, and narcissism, among other traits.

During the 1990s, popular media picked up on these traits and began representing them in various films, television programs, and other outlets. In the 1991 film *Slacker*, Richard Linklater presents a group of disaffected twenty something outcasts meandering through their lives during a single day in Austin, TX. In his 1994 film *Reality Bites*, Ben Stiller examines a group of recently-graduated Gen-Xers struggling during their post-college years. Ethan Hawke plays Troy Dyer, a college-educated twenty something who works a menial job, is cynical about his future, occasionally plays in a band at a coffee shop, shows little-to-no ambition, and occasionally dates Lelaina, played by Winona Ryder. Lelaina, an aspiring TV production assistant, has to settle for what she considers demeaning work that she believes undermines her artistic integrity. Also, in 1994, Kevin Smith directed and starred in *Clerks*, an irreverent indie film about two slackers who work the counter at a convenience store and a video store, respectively, and who bemoan their lack of job opportunities, ambition, and love lives. These types of slacker figures were later mocked in the brilliant late 1990s animated satire *Daria*, particularly through the character Trent, the brother of Daria's best friend and a twenty something slacker who is just ambitious enough to make band practice occasionally and wake up before three o'clock in the afternoon. What emerged out of these films, as well as numerous other television shows and films like them, are several Generation X archetypes that since the 1990s have figured prominently in popular film and television shows, especially HBO's *Girls*.

I am not suggesting that *Girls* is, in secret, a Generation X product. It is not. While co-producers Judd Apatow and Jenni Konner are Xers, the show's main voice is a Millennial one. As Emily Nussbaum articulates in her rave review of the show and about Lena Dunham's ability to tap into a distinctive millennial voice in *Girls,* the show "was a bold defense (and a searing critique) of the so-called Millennial Generation by a person still in her twenties," she wrote.[30] "As my younger colleague Willa Paskin put it, the show felt, to her peers, FUBU: 'for us by us.'"[31] Yet, even though *Girls* very much taps into the millennial zeitgeist, it does so by appropriating what I have defined as Generation X archetypes, cultural touchstones, images, and patterns that emerged in Generation X popular culture during the 1990s. As Frye suggests, these archetypes serve a narrative function in that not only are they an unconscious act on the part of the creator—in this case Lena Dunham—but these archetypes serve to signify numerous cultural concepts of which both creator and audience are already cognizant. In other words, *Girls* is familiar not just to many Millennials but to many Gen-Xers, as well, because they rely on archetypes that many in her audience are aware of and which, as a result, serve as a foundation to the show's narrative. Prominent among these archetypes are two I plan to explore in *Girls*: one, the overeducated, underachieving male slacker, and two, the twenty somethings more reliant on friends than on parents or other authority figures. In addition, I will address the image of the adult, settled Gen-Xer in *Girls*, in the figure of Joshua from the episode "One Man's Trash," a figure who suggests for Hannah and for the show's other Millennials that they ultimately will not be stuck permanently in their twenty something malaise. All three perspectives—the male slacker, the twenty something relying on friends, and the settled, more adult Gen-Xer—I would argue, have emerged as current cultural archetypes being appropriated, unconsciously or not, by *Girls*.

One of the common Generation X archetypes that emerged in the 1990s and has become a cultural touchstone since is the male slacker. In his book *Men to Boys: The Making of Modern Immaturity*, Gary Cross argues that many men in contemporary culture "refuse to grow up."[32] Naming these figures "boy-men" Cross argues that "the boy-man has become a central character in our culture and, even if men do find ways of meeting their economic and even social obligations, the culture of immaturity has become the norm rather than the exception."[33] Cross identifies the roots of this shift in the men of the "Greatest Generation," men he argues who might have embraced their role as providers but were ultimately confused by the contradictions and expectations of modern fatherhood. Their uncertainty, he suggests, gave birth to the Beats and to men who indulged in childhood hobbies and boyish sports. This indulging of adolescence pursuits, Cross argues, fashioned a new kind of manhood, one in which men from the Baby Boomer generation are engaged in a constant struggle to hold onto their youth and, when that was gone, embrace, among other quick fixes, Viagra. As such, Cross points out in his book that once Generation X came of age in the late 1980s and 1990s, they were left without mature role models to emulate or rebel against, and as a result, turned to cynicism and sensual intensity. At the same time, the media fed on this Generation X longing and transformed what would otherwise be merely a life stage into a highly desirable lifestyle. Cross, thus, suggests that this hardening of a life stage into a life style took place just as Gen-Xers were entering the stage in the 1990s. He notes that the term "slacker" was "a characterization given these Generation X males when the term was first invented in the late 1980s."[34] Furthermore, he also suggests that this image of the Gen-X slacker is a complicated one because the image of the slacker belies the reality of most Xers being more active and innovative than previous generations. Cross writes about his own Generation X sons and their counterparts:

> Despite the common image of the couch-potato Gen Xer fixed zombielike to the ubiquitous screen, my sons' generation is, if anything, more active, more open to innovation than mine. This means not only a focus on fitness and an adaptability to change but a longing for immersion in the intensity of sensual experience, which has become almost a defining trait of Generation X. This quest for excitement has perhaps always had its appeal to adolescents and youths. Since the late 1970s and especially since the 1990s, however, it has become progressively a longing that extends into manhood.[35]

Here, Cross recognizes the image of the slacker as associated with Generation X that developed in popular culture during the 1990s and, as a result, solidified into a defining characteristic of manhood not just for Gen-Xers but for Millennials as well. Yet, he also recognizes the limits of this image by showing that most Xers rarely fit that image—an idea I will address further in my analysis of the *Girls* episode "One Man's Trash." This "longing for immersion in the intensity of sensual experience" refers to what Cross sees as Generation X's desire for thrills generated by such manufactured experiences as video games, among other outlets. However, I would suggest that this desire for the "intensity of sensual experience" as a defining marker of the Generation X "slacker" has been appropriated by the image of the "slackers" in HBO's *Girls*. While the men of *Girls* are not shown playing video games, they do participate in other adolescence-extending activities that draw from and play on the archetype of the male slacker developed in the popular culture of the early 1990s.

The main character from *Girls* who fits this archetype the most is Hannah's on-again, off-again boyfriend, Adam Sackler. Adam's last name is not only an anagram on "slacker," but he is portrayed in many of the archetypal conventions of the brooding, anti-social, directionless, well-educated twenty-something male made popular in 1990s Generation X culture. For example, Adam appears directionless, does not hold a steady job, and gives little-to-no indication he wants one. Early in season 1, for example, he tells Hannah, after she informs him that her parents are no longer supporting her financially, that "you should never be anyone's fucking slave" ("Pilot"). We soon learn that Adam, of course, is supported by his grandmother who provides him with $800 a month. He tells Hannah that in addition to this money, he supplements, but the viewer never really sees how he earns any additional income. Adam is a struggling actor who is also building a boat to use to sail down the Hudson, although for what purpose is never really clarified. In much of the early episodes of *Girls*, Adam refuses to meet Hannah's friends, rarely (if ever) returns her text messages, and lives in a slovenly Brooklyn apartment. He often wears only jeans and no shirt, and when we do see him out in social settings, he appears awkward and uncomfortable in his own skin. He would also appear to be somewhat well-educated. Although we never learn where or if Adam attended college, he demonstrates a nuanced understanding of George Bernard Shaw's *Major Barbara,* after landing a role in a Broadway production of the play, and in one scene borrows *Little Women* from Ray. He is not unlike many of the slackers made popular in Generation X films and TV. For example, Adam's spiritual godfather would appear to be someone like Troy from *Reality Bites*. In that film, Troy is well-educated, works menial jobs, and harbors artistic ambitions by performing guitar in a coffee shop. Like Adam's relationship with Hannah, Troy also engages in an on-again, off-again romance with the main character Lelaina, played by Winona Ryder. While *Girls* is a more complex, complicated, and better written offering than *Reality Bites*, the male slacker figure represented by Adam underscores many of the archetypal elements of this Generation X male figure that the film helped make a part of the pop cultural landscape. However, he's a surprising slacker *revisited*: we think Adam holds no gainful employment and that he only occasionally pursues his artistic outlet, yet he works and holds true to his artistic values, reaching his dream of performing on Broadway. We initially think Sackler's a slacker, absentee boyfriend, yet he develops into a loving, devoted, imperfect partner to Hannah.

Another Generation X archetype that *Girls* uses is the image of the twenty something relying on friends and not parents. One of the common descriptions of Gen-Xers is that many come from parents who divorced and, as a result, wound up relying more on their friends for emotional and financial support. Divorce, indeed, occupies much of the Generation X *ethos.* For many Gen-Xers, divorce was common. Many Xers spent less time with their parents than previous generations of children had, often under the moniker of "latchkey kids." During the 1970s and 1980s, many Xers found themselves home alone and taking care of themselves and their siblings, while their parents worked, and were not coddled for every emotional need and want—a common description of many Millennials. According to a 2011 *Wall Street Journal* piece, for instance, the divorce rate peaked in 1980 with 22.6 per one thousand married couples divorcing.[36] Thus, many TV shows and films during the 1990s that portrayed Generation X made appeals to this *ethos* and featured young people in tensions with their parents, showed them relying on their friends for support, and at times even cut parents out altogether. As a result of these cultural representations, a Generation X archetype of the young person alienated from his or her parents developed. Examples include, of course, NBC's *Friends*, a show that features six Gen-Xers in their twenties living in New York City, relying on one another for emotional, social, and sometimes financial support. In the Pilot episode, for example, Monica reconnects with old high school friend Rachel who has been cut off from her well-off parents because she broke off her engagement on the eve of her wedding. Subsequently, Rachel moves in with Monica, starts working in a coffee shop, and tries to make it on her own with the help of her friends. At Lelaina's college graduation dinner in *Reality Bites*, Lelaina's father Tom, played by Joe Don Baker, gives her a gasoline credit card that he will pay for one year, and his new wife's used BMW. Tom's new wife no longer needs the car since he just bought her a brand new one. While Lelaina is not cut-off completely financially by her parents, her father does tell her, "little darlin', after you've been in the real world for a while, you're gonna appreciate that car."[37] In both examples, but in especially *Friends*, parents are often portrayed as clueless, absentee, unreliable, or just plain buffoonish. Chandler's father, for instance, undergoes a sex change operation, a running gag that is often played merely for laughs and hijinks. As such, a Generation archetype of the twenty something more dependent on friends rather than family emerged, one that *Girls* ultimately appropriates for its own narrative structure.

Girls, of course, is a show by Millennials for Millennials. Yet, for a cultural text very much about Millennials, its portrayal of parents appears to be more in line with Generation X than it would with fellow Millennials. A common description of Millennials suggests that they are very close to their parents and that they rely on them for emotional and financial support, and that they see their parents almost more as friends than authority figures, so much so that the parents of Millennials are often referred to as "helicopter parents," a parent who pays extremely close attention, hovering overhead throughout the different stages of a child's life. A recent *New York Times* article cites a Pew research study that suggests Boomers and Millennials "feel a duty to care for each other."[38] The article also points out that both generations expect to take financial care of the other: "The vast majority of 18- to 29-year-olds polled—84 percent—said adult children have a responsibility to provide financial assistance to an elderly parent if he or she needs it. And 54 percent of the 50- to 64-year-olds said that parents have a responsibility to provide for their adult children."[39] This report, then, appears to reinforce the mainstream understanding of the entitled Millennials relying on the enabling, helicopter Boomer parents.

However, *Girls* appears to portray the relationship between its millennial characters and their Boomer parents very differently. I would argue that *Girls* appropriates the Generation X twenty something relying more on friends than parents, much more than it does the relationship between Boomers and Millennials, as reported in such studies as the Pew Research Center report. One reason for this portrayal may be that the patterns, images, and characteristics of young people that developed in the 1990s now acts as a type of archetype. In some ways, this image of the Gen-Xer relying more on friends than family, as well as the male slacker, have become cultural myths that, as

Frye points out, "*is* the archetype."[40] For instance, in the Pilot episode of
Girls, Hannah is cut off financially from her parents. Hannah is working on
her first book, while working at a publishing company as an unpaid intern.
While Hannah's mother (Loreen) is all for cutting her off financially and is
quite blunt in her announcement, Hannah's father (Tad) hems and haws and
is less sure about the move. When her parents give her the news, she is
stunned and scared and appears to act in a way consistent with mainstream
understanding of Millennials:

> LOREEN: We're not going to be supporting you any longer.

> TAD: You see, I wasn't going to phrase it like that, Loreen, the way you
> phrased it.

> HANNAH: But I have no job.

> LOREEN: No, you have an internship that you say is going to turn into a
> job.

> HANNAH: I don't know when.

> LOREEN: You graduated from college two years ago. We've been sup-
> porting you for two years, and that's enough.

> HANNAH: Do you know how crazy the economy is right now? I mean,
> all my friends get help.[41]

In this scene, neither Hannah or her parents look particularly good. Hannah is
incredulous that her parents are cutting her off, despite graduating from
college two years earlier. And, the sudden way her parents, especially her
mother, announce the news is alarming. On the one hand, the portrayal of
Hannah and her parents appears to reflect the relationship between Boomer
parent and Millennial child in that Hannah's parents have supported her, it
would seem, more than enough in her post-college years. And, Hannah's
reaction is one very much consistent with mainstream understanding of post-
college Millennials. Later in the episode when Hannah confronts her parents
in their hotel room about needing $1100 a month for the next two years to
complete her book, her mother demands she get a job or start a blog and calls
her spoiled. When Hannah asks, "Yeah, well, whose fault is that, Mom?"
Loreen answers, "Your father's."[42] Here, both Hannah and her mother are
blaming one another for the entitled/enabling cycle common among Millennial-Boomer relationships. When Hannah passes out in front of her parents,
Tad says she needs a cup of coffee, but Hannah responds with "Coffee is a
grown up drink," suggesting that she is still not ready to assume adult respon-

sibilities. [43] Loreen continues to blame Tad for coddling her and, in short, what emerges from this scene is the debate between Boomer parents over how to support their Millennial daughter.

On the other hand, what ultimately ensues not just in this episode, but in the series as whole, is a development in both Hannah and her parents that is more consistent with Generation X portrayals of parent-child relationships, one that stems from archetypal behavior seen in 1990s Generation X popular culture. Later in the scene, a frustrated Loreen screams out, "I want a lake house! I work hard! I want to sit by a fucking lake!" [44] Here, Loreen appears to reinforce all stereotypes of the selfish Boomer, as perpetuated in much Generation X popular culture. But, more importantly for Hannah, while she continues to display some of the entitled, selfish traits often associated with Millennials, traits that were also used to describe Gen-Xers in the 1990s, she ultimately begins relying on her friends for emotional and financial support. She takes a job working in her friend Ray's coffee shop, not unlike Rachel in *Friends*. She lives with her best friend Marnie, and she continues to pursue her book and, by the end of season 3, has been accepted into the prestigious Iowa's Writer's Workshop. And, while *Girls* still shows her interacting with her parents in various episodes, their relationship is often an alienated one, not unlike the alienation portrayed in Generation X popular culture.

The other millennial characters in *Girls* also demonstrate relationships with parents that undermine mainstream understanding of Millennial-Boomer relationships and suggest a kinship more in line with their Generation X predecessors. We never see or hear from Shoshanna's parents until briefly in season 4, and the only time Adam mentions his parents is when he tells Hannah in the pilot episode that he "wouldn't take shit from my parents. They're buffoons." [45] The only other main characters whose parents we meet are Jessa and Marnie, and here we only meet one each. In the episode, "Video Games," Jessa takes Hannah to her estranged father's house where he is living with his new-age wife and their teenage son. Jessa's father, like her, is unreliable and an addict who neglects to pick up Jessa and Hannah to take them to the train station at the end of the episode. Jessa also meets a father figure in rehab, Jasper, played by Richard Grant. But, he too is unreliable as evidenced by the fact he has neglected his own daughter. Earlier in season 2, we meet Marnie's mother Evie, played by Rita Wilson. Through Marnie, we learn her father left Evie and the family years earlier. Yet, Marnie and Evie are not portrayed as particularly close. For example, when Marnie loses her job early in season 2, shortly after losing her boyfriend Charlie, she visits Evie who tells her she's looking old and that she misses "the softness in your face." Marnie reminds her mom of the stress she's been under lately. [46] Not showing much sympathy for her daughter, Evie criticizes Marnie's and Hannah's body and eating habits: "Don't say fired," Evie scolds Marnie. "You're transitioning. They downsized. Jesus, your father will tell you that, if he ever gets out from under his pillow . . . All you girls think you look really good, but you just look like floats in the Macy's parade—these big heads on these tiny bodies."[47] Again, the relationships between these Millennial twenty somethings and their Boomer parents undermines the culture's typical understanding of Millennials and their parents. Rather than reinforce the stereotype of the enabling Boomer and the entitled Millennial, *Girls* rather relies on the Generation X archetype of the post-college twenty something with divorced parents who relies more on friends than parents and other authority figures.

This chapter is not suggesting that *Girls* is merely a repeat of earlier programming such as *Friends*, *Reality Bites*, or other Generation X popular culture. Those shows, for all their cultural influence, were not nearly as complex, as well written, or as complicated as what Lena Dunham and her colleagues have achieved in *Girls*. *Girls*, while technically a comedy, pulls no punches in its portrayal of how post-college Millennials survive and thrive in New York City. Their apartments, for instance, are certainly more realistic than anything in *Friends*. Their relationships with one another, while strong and loving, also show strains and difficulties. Hannah, as Nussbaum points out, is "spoiled and self-destructive," suggesting that *Girls* shows young people in a much more raw, flawed, and in general realistic way than most shows of its kind.[48] Indeed, *Girls* portrays a period of life, as Dunham points out, "lived as a rough draft—something well intentioned, possibly promising, but definitely begging for cruel critiques" that both celebrates and critiques the choices young people make during this often confusing, often difficult time.[49]

But, one of the interesting parts of *Girls*, and one that connects it with current manifestations of Gen-Xers now in their thirties, forties, and approaching their fifties, is that it implies that this time of one's life is not, as Gary Cross may argue in *Men to Boys*, a permanent lifestyle but rather a phase. As noted in the above discussion of the Boomer parents on *Girls*, the show appears to feature no reliable adult character, or that the adults and parents who do show up tend to be narcissistic, unreliable, and disinterested in their children's lives. In the season 2 stand-alone episode "One Man's Trash," Hannah spends a weekend with Joshua, a forty-two-year-old physician who lives alone in a well-heeled brownstone and offers a glimpse into what may be Hannah's future as a part of conventionally successful adult life. Joshua is not the first Gen-Xer on *Girls*. In season 1, we meet Jeff Lavoyt, an out-of-work married man whose children Jessa occasionally nannies. The episodes suggest that Jeff wants to hit on Jessa, and he even follows her to a warehouse party attended mostly by teenagers and twenty somethings. Jeff would appear to reinforce Cross's argument about the transitional period between adolescence and adulthood becoming a permanent state. The presence of Joshua on *Girls* complicates that argument. As a Gen-Xer, Joshua is, I would suggest, the series' first real adult. Unlike Hannah's often-exasperating parents and Marnie's self-absorbed mother and absent father, Joshua comes across as level-headed, content, and as a good listener for Hannah's concerns. Even though he is single and lonely—the episode never clarifies if Joshua is divorced or a widower—he appears comfortable in his own skin and is uncomplicated, unlike Adam, secure in his life, is relatively happy, and acts toward Hannah with no alternative motivations, unlike the majority of Hannah's friends and boyfriends. In other words, Joshua appears to represent the contentment felt by many Gen-Xers now in their thirties and forties, as described by Miller in his University of Michigan study. Indeed, this contentment seems to suggest a new understanding of Generation X as manifested by Joshua; gone are the cynical slackers, replaced by balanced, content adults.

This sense of contentment opens Hannah's eyes to what may be in store for her future. The episode begins with Joshua confronting Ray to complain about someone from Ray's coffee shop dumping trash in his garbage cans. Hannah visits Joshua to confess it was her dumping the garbage, and after hearing Hannah's apology, Joshua invites her into his brownstone home, where they proceed to embark on a weekend tryst. As such, it is a stand-alone episode that takes a break from the weekly adventures of Hannah and her friends. While some critics argued that it was unrealistic for someone like Joshua to have a weekend affair with Hannah, that is not the point of this episode. Indeed, *Slate*'s Hanna Rosin notes it is supposed to be unrealistic because the episode is a fantasy, "and fantasies are often unrealistic. You could tell because it stood apart from the rest of the series, like a standalone play in three tiny succinct acts."[50] The point of the episode, at least in terms of the relationships between Gen-Xers and Millennials, is that it allows Hannah to question her previous motivations and to catch a glimpse into a future where she, too, might find happiness, contentment, and success after the uncertainty of her post-college twenties. The two spend the weekend making love, playing ping pong, cooking and eating, reading the paper—in general, acting like a successful, happy, married couple. Near the end of their time together, Hannah has a minor breakdown and begins to question her purpose in life and what it means to be happy. As TV critic Alan Sepinwall notes in his review of the episode, it "builds to a big epiphany for Hannah about how she wants a normal life more than she would care to admit to anyone, but it takes a long time getting there."[51] Near the episode's end, Hannah has an epiphany about her own sense of happiness and what she expects from her life. Joshua and Hannah are sitting in bed, talking, after Hannah has passed out in the shower. Joshua is taking care of her, caressing her hair, asking if all is okay, reminding her that if she needs help the next time, to call him. In other words, he is caring, rational, and adult. Then, Hannah begins crying, visibly upset about something, and opens up to Joshua:

HANNAH: Please don't tell anyone this but . . . I want to be happy.

JOSHUA: Of course you do. Everyone does.

HANNAH: Yeah, but I didn't think that *I* did. I made a promise such a long time ago that I was going to take in experiences, all of them, so that I could tell other people about them and maybe save them, but it gets so tiring trying to take in all the experiences for everybody, letting anyone say anything to me. Then I came here, and you've got the fruit in the bowl and the fridge with the stuff . . . the robe, and you're touching me the way that—I realize I'm not different. You know? I want what everyone wants. I want what they all want. I want all the things. I just want to be happy.[52]

Here, Hannah, in her twenty something self-centeredness, experiences an epiphany about her life and about what she wants from it. On the one hand, she has always assumed she was different from everyone else and that she has taken it upon herself to live various experiences and tell others in her writing about what they mean. This desire to live intensely, she assumes, is anathema to true happiness. On the other hand, after spending the weekend with Gen-Xer Joshua, she realizes that she, ultimately like everyone else, just wants happiness and contentment, seeing these things represented by the material trappings of Joshua's lifestyle. Rather, Hannah is living her twenties with an intense amount of angst, carelessness, and alienation common for many twenty somethings.

Yet, *Girls* presents this angst in an archetypal framework that hearkens back to popular culture's mainstream manifestations of these archetypes— Generation X in the 1990s. I don't think it is an accident that in this episode Joshua is forty-two and Hannah is twenty-four. They mirror one another: On one hand, although lonely, Joshua is stable, content, and successful. Hannah's life, on the other, is rocky and often unstable, and she appears hungry for the happiness and stability Joshua's life presents. One gets the sense that Joshua's loneliness is something that has been with him for a long time and that he, too, had his fill of angst and instability in his twenties and that Hannah, too, will eventually figure *it* out and find a measure of stability and happiness as she ages. But, right now Hannah is still a self-absorbed twenty something. After telling Joshua that at age three she lied to her mother about the babysitter touching her vagina, Joshua replies with an equally intimate story about an awkward sexual experience he had at age nine. But, Hannah immediately dismisses it because as she puts it "well, I think that's pretty different 'cause you let him, and this wasn't my choice."[53] Hannah is still so self-involved in her own experiences that not only can she not empathize with Joshua's experience but dismisses it, because she simply cannot control her own impulses, a common feeling for many still in their twenties. So, while Hannah has this important empathy about herself, she is still Hannah. When Joshua tells her he has to go to bed because he has to get up early for work the next day, Hannah seems shocked to learn that he has to go to work. "You're going to work tomorrow?" she asks, surprised by his announcement. He replies with, "Well, I gotta."[54] The implication here is that Hannah has yet to understand that one of the characterizations of being an adult is that you go to work, even if you don't want to. The rest of that scene plays out with Hannah confused about whether Joshua is playing games with her, her complaining that he did not open up emotionally to her—even though when he did, Hannah in her self-absorption dismissed it or just did not listen—and with her expecting him to act like others in her life: immature and passive aggressive. Joshua, though, is reasonable, forthright, and honest. In other words, an adult. In the last scene of the episode, we see Hannah wake up in Joshua's house alone, make herself breakfast, read the paper, walk through the home contemplating the different material trappings of adulthood: she looks at Joshua's closet full of suits, she makes the bed, and takes out the garbage. She quietly walks away, wearing the same outfit she had on when she arrived, back to her own post-college reality but perhaps armed with the knowledge that she, too, will find her way to a life of stability and happiness, as portrayed by the Gen-Xer Joshua.

In this chapter, I have argued that the characterization of Generation X in the 1990s, namely the male slacker and the twenty something more reliant on friends than parents—have morphed into archetypes to describe young people in their post-college years. These archetypes have been appropriated by HBO's *Girls* to present a raw, gritty, and complex portrayal of Millennials undergoing a similar transition in post-recession America. While *Girls* shares many similarities with early 1990s popular culture texts, such as *Friends*, *Reality Bites*, and other touchstones of Generation X culture, Lena Dunham's narrative takes these archetypes and transforms them into characters who are more realistic, complicated, and three dimensional than the way their Generation X counterparts were presented in those earlier popular manifestations. In doing so, *Girls*, especially in the episode "One Man's Trash" also seems to suggest that Hannah and her friends will, one day, make it through this difficult period and find the type of contentment many Gen-Xers have found since their own post-college years, years that were described in language and rhetoric not unlike how the Millennials are being portrayed now. Ultimately, *Girls* appropriates these Generation X archetypes and cultural touchstones and re-appropriates them into characters that are at once familiar and at the same time, because they come from the generation portrayed, complicated.

NOTES

1. "Living the dream. One mistake at a time" is the tagline for this HBO series.

2. Alessandra Stanley, "There's Sex, There's the City, but No Manelos," *New York Times,* April 12 2014, accessed June 20, 2014, http://www.nytimes.com/2012/04/13/arts/television/lena-dunhams-girls-begins-on-hbo.html?_r=0.

3. John Kubicek, "*Girls* Review: The Voice of the Worst Generation," *BuddyTV.com,* April 16, 2012, accessed June 25, 2014, http://www.buddytv.com/articles/girls/girls-review-thevoice-of-the-45043.aspx.

4. Jesse Levine, "Don't Shoot the Messenger: HBO's *Girls* Backlash," *Huffington Post,* April 24, 2012, accessed June 23, 2014, http://www.huffingtonpost.com/jesse-levine/dontkill-the-messenger_b_1443100.html.

5. Stanley, "There's Sex, There's the City, but No Manolos."

6. Ibid.

7. Arthur Berger, *Cultural Criticism: A Primer of Key Concepts* (London, SAGE Publications, 1995), 124.

8. Ibid, 58.

9. Ibid, 126.

10. David Richter, *The Critical Tradition: Classic Texts and Contemporary Trends* (New York: Bedford St. Martins, 1989), 645.

11. Frye, "The Archetypes of Literature," in David Richter, 682.

12. Ibid.

13. Ian Balfour, *Northrup Frye* (Boston, MA: Twayne Publishers, 1988), 30.

14. Jon Miller, "Active, Balanced, and Happy: These Young Americans are not Bowling Alone," *The Generation X Report: A Quarterly Research Paper Report from the Longitudinal Study of American Youth,* no. 1-1 (2011): 1.

15. George Masnick, "Defining the Generations," *Housing Perspectives: Research, Trends, and Perspectives from the Harvard Joint Center for Housing Studies,* November 28, 2012, accessed June 23, 2014, http://housingperspectives.blogspot.com/2012/11/defining-generations.html.

16. Ibid.

17. Elwood Watson, ed, *Generation X Professors Speak: Voices from Academia* (Toronto: Scarecrow Press, 2013): vii.

18. Neil Howe and Bill Strauss, *13th Gen: Abort, Retry, Ignore, Fail?* (New York: Vintage Books, 1993).

19. Ibid, 21.

20. Ibid, 25.

21. Ibid, 27.

22. Ibid.

23. Masnick, "Defining the Generations".

24. Miller, "Active, Balanced, and Happy," 2.

25. Ibid.

26. Ibid.

27. Watson, *Generation X Professors Speak,* xviii.

28. Joel Stein, "Millennials: The Me Me Me Generation," *Time.com,* May 20 2013, accessed June 25, 2014, http://www.fandm.edu/uploads/media_items/stein-2013-megeneration.original.pdf.

29. "The Video Generation," *Newsweek,* December 30, 1985, 44.

30. Emily Nussbaum, "It's Different for *Girls,*" *New York Magazine,* March 25, 2012, accessed June 20, 2014. http://nymag.com/arts/tv/features/girls-lena-dunham-2012-4/.

31. Ibid.

32. Gary Cross, *Men to Boys: The Making of Modern Immaturity* (New York: Columbia University Press, 2008), 1.

33. Ibid, 2.

34. Ibid, 3.

35. Ibid, 212.

36. Susan Gregory Thomas, "The Divorce Generation," *Wall Street Journal,* July 9, 2011, accessed June 23, 2014, http://online.wsj.com/articles/SB100014240527023035446044576430341393583056.

37. *Reality Bites,* directed by Ben Stiller (1994; Hollywood, CA, 2004), DVD.

38. Michael Winerip, "Boomers and Millennials Feel a Need to Care for One Another," *New York Times*, December 20, 2012, accessed July 2, 2014, http://www.nytimes.com/2012/12/20/booming/boomers-and-millenneals-feel-a-need-tocare-for-each-other.html?_r=0.

39. Ibid.

40. Frye, "The Artchetypes of Literature," in Richter, 682.

41. "Pilot," *Girls*, television, directed by Lena Dunham (2012; New York City; HBO, 2013), Netflix.

42. Ibid.

43. Ibid.

44. Ibid.

45. Ibid.

46. "It's About Time," *Girls*, television, directed by Lena Dunham (2013; New York City; HBO, 2014), Netflix.

47. Ibid.

48. Nussbaum, "It's Different for Girls," http://nymag.com/arts/tv/features/girls-lena-dunham-2012-4/.

49. Ibid.

50. Hanna Rosin, "*Slate*'s Guys are so Wrong about *Girls*," *Slate.com*, February 11, 2013, accessed June 29, 2014, http://www.slate.com/blogs/xx_factor/2013/02/11/slate_s_guys_on_girls_what_they_get_wrong_about_one_man_s_trash.html.

51. Alan Sepinwall, "Review: *Girls*—'One Man's Trash': Dancin' with Mr. Brownstone," *What's Alan Watching? Inside Television*, February 10, 2013, accessed on June 28, 2014. http://www.hitfix.com/whats-alan-watching/review-girls-one-mans-trash-dancin-with-mr-brownstone.

52. "One Man's Trash," *Girls*, television, directed by Richard Shephard (2012; New York City; HBO, 2013), Netflix.

53. Ibid.

54. Ibid.

BIBLIOGRAPHY

Balfour, Ian. *Northrop Frye*. Boston: Twayne Publishers, 1988.

Berger, Arthur. *Cultural Criticism: A Primer of Key Concepts*. London: SAGE Publications, 1995.

Cross, Gary. *Men to Boys: The Making of Modern Immaturity*. New York: Columbia University Press, 2008.

Frye, Northrop. "The Archetypes of Literature." In *The Classical Tradition: Classic Texts and Contemporary Trends*. Edited by David, 677–85. New York: Bedford St. Martins, 1989.

_____. *Anatomy of Criticism: Four Essays*. Princeton, NJ: Princeton University Press, 1957.

Howe, Neil and Bill Strauss. *13th Gen: Abort, Retry, Ignore, Fail?* New York: Vintage Books, 1993.

"It's About Time." *Girls*. Directed by Lena Dunham. 2013. New York City: HBO, 2014. Netflix.

Jung, Carl, ed. *Man and His Symbols*. New York: Dell, 1968.

Kubicek, John. "*Girls* Review: The Voice of the Worst Generation." *BuddyTV.com*. April 16, 2012. Accessed June 25, 2014. http://www.buddytv.com/articles/girls/girls-review-thevoice-of-the-45043.aspx.

Levine, Jesse. "Don't Shoot the Messenger: HBO's *Girls* Backlash." *Huffington Post*. April 24, 2012. Accessed June 23, 2014. http://www.huffingtonpost.com/jesse-levine/dontkill-the-messenger_b_1443100.html.

Masnick, George. "Defining the Generations." *Housing Perspectives: Research, Trends, and Perspectives from the Harvard Joint Center for Housing Studies*. November 28, 2012. Accessed June 23, 2014. http://housingperspectives.blogspot.com/2012/11/defining-generations.html.

Miller, Jon. "Active, Balanced, and Happy: These Young Americans are not Bowling Alone." *The Generation X Report: A Quarterly Research Paper Report from the Longitudinal Study of American Youth*, no. 1–1 (2011): 1–8.

Nussbaum, Emily. "It's Different for *Girls*." *New York Magazine*. March 25, 2012. Accessed June 20, 2014. http://nymag.com/arts/tv/features/girls-lena-dunham-2012-4/.

"One Man's Trash." *Girls*. Directed by Richard Shephard. 2013. New York City: HBO, 2014. Netflix.

"The One Where Monica Gets a Roommate." *Friends*. Directed by James Burrows. 1994. Burbank, CA: Warner Home Video, 2002. DVD.

"Pilot." *Girls*. Directed by Lena Dunham. 2012. New York City: HBO, 2013. Netflix.

Reality Bites. Directed by Ben Stiller. 1994. Hollywood, CA: Universal Studios, 2004. DVD.

Richter, David, ed. *The Critical Tradition: Classic Texts and Contemporary Trends*. New York: Bedford St. Martins, 1989.

Rosin, Hanna. "*Slate*'s Guys are so Wrong about *Girls*." *Slate.com*, February 11, 2013. Accessed on June 29, 2014. http://www.slate.com/blogs/xx_factor/2013/02/11/slate_s_guys_on_girls_what_they_get_wrong_about_one_man_s_trash.html.

Sepinwall, Alan. "Review: *Girls*—'One Man's Trash': Dancin' with Mr. Brownstone." *What's Alan Watching? Inside Television*. February 10, 2013. Accessed on June 28, 2014. http://www.hitfix.com/whats-alan-watching/review-girls-one-mans-trash-dancin-with-mr-brownstone.

Stanley, Alessandra. "There's Sex, There's the City, but No Manelos." *New York Times*. April 12 2014. Accessed June 20, 2014. http://www.nytimes.com/2012/04/13/arts/television/lena-dunhams-girls-begins-on-hbo.html?_r=0.

Stein, Joel. "Millennials: The Me Me Me Generation." *Time.com*. May 20 2013. Accessed June 25, 2014. http://www.fandm.edu/uploads/media_items/stein-2013-megeneration.original.pdf.

"Video Games." *Girls*. Directed by Richard Shephard. 2013. New York City: HBO, 2014. Netflix.

"The Video Generation." *Newsweek*. December 30, 1985. 44.

Watson, Elwood, ed. *Generation X Professor Speak: Voices from Academia.* Toronto: Scarecrow Press, 2013.

Winerip, Michael. "Boomers and Millennials Feel a Need to Care for One Another." *New York Times*. December 20, 2012. Accessed July 2, 2014. http://www.nytimes.com/2012/12/20/booming/boomers-and-millenneals-feel-a-need-tocare-for-each-other.html?_r=0.

Chapter Eight

Reading *Girls*:
Diegesis and Distinction

Laura Witherington

When Hannah Horvath (Lena Dunham) argues with her parents for their continued financial support of her New York writing endeavors, she declares that she "may be the voice of my generation,"[1] and even when she moderates her bold statement to be "a voice" of her generation, her insistence on representing a particular Millennial experience in her writing emphasizes the potential she believes writing holds to express culture. Although Hannah seeks her own voice through publishing her essays, the series's inter-textuality with popular culture, and especially with literature, extends Hannah's solo into a chorus as other voices harmonize on her themes. *Girls* privileges reading, writing, and books as dominant cultural artifacts, and the series expands the market and "need for" reading and books through establishing their place in hip, twenty something society.

Because of Hannah's intended vocation, the dominance of books as props and topics of discussion seems natural. The series reiterates the image of the text so frequently that it begs examination as a motif. *Girls* uses books in three distinct ways. In some scenes, the effect of stacks of books is curatorial, where the texts appear to have been read previously, even perhaps cherished, and remain in a character's home as a connection to the past. In other scenes, books seem to be part of the decor, chosen to create the appearance of intellectual acquisition, where sometimes there may be none. And in several scenes, characters read from texts that provide insight into the current action or into the character's motivations. This chapter will examine the implications of particular texts on scenes and characters, and will consider how the series's overall attention to literacy generates ideological messages on class and masculinity.

Girls is so richly inter-textual that just listing the texts that appear or are alluded to creates a dizzying expanse of genre, period, and ideology. Some texts are easily identifiable from their position on set and camera focus, while others contribute more directly to scenes and understanding characters' motivations. In "Dancing on My Own: Popular Music and Issues of Identity in *Girls*," Chloé H. Johnson analyzes how integration of music in key scenes expands the viewers' understanding of characters' interior monologue. She writes, "music, used within the diegesis, functions on a particular level that allows us a more in-depth immersion into the fictional world of the characters. . . . A moment of bonding kicks in when we hear a song we know, generating a kindred connection with the character."[2] Johnson further contends that music's unique affective nature and the contemporaneity of the soundtrack for *Girls* invites deeper viewer identification with the characters and absorption in the episodes. Through both the lyrics and the tunes themselves, viewers join Hannah as she spins wildly at a club or bonds with Marnie (Allison Williams) through the intimacy of cathartic dance when they have both suffered disappointments. In the first example, Icona Pop's "I Love It" (2012) conveys Hannah's and Elijah's (Andrew Rannells) feral abandon as Hannah tries cocaine for the first time in order to narrate the experience later for a JazzHate essay. In the second, Robyn's song "Dancing on My Own" (2010), emphasizes the strength Hannah and Marnie draw from each other after Hannah comes to terms with her HPV diagnosis and Marnie is challenged by her relationship with Booth Jonathan (Jorma Taccone). In both cases, the song selections enhance the viewers' understanding of the characters' feelings and their thematic implications.

In this way, texts read by characters expand the meaning of each scene. Instead of the near-universal engagement of popular music, books establish distinctions between viewers who have read them and those who have not. Johnson establishes that viewers are likely to have "encountered popular songs"[3] and therefore find connections between characters' experiences and their own, but even when the songs are new to viewers, the "text" of the song—its lyrics and tune—are immediate. Allusions to texts rely on viewers having read the books or their knowing of them. Thus, the texts can be "read" in three broad ways. First, viewers who have read the texts make connections between the content and the episode. Also, viewers who know *of* the texts but have not read them bring their perceptions or assumptions to their understanding of the texts' meaning in the context of the episode. Finally, viewers who know nothing of the text see merely the act of reading, an act imbued with many cultural interpretations and class distinctions. This final category of viewers/non-readers will be addressed later in this chapter, but it is worth first considering how prominently featured texts convey meaning to viewers who are also informed readers and recognize the texts and their expanded meaning of scenes.

PRIVILEGED TEXTS

The pilot episode opens with Hannah's parents withdrawing their financial support. Needing to support herself, Hannah approaches her employer to request that her unpaid internship be upgraded to a paid position. The publishing house is not identified, but viewers quickly struck out to identify it based on the covers and titles on display in the office set. The pilot aired on 15 April 2012 and on 24 April, the *Los Angeles Times* online edition addressed the identity of the publisher in "*Girls*'s Lena Dunham Interned at Soft Skull, Not at Melville House." The detective work was simple for readers who could recognize *EEEEE EEE EEEE* by Tao Lin, which is featured prominently on a shelf behind Hannah's editor and boss, Alistair (Chris Eigeman). Carolyn Kellogg explains that although Melville House's distinctive book jackets suggest it is the site for Hannah's internship, Lena Dunham actually interned at Soft Skull her first year after graduation from Oberlin. Kellogg cites Richard Nash, Dunham's actual supervisor at Soft Skull, saying that the scene was "autobiographical in the vaguest way."[4] Implicit in this explanation is the argument that connecting the fictional setting to Dunham's personal experience is worthwhile. The series' brand of realism inspires viewers and critics to watch and research with a detective's eye for clues and connections in the "real," not fictional, world. It is important to consider the impact of realistic details, not merely identify them on a treasure hunt. Representation of Melville House conveys a sense of Hannah's aspirations, as she reveals in the scene that she intends to send her to-be-finished manuscript there for review. Melville describes itself as "an independent publisher" that is "well-known for its fiction" and its "world-wide reputation for . . . rediscovery of forgotten international writers."[5] Beyond investigation to determine the represented publisher, since Dunham was not fired from her internship as Hannah is, the more important connection in the scene is the impact of the characteristic book jackets.

Kellogg references *Publishers Weekly* and its article of 24 April 2012, too, "Melville House Has a Friend in Lena Dunham." Here, Rachel Deahl explains the practicalities in placing those Melville titles so prominently. The show requested to use actual Melville offices, but settled for "renting thousands of Melville House titles for filming."[6] The identifiable titles are significant to the series, with *EEEEE EEE EEEE* being the most obvious. Tao Lin's 2007 absurdist tale follows Andrew, a disgruntled pizza deliverer, as he daydreams about a romantic interest and hallucinates about talking animals. The novel's title refers to the speech of a dolphin who converses with Andrew. If *Girls* intentionally chose Melville House as a setting and was thoughtful enough about its branding to rent thousands of books, the display of *EEEEE EEE EEEE* should indicate its relevance to Hannah and her situation. Like Andrew, Hannah finds herself disoriented in the adult world. She

cannot find a fulfilling job, despite her ambitious career goals. She is financially strapped and her series of jobs beginning with the publishing internship, moving to clerical work in a law office where sexual harassment is the
norm, and then temporarily serving at Café Grumpy, moves her from one
absurd situation to another. Season 3 finds her in a well-paid position writing
at *GQ Magazine*, but even there, she fails to acclimate to the adult world.
Despite her gratifying paycheck and perks like a night at the Gramercy Park
Hotel, she continues to condescend to the other writers and their assigned
topics. The real world becomes surreal to her in every situation, even if it is
not to the bizarre end of hallucinating that animals talk.

Other books in the fictional version of the Melville House office include
Joseph Conrad's *Freya of the Seven Isles* (1911), Samuel Johnson's *The
History of Rasselas, Prince of Abyssinia* (1759), Mary Shelley's *Mathilda*
(1819), and Christopher Morley's *Parnassus on Wheels* (1917). It is interesting that these texts are much older and from canonically respected authors.
The effect is to situate Lin's *EEEEE EEE EEEE* within the greater historical
context, which is Hannah's goal—to finish her book draft and submit it to
Alistair for publication. Thus, the titles chosen for set design also contextualize Hannah's own writing. In a figurative way, Hannah needs to situate
herself in the greater historical context, not just as a writer, but as an adult.
The title of the series, after all, is "Girls," not "Women," and its *bildungsroman* elements suggest the need for Hannah to discard the illusions of youth
and accept the realities of maturity.

At the end of the pilot, Hannah appears in her parents' hotel room, intoxi-
cated by opium tea. She restates her case for their financial support using the
argument suggested by Jessa (Jemima Kirke)—that she is an artist like Flaubert writing in an attic. Hannah's parents, Loreen (Becky Ann Baker) and
Tad (Peter Scolari) Horvath, are both professors, but the series does not
divulge their appointments or disciplinary specialties. It is clear, though, that
they are both well-read, something suggested in this final scene of the pilot
with a book Tad lays aside when Hannah enters the room. The book is Gary
S. Becker and Richard A. Posner's *Uncommon Sense: Economic Insights,
from Marriage to Terrorism* (2009). This particular text's positioning in the
episode supports the senior Horvaths' position that Hannah should work and
support herself. Loreen laughingly rejects Hannah's request for "Eleven hundred dollars a month for the next two years" and instructs her instead to get a
job and start a blog. Blogging was the source of Becker and Posner's book.
Their introduction situates the printed text in the context of its original online
source:

> Blogging is a major new social, political, and economic phenomenon enabled
> by the Internet. . . . Information on the Internet comes from many sources. It is
> a fresh and striking exemplification of Friedrich Hayek's thesis that the knowl-

edge essential to society . . . is widely distributed among people and that the social challenge is to create mechanisms for pooling that knowledge. The mechanism that was the focus of Hayek's work, as of economists generally, is the price system. . . . The blogosphere differs from a system with explicit prices and monetary compensation because information in this sphere is usually made available without expectation of any monetary compensation or other financial rewards, although some bloggers have managed to attract advertising revenues and others (present company included) have made book deals.[7]

The pair started the *Becker-Posner Blog* in December 2004 with weekly postings on whatever they found interesting. The book collects forty-one of the early essays, grouping them by subject matter, with few editorial changes. The blog remains extant, so that readers of the book can find the original blog posts and their attending comments.

Placing the Becker-Posner text in the room when the Horvaths lecture Hannah on realistic ways to support herself both underscores and undercuts their argument. It is easy to see where Loreen and Tad find the idea they provide to Hannah, and *Uncommon Sense* provides a model for producing a book from a collection of blog essays. However, Becker and Posner's experience at the time of publication far surpassed Hannah's. The introduction describes Becker as "a Nobel-prize-winning economist who in addition to scholarly publications on a wide range of economic issues including education, discrimination, labor, the family, crime, addiction, and immigration, for many years wrote a monthly column for *Business Week*."[8] Posner is described as "a federal appellate judge and also a writer of books and articles in a variety of fields, including antitrust, intellectual property, and other fields in which economics is applied to law, but also topical fields such as impeachment, contested elections, and national security issues."[9] Becker and Posner were established professionals *before* beginning their blog. While their argument for the democratizing characteristics of the Internet and blogging is sound, their own cumulative expertise makes the process appear more accessible than it should for relatively inexperienced Hannah.

Hannah's lack of experience and her quest to gain experiences is a theme in the series. She wants to try new things and explore possibilities, and she pushes herself in this direction specifically so that she has something interesting to write about. The JazzHate editor in "Bad Friend,"[10] Jame (Angela Featherstone), exhorts her to pursue wild opportunities in order to have something to write about. She tells her to have a threesome with strangers off Craigslist or do cocaine for the first time. Hannah tells Shoshanna (Zosia Mamet) and Ray (Alex Karpovsky) that she "wants to do everything."[11] Hannah eventually does land a print book deal from her essays, but the path suggested by Becker and Posner, and then Loreen Horvath, is not as simple as it sounds. Becker and Posner serve as an aspirational model for publication, but not a blueprint for the uninitiated.

The second episode reinforces the use of books for diegetic narrative. Hannah and Adam (Adam Driver) discuss his aversion to condoms after they have had sex in Adam's apartment, which is cluttered and conspicuously undecorated. His mattress rests on pallets, and a stack of several books sits beside the bed. Most of the books are unidentifiable, but one stands out, Saul Bellow's *Him with His Foot in His Mouth*. The collection of stories was published in 1984, with the eponymous novella setting the tone with its narcissistic apologist explaining his insult to a librarian in the 1940s. The thirty-five-year-old wisecrack by Dr. Herschel Shawmut to the passing Miss Carla Rose followed her complimenting his cap by saying that he looked "like an archeologist." Shawmut answers that Miss Rose looks "like something I just dug up."[12] While apologizing for the likely-forgotten insult is the supposed purpose of the epistle, the narrative follows Shawmut's many conversational missteps in the name of his "lifelong weakness for this sort of Jewish humor,"[13] which land him in Canadian expatriate isolation following financial ruin. While *Vogue* describes Adam Sackler in season 3 as "inveterately bizarre, but true-of-heart,"[14] in season 1 only the bizarre is evident, not the true-of-heart, and in many ways he is much like Herschel Shawmut.

In the pilot, Adam seems to tolerate Hannah only because she is willing to perform sexually in ways that satisfy his unusual desires. He lies about using condoms, concocts stories for their dirty talk that involve pedophilia and drug addiction, and he texts pictures of his genitals to other women. His mistake in texting Hannah an explicit photo intended for another girl seems like the sort of mistake a twenty-first-century Shawmut might make. Hannah is shocked, but also a bit flattered, when she receives the pornographic image; however, Adam quickly follows up with a text, "Sorry, that wasn't for you."[15] While the picture was shocking, Hannah is offended that he intended it for someone else, but also that he freely shares that information with her. In her initial giddiness over the picture, Hannah shares it with Marnie (Alison Williams) and Charlie (Christopher Abbott), and Marnie lectures Hannah against Adam's treatment when he follows up with the confession that the picture was meant for another woman.

Adam's insensitive gaffs are verbal, as well. In the pilot, Adam and Hannah's post-coital conversation centers on the origin of her tattoos, which leads to discussion of her weight. She explains that she sought tattoos as a way of "taking control of [her] own shape"[16] after gaining weight. Adam responds that she can always have them lasered off. He does not acknowledge her courage in reclaiming her body nor does he inquire further about the inspiration of the "illustrations from children's books" from which the images are copied.[17] In the third episode, Adam squeezes together Hannah's flesh in a way that makes her self-conscious again about her weight. He claims that he, too, has belly fat, and invites her to reciprocate the squeeze; however, his thin frame does not provide enough flesh to make his point, leaving Hannah even more self-conscious.

Adam's casual tone in these encounters reveals how little he cares for Hannah, and yet by the end of the second season, Adam redeems himself by confessing his love for her and rushing to her aid when she cowers under the covers in an anxiety attack exacerbated by her obsessive-compulsive disorder. The Adam of season 1 is much different from the Adam from the end of season 2, and seeing his heroic side in "Together" and his consistent kindness toward Hannah in season 3 forces the viewer to reconsider the character's actions in season 1. Bellow's Hershel Shawmut expands Adam's season 1 characterization by aligning him with the intentionally insensitive protagonist; however, Adam's choice of texts, and his avid reading habits in general[18] should indicate the "true-of-heart" side of him that is not immediately apparent to the audience or Hannah's friends.

Characters' reading choices can also demonstrate their inconsistencies through diegetic inter-textual discourse. Consider Ray's violation of Hannah's privacy by reading her journal and then judging both her writing and her thoughts. In "Hannah's Diary," Ray and Charlie are left alone in Hannah and Marnie's apartment. Ray suggests they snoop, and although Charlie is initially reluctant, he succumbs to curiosity and watches as Ray rummages through drawers. Ray finds the journal lying on the bed and remarks, "Of course she keeps a journal, like all girls who listen to Tori Amos and masturbate." But when he begins to read it, he admits, "She's *kind* of funny. I don't really care how she feels about keeping bread in the house, but she's *kind* of funny." Charlie's reservations are overcome when his interest is piqued by Ray's silent absorption in the text. Ray tries to redirect Charlie's attention, but Charlie reads the passages in which Hannah criticizes his devotion to Marnie. Although the journal is Hannah's and not Marnie's, Charlie and Ray transfer the blame to Marnie. Their later musical performance as Questionable Goods includes a song titled "Hannah's Diary," which castigates both Hannah and Marnie with lines taken from the journal.

The four later argue about passages in the journal and about the purpose and nomenclature of the text. Charlie calls it a journal; the song called it a diary; Hannah argues it is a "notebook" because "journal sounds too juvenile." A later episode, "She Did," finds Ray reading another sort of journal. At work at Café Grumpy, Hannah stands behind the counter reading celebrity gossip magazine *Us Weekly* while Ray leans on the counter reading *I Capture the Castle*, by Dodie Smith. Ray mutters to himself, "This book is fucking incredible. Anything by a British woman is just . . . fuck."[19] Smith's epistolary novel proclaims itself a journal early, when the protagonist and narrator Cassandra Mortmain writes,

> I am writing this journal partly to practise my newly acquired speed-writing
> and partly to teach myself how to write a novel—I intend to capture all our
> characters and put in conversations. It ought to be good for my style to dash
> along without much thought, as up to now my stories have been very stiff and
> self-conscious. The only time father obliged me by reading one of them, he
> said I combined stateliness with a desperate effort to be funny. He told me to
> relax and let the words flow out of me.[20]

Like Hannah, Cassandra journals to practice narrative skills for a future
novel, and both characters share their work with their fathers. Although Ray
complains that Hannah uses her journal to express her feelings on topics as
trivial as bread, Cassandra extensively logs descriptions of food, usually
bread for afternoon tea, and because the Mortmain household lives in penury,
she writes, "I thank heaven there is no cheaper form of bread than bread."[21]
Ray criticizes Hannah's food descriptions while he enjoys Cassandra's
Smith's tale.

While Hannah's and Cassandra's situations differ substantially, their stories follow similar coming of age tropes of exploration, including romance,
betrayal, and self-assessment. The yardstick for both Hannah and Cassandra
in self-assessment is fictional heroines, particularly Jane Austen's heroines.
For example, in addition to multiple allusions to Austen's costuming ("Jane
Austen dresses and crinolines and bustles")[22] and settings ("Jane Austen
wrote in the sitting-room"),[23] Cassandra transcribes the vicar's description of
her as "the insidious type—Jane Eyre with a touch of Becky Sharp. A
thoroughly dangerous girl."[24] Cassandra describes herself and her sister Rose
as "two Brontë-Jane Austen girls, poor but spirited, two Girls of Godsend
Castle."[25] Dodie Smith models the habit the girls of *Girls* have of describing
themselves in terms of fictional heroines.

In the pilot episode, Jessa has returned from overseas travels and chats
with her cousin Shoshanna, who is in awe of her free-spirited ways. Shoshanna references her *Sex and the City* poster and she discusses the film and the
television series, but neglects to mention the Candace Bushnell book (1997)
of the same name on which both are based. Shoshanna begins her recurring
practice of classifying friends in terms of the characters: "You're funny,
because you are definitely like a Carrie, but with, like, some Samantha aspects and Charlotte hair." She classifies herself as "a Carrie at heart, but like
sometimes . . . sometimes Samantha kind of comes out," though at school she
wears her "Miranda hat."[26] Like Cassandra Mortmain, Shoshanna bases her
identity on which characters she feels most like, taking elements from several
to construct a unique composite.

Ray finds his own literary identity with Shoshanna's and Hannah's help
in "Boys." Ray demands that Hannah return his copy of *Little Women* and
refuses her offer to purchase him a new one instead of retrieving it from
Adam's apartment. He insists on securing the copy his godmother gave him

because she "writes notes in the back of books explaining how they relate to [his] shit." Shoshanna challenges the idea that *Little Women* relates to Ray, asking "Does she think you are a Marmee or an Amy?" Ray cannot answer because he has not read the book, but speculates he is a Marmee, which Hannah corrects: "You aren't a Marmee. You are probably the dad who dies of influenza at the war."[27] She seems unwilling to transgress gender assignments, but does not consider other possible matches for Ray, like Laurie, Mr. Brooke, Frederick, or Mr. Laurence. Shoshanna's taste in literary allusion tends toward popular culture. While helping Marnie choose an outfit for a dinner party with Booth Jonathan (Jorma Taccone), she says, "Oh my God, that's so fabulous. You're like Bella Swan from *Twilight*, and I'm like her weird friend who doesn't understand how fabulous her life is because my boyfriend won't spend four dollars on tacos."[28] While literary classification seems to be a quirk of Shoshanna's, others enjoy the game, and she is not alone in the habit. There are many online quizzes to determine how the subject fits into a fictional world from film or literature, including several based on *Girls*, ready to classify the subject as a Hannah, Marnie, Jessa, or Shoshanna.[29] The impulse for literary comparison is popular and not original to Shoshanna or the Internet. It is another way, in addition to epistolary practice, that *I Capture the Castle* mirrors motifs in *Girls*.

Hannah's habit of borrowing books provides the opportunity for another diegetic expansion of her short-lived relationship with Sandy (Donald Glover) in season 2. "It's About Time"[30] ends with Hannah stopping by Sandy's apartment on the way home from a visit to nurse injured Adam. Since it is the middle of the night, Sandy opens the door by sweetly chiding her about the lateness of her appearance. She responds, "Can I borrow *The Fountainhead*?" which he goes to claim from his "library." Hannah walks in the other direction, toward his bedroom, where she undresses and collapses on the bed. Her request for the book seems to be a ruse to gain entry to his apartment at an unusual time for sex. Sandy's identity as a Black Republican becomes central to his character's short arc on the series, and his ownership of *The Fountainhead*—and Hannah's certainty that he owns the book—is emblematic of his conservatism.

If any literary work stands as an aegis for conservatism, it is *The Fountainhead*. Richard Lingeman labels it the right's "utopian novel."[31] Ayn Rand biographer and critic Jennifer Burns writes, "The story of Ayn Rand is also the story of libertarianism, conservatism, and Objectivism, the three schools of thought that intersected most prominently in her life,"[32] though she later folds the three together, saying, "The greatest contribution of Rand's Objectivism was to moor the libertarian movement to the right side of the political spectrum."[33] In addition to Rand's legacy as poster-girl for alienated intellectual youth, Burns describes the political left's use of Rand since the 2008 financial crisis as an opportunity to blame the "economic devastation" on Objectivism's "ideas about free markets and selfishness."[34] *The Fountainhead* deepens our understanding of Sandy and Hannah's fledgling romance, as she uses the excuse to borrow the book to gain entry to his apartment, and he accepts the flimsy excuse without question. *Girls* uses Hannah's request to substantiate Sandy's political classification. Since Sandy himself does not initiate political discussions, his easy access to *The Fountainhead* labels him instead. His blackness is easily read on-screen, but his conservatism might not be so easily determined without awkward conversations that would also make him a less likeable character. Sandy's conservative beliefs are as central to his relationship with Hannah as his race.

Nikita T. Hamilton comments on the treatment of race in *Girls* in "So They Say You Have a Race Problem? You're in Your Twenties, You Have Way More Problems Than That." While she focuses on Hannah's self-conscious tone-deafness regarding race when she says she "never even thought about the fact that [he was] Black,"[35] we might consider Hannah's approach to Sandy's politics the same way. Sandy accuses Hannah of racial tourism, or dating a "Black guy" for the novelty of the experience, but Hannah's own discussions of Sandy center more on his being a Republican. She does not mention to her friends that he is Black, but she does tell Elijah that he is the "kind, sexy, responsible boyfriend" she has always wanted. Elijah responds that he is "also a fucking Republican," and Hannah halfheartedly defends him, saying, "I don't get why that's such a big deal."[36] Later, Hannah confesses to Jessa that Sandy is "nice and funny" but "kind of a Republican." Although the argument that ends in their break up hinges on Hannah's citation of statistics on race and incarceration,[37] she's self-conscious about Sandy's politics in a way that is more obvious than her concern about race, transforming the racial tourism into partisan tourism. During their final argument, Sandy and Hannah sit on a sofa in his apartment, and on the end table are two books: one with the title *America* and the other John McCain's *Faith of My Fathers*. It is as if Sandy's commitment to conservative ideology requires more proof than Hannah's discussion of it, although his values never interfere directly with Hannah or their relationship. Instead, her ideas about his ideology doom their romance.

Viewers are introduced to Sandy at the beginning of "It's About Time" during Hannah and Sandy's first sexual encounter. Their next scene has them playing chase in Spoonbill & Sugartown Booksellers before they stop to talk about their relationship. Hannah proclaims her intention to behave differently from her usual approach to relationships by not knocking "on your door in the middle of the night" or making up "weird excuses just to see you,"[38] although this is exactly what she does by the end of the episode. Since the scene is set in a bookstore, they are surrounded by texts, but when the game of tag pauses for their discussion, one book remains in focus behind Hannah, André Leon Talley's *A.L.T. 365+*. Its placement seems unremarkable until it reappears in "I Saw You,"[39] when it occupies a similar position in a scene set in Soojin's (Greta Lee) new gallery, in which Marnie has obtained a job. A small ledge holds several books, including *A.L.T. 365+* and *Starstruck: Vintage Movie Posters from Classic Hollywood* by Ira M. Resnick and Martin Scorsese. *A.L.T. 365+*'s appearance in both the first and third season lends little to the plot of either episode, but instead opens for consideration the contrast between style and substance.

Talley's photography monograph follows his adventures for a little over a year as he catalogues celebrities through disposable Kodak cameras. The often grainy and unfocused images accompany text about each photographed figure. Subjects include Diana Ross, Mariah Carey, and Will Smith, but more prominent are names from fashion and couture: Ralph Lauren, Christian Dior, Alexander McQueen, and Helmut Lang. The designers themselves sometimes appear, but more photographic real estate is allotted to their models and designs. Manolo Blahnik boots, sandals, and stilettos laid out with their boxes claim a two-page spread. It is a book more likely to appear in *Sex and the City* than *Girls*, and perhaps that is the point. The *A.L.T. 365+* experience is the life of Carrie Bradshaw (Sarah Jessica Parker), not Hannah Horvath. New York has been called the fifth lead character of *Sex and the City*, but Hannah's New York is Brooklyn, not Manhattan, and her experiences do not involve Manolo Blahnik heels. *A.L.T. 365+* serves as a reminder of the proximity of a very different New York. Appearing in the background to Hannah and Marnie, the book suggests that their hipster Brooklyn lives occur in a parallel universe to the lives of celebrity and fashion elite, and yet, this is not a comment on their desire for high-end consumer goods. The allusion to couture society demonstrates *Girls* perspective on bourgeois consumption, which is to step away from the table. Instead of envying the Manolo Blahniks, *Girls* observes, catalogs, and critiques them with anthropological remove. Like the topics in Hannah's journal, high-end fashion is a subject for observation and comment.

THE ACT OF READING

Girls includes many scenes of characters reading, so many that the act of reading itself becomes a motif. The series shows characters engrossed in texts, as when Ray exclaims over *I Capture the Castle* or Jasper's (Richard E. Grant) absorption in *The Woman in White*. The image of the reader itself must be read, for as Roger Chartier writes, "reading [. . .] can never be reduced to what is read."[40] Situating the act of reading as Pierre Bourdieu suggests, as any other cultural practice, means that the ritualization of reading as seen in *Girls* imbues it with symbolic meaning beyond the act of literal comprehension for information or entertainment.

Bourdieu explores the heuristics implied by aesthetic taste extensively in *Distinction: A Social Critique of the Judgement of Taste*. He claims in "Reading as a Cultural Practice," "[r]eading obeys the same laws as other cultural practices,"[41] and in *Distinction*, Bourdieu maps reading onto the geography of those other cultural practices. After he begins his argument on distinction and taste by examining the likelihood that workers in different professions will recognize particular songs like "Rhapsody in Blue" and "Well-Tempered Clavier," Bourdieu moves to consider how books follow the template for cultural taste. He claims that all cultural products "yield a profit in distinction proportionate to the rarity of the means required to appropriate them, and a profit in legitimacy, the profit par excellence, which consists in the fact of feeling justified in being (what one is), being what it is right to be."[42] The "rarity of the means required to appropriate them" must be paired with the feeling of "what it is right to be," or in other words, rarity itself is not enough to convey distinction. There must be cultural agreement on the value of the object by "class societies" that the object can "express or legitimate domination."[43] Since books as objects are relatively inexpensive (excluding "rare" editions or collector's items, which are not at stake in *Girls*), the "rarity of means" is not the cost of the book as an object, but the education or experience needed to comprehend the book for the reader's purpose.[44] Bourdieu describes culture's "disgust at the 'facile'" as "refusal of what is easy in the sense of simple, and therefore shallow, and 'cheap,' because it is easily decoded and culturally 'undemanding.'"[45] In this way, culture adheres to the "Platonic prejudice . . . in favour of the 'noble senses.'"[46] An example would be Tao Lin's *EEEEE EEE EEEE*, which eschews standard linear narrative in favor of surreal talking animals and stream of consciousness jumps in temporaneity. Tao Lin's "refusal of the *facile*" classifies the text as one with Kant's "taste of reflection" as Bourdieu describes.[47]

Girls associates many of its characters with books in the "taste of reflection" category: Adam with *Him with His Foot in His Mouth* and *Aristotle's Poetics,*[48] Ray with *I Capture the Castle*, Tad with *Uncommon Sense*, and Jasper (Richard E. Grant) with *The Woman in White*.[49] It is not just the number of books that characters keep, although several of their apartments sport shelf after stuffed shelf, in addition to the stacks of books on tables and around beds. It is their taste in choosing and reading these books. *Girls* features counter-examples of poor taste, too, particularly in Hannah's stint working at *GQ Magazine*. She explains to Ray in "Free Snacks"[50] that one of her online pieces has attracted the interest of the "literary institution," which in turn landed her a writing job. He instantly corrects her gloating, since her contributions to the new section "Field Guide to the Urban Man" will be an "advertorial," which he considers "creatively bankrupt." Her new co-worker, Joe (Michael Zegen) confirms Ray's assessment when he describes the difference between editorial and advertorial writers, since the former do not qualify the latter as writers. Hannah is assigned an interview with Patti Lu-Pone, but she must center the conversation on bone density for the advertisement instead of exploring any of LuPone's creative work. Hannah finds that her co-workers are serious "writer writers" too, with achievements ranging from "a Yale Series of Younger Poets Prize in 2009" to publication in *n+1* and the *New Yorker*. While Hannah's goal is to sell her work and make her living as a writer, she does not want to be a "corporate writer," in part because she finds the bourgeois and commercial distasteful, even though she seems to enjoy the actual work.

We also find a counter-example of "taste of reflection" in reading done by women on the series. When Ray reads *I Capture the Castle* in Café Grumpy, Hannah, too, takes a "reading break," even though it is unauthorized. However, *she* reads *Us Weekly*, a celebrity gossip magazine. She reads frivolous material other times, too, as she admits in "Vagina Panic" (season 1, episode 2) to having read *Listen Ladies: A Tough Love Approach to the Tough Game of Love* in an airport once. Shoshanna touts the fictional book as a good source of advice to single women, though her description of it sounds like the much maligned *The Rules: Time-tested Secrets for Capturing the Heart of Mr. Right* by Ellen Fein and Sherrie Schneider, from 1995. While Jessa and Hannah deride the advice given by the fictional *Listen Ladies*, Hannah's admission to airport reading suggests that she reads widely, often from spurious sources, and that reading in an airport need not follow the rules of ordinary reading habits and taste. Hannah's online reading is questionable, too, as she defends searching for information on her editor David Pressler-Goings's (John Cameron Mitchell) death on *Gawker*. Even though the irreverent title of the article is "Goings, Goings, Gone," Hannah supports the source, describing it as "a web portal that celebrates the written word, and its sister site *Jezebel* is a place where feminists can go to support one another."[51] Each of these popular readings is presented as tasteless reading, and characters are required to justify their selection of material. The series, in general, promotes thoughtful literacy.

The introduction of less respectable texts complies with Bourdieu's argument that texts constantly rearrange themselves on the ladder of cultural credibility. As part of his structuralist argument on the behavior of all objects, and books in particular, Bourdieu writes, "Thus the tastes actually realized depend on the state of the system of goods offered; every change in the system of goods induces a change in tastes."[52] We might consider the books "offered" or on display in *Girls* as part of two systems. The first system is the system that includes all other books. When viewers see *Us Weekly* in "She Did," they place it in context not only with Ray's reading of *I Capture the Castle*, but with other gossip magazines like *People Magazine*, with other magazines likely to appear at the grocery checkout lane like *Na-*

tional Enquirer and *O Magazine*, and with all other books and texts. An individual heuristic is generated to determine the quality of the magazine and assign the relevant cultural markers of taste to the reader, in this case, Hannah.

The second system of goods offered is the closed system within *Girls.* Within this system, only the books "offered" by the series populate the heuristic. The system includes the fictional *Listen Ladies* as well as texts that appear, but are not discussed, such as *At Dawn We Slept: The Untold Story of Pearl Harbor,* which sits beside Adam's bed as he and Hannah watch television in "It's About Time"[53] or *A Daughter's Love*, which is easily identifiable on Shoshanna's dresser in the same episode. In the closed system, viewers must assign the texts value based on knowledge of the characters instead of deriving information from the texts. Each time a real or fictional text is introduced to the series, the others shuffle their positions in relation to it. For example, Hannah swells with satisfaction when David Pressler-Goings offers her an electronic book deal in "Boys,"[54] but her happiness is soon dashed when she meets a man at a party who tells her to talk to another party-goer who is writing a book, also, with the caveat, "well, just an e-book, but that's a book, too, right?" At this point, Hannah and the viewer reduce the value of her e-book deal in relation to the never-seen party-goer's book.

The closed system of offered books is also a closed system of readers. While reading is discussed often, from Hannah chastising Loreen's surprisingly patriarchal view on marriage by asking, "What are you even talking about in your women's book group?"[55] to Jessa's claim to have seen Shoshanna reading the newspaper before,[56] the girls in *Girls* discuss the act of reading, usually without discussing the actual texts, and scenes of women reading are few and rarely demonstrate the "taste of reflection." For example, there is the already referenced scene of Hannah reading a magazine, and there are several scenes that involve Shoshanna reading a textbook for a college class. In contrast, men are shown reading often and widely from texts that reflect cultured taste. Adam, Ray, and Tad are particularly visible readers. The effect is to masculinize reading and feminize writing, since Hannah is the only productive writer of "reflection" in the cast. There are images of her writing—often with difficulty, but still writing—and there are images of men reading well-selected books. Dunham has said of Driver that he is "the sexiest man alive"[57] and the series demonstrates his character's sex appeal through his reading habits and by surrounding him with images of literacy. His bed is surrounded by books and books pile up around his apartment. He reads in bed, wearing only his underwear. By turning the tables on historical gender roles of production and consumption of texts, *Girls* makes reading— and reading "good" books—attractive and masculine.

NOTES

1. "Pilot," *Girls*, directed by Lena Dunham. New York: Home Box Office, April 15, 2012.
2. Chloé H. Johnson, "Dancing on My Own: Popular Music and Issues of Identity in *Girls*," (191).
3. Ibid.
4. Kellogg, Carolyn. "'Girls'' Lena Dunham Interned at Soft Skull, Not at Melville House."
5. "About," *Melville House*, Melville House, Web, October 7, 2014.
6. Rachel Deahl, "Melville House Has a Friend in Lena Dunham," *Publishers Weekly*, April 24, 2012.
7. Gary S. Beckner and Richard A. Posner, *Uncommon Sense: Economic Insights, from Marriage to Terrorism* (Chicago: University of Chicago Press, 2009): 1.
8. Ibid, 2.
9. Ibid, 3.
10. "Bad Friend," *Girls*, directed by Jesse Peretz, New York: Home Box Office, January 27, 2013.
11. "Boys," *Girls*, directed by Claudia Weill, New York: Home Box Office, February 17, 2013.
12. Saul Bellow, *Him with His Foot in His Mouth* (New York: Penguin Books, 1974), 8.
13. Ibid., 5.
14. Nathan Heller, "That Girl," *Vogue*, January 15, 2014: 196.
15. "Hannah's Diary," *Girls*, directed by Richard Shepard, New York: Home Box Office, May 6, 2012.
16. Ibid.
17. Dunham admits that the scene reveals her real reasons for getting tattoos. The large image on her back is from *Eloise* by Kay Thompson. Others include, "*Ferdinand the Bill*, a book called *Pals* which no one has ever heard of, and a Scottish book called *Fairwater*" ("Q&A with Lena Dunham").
18. In "Welcome to Bushwick a.k.a. The Crackcident," Adam's friend Tako (Roberta Colindrez) discusses his alcoholism with Hannah: "That's like the main defining thing about him, isn't it? That and his love of books."
19. "Hannah's Diary" *Girls*.
20. Dodie Smith, *I Capture the Castle* (New York: St. Martin's Press, 1948): 4.
21. Ibid., 10.
22. Ibid., 84.
23. Ibid., 26.
24. Ibid., 111.
25. Ibid., 197.
26. "Pilot," *Girls*.
27. "Boys," *Girls*.
28. Ibid.
29. See "Which HBO Girls Character Are You?" www.huffingtonpost.com/joanna-popper/hbo-girls-characters_b_1573533.html; "Which Girls Character Are You?" www.quibblo.com/quiz/h_TpIMJ/Which-Girls-Character-Are-You; "Which 'Girls' Character Are You?" www.buddytv.com/personalityquiz/girls-personalityquiz.aspx?quiz=500000144.
30. "It's About Time," *Girls*, directed by Lena Dunham, New York: Home Box Office, January 13, 2013.
31. Richard Lingeman, "Nader's Road to Utopia," *The Nation,* October 12, 2009: 6.
32. Jennifer Burns, *Goddess of the Market: Ayn Rand and the American Right* (New York: Oxford University Press, 2009), 4.
33. Ibid., 248.
34. Ibid., 283.
35. "I Get Ideas," *Girls*, directed by Lena Dunham, New York: Home Box Office, January 20, 2013.

36. Elijah later tries to rile Sandy by suggesting he is too busy reading "Republican Quarterly" to read Hannah's essay.

37. Although her approach conveys her self-consciousness about race, the discussion could also be considered a critique of his politics.

38. "It's About Time," *Girls.*

39. "I Saw You," *Girls*, directed by Jesse Peretz, New York: Home Box Office, March 16, 2014.

40. Todd W. Reeser and Steven D. Spalding, "Reading Literature/Culture: A Translation of 'Reading as Cultural Practice.'" *Style* 36, no. 4 (2002): 662.

41. Ibid., 662.

42. Pierre Bourdieu, *Distinction: A Social Critique of the Judgement of Taste*, trans. Richard Nice (Cambridge: Harvard University Press), 1984: 228.

43. Ibid.

44. Consider again Johnson's argument regarding popular music in *Girls*. The lyrics and the effect of the tunes are more readily accessible than books because they are immediate. The viewer experiences them as the characters do. Books require a much greater investment of time and intellectual energy.

45. Ibid., 486.

46. Ibid., 486–87.

47. Ibid., 488.

48. "Role-Play," *Girls*, directed by Jesse Peretz, New York: Home Box Office, March 9, 2014.

49. "Truth or Dare," *Girls*, directed by Lena Dunham, New York: Home Box Office, January 12, 2014.

50. "Free Snacks," *Girls*, directed by Jamie Babbit, New York: Home Box Office, February 9, 2014.

51. "Dead Inside," *Girls,* directed by Jesse Peretz, New York: Home Box Office, January 26, 2014.

52. Pierre Bourdieu, *Distinction: A Social Critique of the Judgement of Taste*, trans. Richard Nice (Cambridge: Harvard University Press), 1984: 231.

53. "It's About Time," *Girls.*

54. "Boys," *Girls.*

55. "Flo," *Girls*, directed by Richard Shepard, New York: Home Box Office, March 2, 2014.

56. "Beach House," *Girls*, directed by Jesse Peretz, New York: Home Box Office, February 16, 2014.

57. Sheila Heti, "Lena! Girls' Girl," *Glamour* , April 2014: 218.

BIBLIOGRAPHY

"About." *Melville House*. Melville House. Web. 7 October 2014.

Alcott, Louisa May. 1869. *Little Women*. New York: W. W. Norton & Company, 2003.

Beckner, Gary S., and Richard A. Posner. *Uncommon Sense: Economic Insights, from Marriage to Terrorism*. Chicago: University of Chicago Press, 2009.

Bellow, Saul. *Him with His Foot in His Mouth*. New York: Penguin Books, 1974.

Bourdieu, Pierre. *Distinction: A Social Critique of the Judgement of Taste*, trans. Richard Nice. Cambridge: Harvard University Press, 1984.

Burns, Jennifer. *Goddess of the Market: Ayn Rand and the American Right*. New York: Oxford University Press, 2009.

Collins, Wilkie. *The Woman in White*. 1859. London: Penguin, 2003.

Deahl, Rachel. "Melville House Has a Friend in Lena Dunham." *Publishers Weekly*. 24 April 2012. Accessed June7, 2014.

Guy, John. *A Daughter's Love*. Boston: Houghton Mifflin Harcourt, 2009.

Hamilton, Nikita T. "So They Say You Have a Race Problem? You're in Your Twenties, You Have Way More Problems Than That." In *HBO's* Girls: *Questions of Gender, Politics, and Millennial Angst*. Edited by Betty Kaklamanidou and Margaret Talley. 43–58. Newcastle: Cambridge Scholars Press, 2014.

Heller, Nathan. "That Girl." *Vogue*. January 15, 2014, 194–204.

Heti, Sheila. "Lena! Girls' Girl." *Glamour*. April 2014.

Johnson, Chloé H.. "Dancing on My Own: Popular Music and Issues of Identity in *Girls*." In *HBO's* Girls: *Questions of Gender, Politics, and Millennial Angst*. Edited by Betty Kaklamanidou and Margaret Talley. 186–198. Newcastle: Cambridge Scholars Press, 2014.

Kellogg, Carolyn. "'Girls''s Lena Dunham Interned at Soft Skull, Not at Melville House." *LA Times Blogs—Jacket Copy*. April 24, 2012. Accessed June 17, 2014.

Lin, Tao. *EEEEE EEE EEEE*. New York: Melville House, 2007.

Lingeman, Richard. "Nader's Road to Utopia." *Nation*. October 12, 2009.

Prange, Gordon W. *At Dawn We Slept: The Untold Story of Pearl Harbor*. New York: Penguin, 1981.

"Q&A with Lena Dunham." *HBO Connect*. Accessed May 28, 2014. http://connect.hbo.com/events/girls/lena-dunham/.

Rand, Ayn. *The Fountainhead*. New York: Plume Books, 1994.

Reeser, Todd W., and Steven D. Spalding. "Reading Literature/Culture: A Translation of 'Reading as Cultural Practice.'" *Style* 36, no. 4 (2002): 659–76.

Smith, Dodie. *I Capture the Castle*. New York: St. Martin's Press, 1948.

Talley, André Leon. *A.L.T. 365+*. New York: Powerhouse Books, 2005.

Chapter Nine

Lena Dunham: The Awkward/ Ambiguous Politics of White Millennial Feminism

Elwood Watson

Since its debut in April 2012, the controversial series *Girls* has become a hot popular-culture topic, and major publications from *Harper's Magazine* and *Salon*, to the *National Review* and the *New Republic* have become obsessed. *Huffington Post* assembled a group of cultural critics to discuss weekly episodes.[1] Even the *New York Times* ran seven articles per week during the show's first three months.[2] Not since *Friends* has a program featuring young people garnered such intense scrutiny from the media and public.[3] The show has also raised questions regarding racial inclusion and exclusion, post-feminism, and representation of millennial women on television.

As a Black male college professor from generation X, I did not pay much attention to *Girls* at first. It was evident that I was not in the show's target demographic. In fact, the show was not likely marketed to anyone over thirty-five, regardless of gender or race.[4] However, as commentary intensified among media and my students, I realized that any socially conscious viewer could identify that the show was in every way imaginable White.

Dunham has earned considerable praise for what critics see as boldness and avant-garde creativity, but the show has also faced intense criticism for its seemingly whitewashed version of Millennials—where non-whites exist on the periphery at best, and men are shiftless, dimwitted narcissists. Detractors have argued that the popularity of *Girls* is merely another instance of mainstream media routinely fawning over a television program about college-educated, middle and upper-middle class, idealistic, single white women in their twenties navigating the minefields of life.

The show belongs to a decades-old genre of television focusing on the sex lives of young white women, and Dunham's awkward response to criticism is demonstrative of the millennial generation's discomfort with discussing race. This discomfort is perhaps most evident in Dunham's writing of the character and romantic interest, Sandy, to temper media critics. This essay offers writers, producers, and directors ideas for addressing issues of racism, marginalization, and exclusion in television.

Sex and the Single White Girl

When Helen Gurley Brown (1922–2012) penned *Sex and the Single Girl* in 1962, and later became editor of *Cosmopolitan* magazine in 1965, she was probably unaware of the impact her book would have on American popular culture. *Sex and the Single Girl,* an advice book that was in sync with many of the values of second wave feminism of the 1960s, yet in conflict with others, encouraged women to become financially independent and experience sexual relationships before or without marriage. In the fifty years since its publication, many television series have chronicled the lives of young single adult women dealing with the same issues as Brown's book. Lena Dunham's *Girls* is the latest version of this genre. In fact, in her recent bestselling book *Not That Kind Of Girl*, Dunham credits Gurley Brown as a role model and inspiration.[5]

Girls is the intersection of *Gossip Girl* (2007–2012), without the wealth, and *Dawson's Creek* (1998–2003) without the North Carolina setting; a hybrid comedy-drama that bears resemblance to a number of previous television programs showcasing young single women, including *That Girl* (1966–1971), *Mary Tyler Moore* (1970–1977), *Rhoda* (1974–1978), *The Days and Nights of Molly Dodd* (1987–1991), and *Ally McBeal* (1997–2002). Critics also describe *Girls* as a millennial version of *Sex and the City* (*SATC*) (1998–2004), another wildly popular HBO series that chronicles the lives of four New York women and their extravagant consumption of men and luxuries.[6] However, Dunham rejects such comparison.[7]

While *SATC* and *Girls* both focus on the lives of four women and their sexual exploits in New York City, here is where the commonalities end. The women of *SATC* are older, have successful careers, and are much more confident than the four main characters portrayed on *Girls*.[8] Hannah Horvath (Dunham) is an aspiring writer, not established like *SATC*'s protagonist Carrie Bradshaw. She is clueless, largely unsuccessful in utilizing her degree, and reliant upon the altruism of her parents to make ends meet—until they cut her off in the first episode. Hannah's so-called boyfriend, Adam, is a narcissistic, sexually immature, manipulative, and sporadically violent bodybuilder. He is largely indifferent to Hannah's feelings, has a love/hate relationship with her, and until the final episode of season 2, treats her like the under-sole of a shoe. Friendships, especially between single people in their twenties, male and female, can be complicated, confusing, and downright tormenting, but Hannah and her hipster sisters take dysfunction, indecision, and confusion to new heights. As a result, they eagerly embrace co-dependency. These characters and their plights mirror the media-held narrative that a disproportionate segment of Generation Y (Millennials) prolongs adolescence to avoid facing the responsibilities of adulthood.

Still, Hannah has a few things in common with her Generation X and Baby Boomer counterparts Molly Dodd and Ally McBeal: indecision, flightiness, and insecurity, to name a few. Most interestingly, all three have been romantically involved with Black men. During the late 1980s, interracial relationships on television were not as common as today. Molly, a well-educated female WASP, exists in a progressive but restricted social circle. Therefore, her liaison with Black detective Nathaniel Hawthorne is groundbreaking for its time. Ally McBeal's involvement with Black physician Dr. Greg Butters is less so because America was more accepting of interracial dating by the late 1990s. Diversity and other forms of cultural pluralism had become more widespread. Ally's whole life seemed racially integrated, from her workplace to her roommate, Black and sexually-vibrant district attorney Renee Raddick. While *The Days and Nights of Molly Dodd* and *Ally McBeal* occasionally received feminist criticism, both characters and their respective shows were certainly racially progressive. The same cannot necessarily be said for Hannah Horvath or for *Girls*. Non-white characters are often transient men and women—disposable figures quickly dismissed, or at the very least marginalized, by her group.

Some observers attribute the show's seeming indifference regarding race to Judd Apatow, producer of the critically acclaimed TV show *Freaks and Geeks* (1999–2000) and comedy films *Superbad* (2007), *Knocked Up* (2007), and *Forgetting Sarah Marshall* (2008). As a producer, Apatow has been faulted for the absence of people of color in his work. In fact, the only non-white to inhabit a lead role in any Apatow film or television series is Maya Rudolph, star of megahit *Bridesmaids* (2011). Rudolph is a racially ambiguous-looking woman, whose Blackness is not obvious to the eye, and her inclusion does little to rebut Apatow's indifference to racial matters. *Girls* is a continuation of Apatow's unwillingness to embrace diverse casting and diverse themes.

Dunham's Critics and Supporters Awkwardly Square Off

After its premiere, Lena Dunham and *Girls* faced criticism from various quarters for its failure to represent people of color. Journalist and cultural critic Francine Latour lamented the show's demographically skewed setting:

The problem I have with Dunham is that the vision of New York City she's offering us in 2012—like *Sex and the City* in 1998 and for that matter *Friends* in 1994—is almost entirely devoid of the people who make up the large majority of New Yorkers, and have for some time now: Latinos, Asians and blacks. It's a zeitgeist so glaring and grounded in statistical reality that Holly-wood has to will itself not to see it: America is transforming into a majority-minority nation faster than experts could have predicted, yet the most racially and ethnically diverse metropolis in America is delivered to us again and again on the small screen as a virtual sea of white. The census may tell us that blacks, Latinos and Asians together make up 64.4 percent of New York City's population. Much of *Girls* is actually set in Brooklyn, a borough where just one-third of the population is white. Yet as Dunham's character, 24-year-old unemployed writer Hannah Horvath, and her friends fumble through life with cutting wit and low self-esteem, they do it in a virtually all-white bubble. [9]

Dunham is not the first person to be taken to task for portraying the Big Apple as virtually all white, middle- and upper-class, and disproportionately populated with hipsters, coffee shops, trendy bistros, and other amenities largely associated with young affluent white people. Oscar-winning writer, producer, and director Woody Allen has also endured similar criticism for his less than diverse depiction of NYC. Nonetheless, the sea of virtual whiteness that Dunham and her contemporaries showcase is largely bereft of reality. Latour's argument reflects the critics who resent that Dunham portrays a New York City whose demographics resemble Montana, Idaho, Maine, Ver-mont, and New Hampshire as opposed to the cultural diversity that is the city's hallmark.

Dunham's failure to depict an ethnically diverse New York City—both outside and inside Hannah Horvath's social circle—excludes people of color in the audience, even if they otherwise relate to the characters. African-American contemporaries Phoebe Robinson[10] and Kendra James[11] levied charges of white-feminist racism against Dunham and *Girls*. In her often quoted essay "DEAR LENA DUNHAM I EXIST," James notes that she and Dunham both attended an elite public high school and Oberlin College with only two years separating them. Throughout her widely retweeted article, James eloquently illustrates that the situations and experience of both women are remarkably similar and her dismay that two individuals from similar cultural and educational pedigrees could harbor such diametrically diverse images of New York City. "Why would I feel so ill-at-ease with her critics essentially declaring her as my voice."[12] James's analysis was revelatory, exposing the fact that Lena Dunham and her supporters see Black women from an obscured perspective and, in some cases, do not see them at all. For Black women like James, Dunham's show represented the inauthentic urban female experience.

The *New York Times* technology reporter and cultural critic Jenna Wortham also expressed her disappointment with the absence of women of color:

> Because these girls on *Girls* are like us, they are like me and they are like you, they are beautiful, they are ballsy, they are trying to figure it out. They have their entire lives ahead of them and I can't wait to see what happens next. I just wish I saw a little more of myself on screen, right alongside them. [13]

Wortham and her fellow Black colleagues make the case that they have a lot in common with Dunham and her co-stars, yet are distressed that they have not been invited along on the journey of Hannah Horvath and her white friends. However, the "I, too, am Lena Dunham" argument is problematic, as it implies that not being included in Hannah's posse delegitimizes women of color. What Wortham and her cohorts are saying, probably unconsciously, is that even though they indeed have characteristics and experiences similar to Hannah and her white costars, they do not actually exist without recognition from white women. It is as if they are looking for white validation.

Dunham's supporters also provide awkward and debatable defense of her artistic decisions. Hilton Als of the *New Yorker* argues that critics of Lena Dunham's exclusionary behavior are misguided:

> [I]sn't Dunham doing women of color a favor by not trying to insert them into her world where ideas about child-rearing, let alone man and class aspirations, tend to be different? John Lennon once said if you want your kids to stay white, don't have them listen to black music. And I think it's crazy to assume Dunham hasn't. She grew up in New York, and you can see it in her clothes and body: no white girl allows herself to look like that if she didn't admire the rounder shapes, and more complicated stylings, that women of color tend to pursue as their idea of beauty. [14]

Therefore, by not including women of color into her racially limited social circle because of supposed diverse viewpoints on parenting, personal relationships, and social goals, and by being a little plump and choosing clothes that most slim white girls (according to Als) would never consider wearing, Dunham is showing solidarity with non-white women. Really? Such disingenuous and nonsensical blather insults a reasonable and conscientious person's intelligence. It is a painfully misinformed and racist stereotype to imply all women of color are overweight, unkempt, and indifferent to their physical appearance. Considering his amalgam of fallacious and careless statements, it is important to emphasize this: white women's shapeliness or atypical wardrobe is not an acceptable stand-in for representation of Black and brown people on television.

Chez Pazienza, another Dunham fan, made the following observation:

> I think that the criticism Lena Dunham's been on the receiving end of from
> some in the black and Hispanic community is unfair. In case you haven't been
> following—and for your own sake, I hope you actually have better things to do
> than concern yourself with this kind of "controversy"—a host of socially con-
> scious journalists of color, many of them female, have complained that Dun-
> ham's show is too "white," that none of the titular girls on *Girls* are black or
> brown. The argument is a little dumb at face value, simply because Dunham
> herself is white and it's not like that's something she can change—and while
> New York City, both real and the depressing hellhole depicted on the show, is
> indeed a melting pot, let's be honest and admit that it's not exactly unlikely
> that people like Dunham's character on the show and her small cadre of
> friends would all be the same shade of white. [15]

Pazienza's argument that the show's producers did not intend for the series to exclude people of color is debatable. While it is probably safe to say that none of the show's writers or producers sat around in meetings deciding how to best exclude or offend non-white people, they did nonetheless, write a program targeting a demographic who would solely identify with the strug-gles of white middle- and upper-class young adults. The problem with this myopic thinking is that there are Black, Hispanic, Asian, Arab, or Indian (*The Mindy Project*, anyone?) young adults everywhere who could relate to many, if not all of the issues their white college-educated, professional peers face. Not all college-educated, career-seeking Hannah Horvaths or Lena Dunhams are white. Such a retrograde assumption on the part of the produc-ers is a classic example of white privilege manifesting itself.

Lena Dunham's creative works and public appearances exemplify this hipster racism, and her awkward and offensive comments and emotive be-havior make her an easy target for criticism. An example of her crass racial insensitivity is evident in a personal essay when she discusses a trip she took to Japan in 2011. She makes the following comment:

> I know I said I could never imagine a Japanese affair, but I've changed my
> mind. Kazu, the art handler hanging my mom's show, is gorgeous like the
> strong, sexy, dreadlocked Mongol in *Crouching Tiger, Hidden Dragon* (caus-
> ing my sister to email the instruction: "Yeah, girl. crouch that tiger, hide that
> dragon. P.S. That's a Chinese movie.").

Throughout the essay, she only relates to Japanese people as objects, arti-facts, or erotic species who are to be consumed and critiqued. To Dunham they are "the other," deviant, unhinged, and not fully human. [16]

The depiction of her mother's sexy Japanese employee brings to mind the final scene of season 1, episode 1, where a Black bum chases after Hannah in a sexually suggestive manner. She quickens her pace and escapes him—the only Black character in the episode. The troubling scene recalls age-old historical stereotypes of Black men as lustful predators in pursuit of young, innocent white females. One can conclude from Dunham's representations of non-white men that she views them as sexualized beings who are ready, able, and willing to sexually satisfy or violate the desires of white women like her.

Dunham's attitude, ineptness and discomfort with race are glaringly apparent in a 2012 interview on the NPR program *Fresh Air*. She empathizes with critics of the show's racial homogeneity and claims that such a situation does not represent her value system:

> I take that criticism very seriously [. . .] this show isn't supposed to feel exclusionary. It's supposed to feel honest, and it's supposed to feel true to many aspects of my experience. But for me to ignore that criticism and not to take it in would really go against my beliefs and my education in so many things. And I think the liberal arts student in me really wants to engage in a dialogue about it, but as I learn about engaging with the media, I realize it's not the same as sitting in a seminar talking things through at Oberlin. Every quote is sort of used and misused and placed and misplaced, and I really wanted to make sure I spoke sensitively to this issue. [17]

Another example of this detached and ambiguous mindset occurs in an interview with *Playboy* journalist David Rensin, where Dunham makes a similar defense of her actions regarding the race criticism that has dogged her and her program:

> I think that's a valid criticism, but we can't let that erase someone's ability to tell a personal story. While being racist and promoting inequality are crimes that should be punished, the sin of writing two Jewish girl characters and two Waspy characters feels less egregious to me. I've tried to be elegant about it and receive the criticism, and I understand what's hard about it. At the same time I'm like, really? [18]

Dunham's comments, which graduate from defensive to mildly offensive, demonstrate the unconscious racism inherent among privileged white females that leaves them open to charges of hypocrisy. She is making a painstaking effort to reassure the audience that she is striving toward racial inclusion and pluralism, and she strives to be non-offensive in her response. Yet her diplomatic response to the issue only reinforces to many critics that she is unsure how to respond. She lacks the language, let alone the interest, to participate in a serious and conscientious dialogue on race.

In response to Dunham's NPR interview, Phoebe Robinson chided Dunham for her reluctance to embrace more racial and cultural diversity in her social life stating "Ms. Dunham: go out and learn some more shit, so you will have more things to write about. It's lazy to stay so self-contained and beyond unacceptable to pass off such a myopic view of the world as the twentieth century experience." [19] While many white female writers and bloggers saw the lack of racial diversity on *Girls* as a problem, it was not so problematic as to prevent them from heaping continuous praise on both Dunham and the series. On the contrary, Dunham's Black female detractors rebuked her for creating a show that was not about girls as they had initially presumed it would be, but rather for producing a series that dealt with the trials, tribulations, and experiences of white girls. Wortham, James, and Robinson were all sincerely surprised and offended by the exclusion of their experiences and those of other non-white women by Dunham. It did not help that Dunham's tepid response to criticism made an already delicate situation more awkward.

The truth is that many whites assume that Black and other non-white people are obsessed with race, thus finding it difficult to understand the level of emotional and intellectual energy that people of color devote to the topic. What whites fail to understand is that white supremacy privileges whiteness as the standard model in our society. Being a member of the dominant culture allows Dunham and others of her privileged world to ignore race. More often than not, the only time they consider or acknowledge race is when they see another person from a different race confronting them or targeting them in a manner they perceive as invasive, impolite, offending their sensibilities, or intruding upon their lives.[20]

To her credit, despite her other issues with race, Dunham does not pretend to understand the Black experience. Unlike some whites (particularly those armchair radicals on the political left), she does not pretend to know what racism feels like. She does not engage in the intellectually dishonest games of sympathy and concern for people of whom she has little, if any knowledge. Nor does she compare her own experiences as a white female to those of non-whites. Indifference to others is not a virtue. In fact, it is problematic. Nonetheless, pretending to harbor concern for people who are seemingly invisible to you is the most perverse form of intellectual dishonesty.

Whites cannot speak with authority about the experiences of people of color, but they can speak of their own experiences of whiteness—which often come with privilege. Comparing their oppressions with marginalized minorities gives whites a dangerously misguided sense that they fully understand the experiences of people of color. Nothing could be farther from the truth. Some whites, in a perverse way, embrace such a position in order to downplay or reject the stories, struggles, and experiences of people of color. Dunham is not entirely representative of this category of people, yet she does reluctantly concede through her comments that she is struggling (however minimally) to become more knowledgeable and sensitive about racism and racial politics.

Mainstream media argues that Generation Y is more racially inclusive than older segments of the American population.[21] Thus, the dearth of racial diversity represented on *Girls* is glaringly notable. The fact remains that there are still more than a few Millennials (1980–1998), Generation Xers (1965–1979), Baby Boomers (1946–1964), and people of the Silent Generation (1925–1945), whose lives are largely segregated. For many, having a segregated life is by choice, for others, circumstance. The reasons for choosing segregation include a number of conditions, such as comfort, discomfort, fear, ignorance, indifference, and in some cases, outright dislike of others who are different. More than a few columnists have echoed this sentiment. As Max Read of *Gawker* put it:

> None of [these factors under criticism] makes *Girls'* portrayal of urban millennial life unrealistic. I've been to plenty of dinner parties where everyone was white, including myself. In fact, I'd argue that the show, taken as a whole, is even more accurate for these shortcomings. It really is the voice of a generation: a generation of white people who suck at talking about race. [22]

Read further argues:

> Dunham, for her part, is not a "hipster racist." When asked about her show's lack of diversity, she's been contrite and open to criticism. But her answers are still awkward, and reveal the other way that the kind of people depicted in *Girls*—should we say upper-middle-class urban millennials?—deal with race: by rendering the non-white members of their community—their "generation"—invisible. [23]

Mr. Read is misguided in his analysis. The fact is that the type of behavior that Hannah Horvath, (Dunham's character), her co-stars, the show's treatment of racial issues, and the real life Ms. Dunham herself engage in is indeed indicative of hipster racism. The often awkward and clumsy attempt to employ irony and satire in an effort to disguise itself. Hipster racism all too frequently involves blatantly racist comments under the assumption that they are outdated, thus inoffensive, or comments made simply to be controversial and edgy. Ms. Dunham and her associates are guilty as charged!

Similarly, Jon Caramanica argues that the lack of racial and ethnic diversity on television is a serious issue, but he suggests the hard truth that many people in their twenties self-segregate:

> *Girls* is hardly alone in its whiteness. Far more popular shows like *Two and a Half Men* or *How I Met Your Mother* blithely exist in a world that rarely considers race. They're less scrutinized, because unlike the Brooklyn-bohemian demimonde of *Girls*, the worlds of those shows are ones that writers and critics—the sort who both adore and have taken offense at *Girls*—have little desire to be a part of. White-dominant television has almost always been the norm. Why would *Girls* be any different? [24]

Each of these arguments rings true. Many Millennials believe the myth that everyone is equal, that color blindness is real, and that racism—and to a degree, sexism—are long-dead injustices. In their minds, any racist or sexist individual is atypical, and they certainly do not see themselves as culpable or capable of harboring such attitudes. Sadly, race—even among whites who consider themselves racially progressive—is an issue that is better off discussed carefully, seldom, or not at all. This sort of racial omission is not surprising. In her groundbreaking narrative, *Playing In The Dark: Whiteness and the Literary Imagination*, Toni Morrison eloquently dissects the historical tendency of whites, including white liberals, to obscure or marginalize the issue of race.

> Evasion has fostered another, substitute language in which the issues are encoded, foreclosing open debate. The situation is aggravated by the tremor that breaks into discourse on race. It is further complicated by fact that the habit of ignoring race is understood to be a graceful, even generous, liberal gesture. To notice is to recognize an already discredited difference. To enforce its invisibility through silence is to allow the black body a shadowless participation in the dominant cultural body.[25]

The implication that non-whites are shadowy creatures who are barely seen and whose voices are rendered invisible is one of profound truth. In interviews, Dunham may recognize the criticisms about racial representation in her show as valid, but by awkwardly sidestepping the issue, she perpetuates this common narrative.

The Awkward and Ambiguous Intersection of Race and Gender

While the early critical discourse on Lena Dunham and *Girls* was passionate, the dialogue remained largely civil until Lesley Arfin, a former writer for the series, tweeted: "What really bothered me the most about the movie *Precious* was the fact that there was no representation of ME."[26] Arfin's callously dismissive response to prior charges of racial exclusion led to social media lambasting Arfin for her racially flippant comments.[27] Under siege, Arfin quickly deleted her tweet and apologized, stating, "Without thinking, I put gender politics above race and class. That was careless." Ta-Nehisi Coates, a columnist for the *Atlantic* who has written eloquently on *Girls* and race, responded to the Arfin controversy: "I don't know Dunham or anyone who writes for *Girls*. Perhaps that was a rogue comment that says nothing about her team. Nevertheless, I think it's only right to ask whether you really want Black characters rendered by the same hands that rendered that tweet. Invisibility is problematic. Caricature is worse."[28] Arfin's brusqueness and indifference to the long, complicated, racial and gender politics of American history are indicative of major dilemmas still haunting white feminism. Her arrogant mindset resembles gatekeeping feminist politics devoid of any sort of pluralism. The fact that Arfin had a history of espousing racially insensitive comments, which is commonplace among hipster racists, did not help matters.

Like many of her white politically left-of-center peers, Dunham is a self-described feminist, yet she appears clueless to the long, recurring history of progressives relegating race to the back burner of discussion.[29] Second-wave feminists argued that both women and Blacks had been oppressed by the white patriarchy; but while white men had oppressed white women, they acknowledged a status higher than men and women of color. The late Black lesbian feminist, warrior, poet Audre Lorde (1934–1992) points out that white women often ignore the built-in privilege and advantages their skin color gives them. They tend to define their experiences as the norm, so "women of Color become 'the other,' the outsider whose experience and tradition is too alien to comprehend."[30] Lorde further declares:

> Women of color in America have grown up within a symphony of anger, at being silenced, at being unchosen, at knowing that when we survive, it is in spite of a world that takes for granted our lack of humanness, and which hates our very existence outside of its service. And I say *symphony* rather than *cacophony* because we have had to learn to orchestrate those furies so that they did not tear us apart. We have had to learn to move through them for strength and force and insight within our daily lives. Those of us who did not learn this difficult lesson did not survive. And part of this is always libation for my fallen sisters.[31]

Betty Friedan's second wave of well-bred, well-wed, well-fed, often well-educated Manhattan, Palm Beach, Southampton, country-club feminism was highly exclusionary. white women were the intended audience. Where were the poor white women? Where were the Black, lesbian, and other non-white women?[32] The exclusion of women of color on *Girls* continues the pattern of a long and tortuous history of division among white and non-white women. Cultural critic and academic Melissa Harris-Perry argues that the myths, behavior, and suspicions Black and white women have historically internalized about one another often impede friendships.[33] In fact, Harris-Perry's public rebuke of *Salon* writer Joan Walsh when she chided Walsh for what she (Harris-Perry) saw as an intellectually dishonest attempt by Walsh to exaggerate the extent of their friendship/relationship when Walsh employed "I am not a racist, I have Black friends" argument when Walsh and other white liberals were critical of President Obama.

> I was shocked and angered. . . . Although I disagree with her, I have no problem with Walsh's decision to take on the claims in my piece. I consider it a sign of respect to publicly engage those with whom you disagree. I was taken aback that Walsh emphasized the extent of our friendship. Walsh and I have been professionally friendly. We've eaten a few meals. I invited her to speak at

Princeton and I introduced her to my literary agent. We are not friends. Friendship is a deep and lasting relationship based on shared sacrifice and joys. We
are not intimates in that way. Watching Walsh deploy our professional famil-
iarity as a shield against claims of her own bias is very troubling. In fact, it is
one of the very real barriers to true interracial friendship and intimacy.[34]

Many Black women (and some Black men) denounced Walsh's comments as
a classic example of misguided white arrogance. Feminist, historian, and
professor emeritus of Northeastern University Winifred Breines concurs that
such divisions have been a major reason for the long historical divide and
mistrust between Black and white feminists.[35]

Lena Dunham, *Girls*, and HBO have been unable to escape this reality of
awkward division as well. It is probably true that Lena Dunham and her co-
stars are not staunch, hate-filled racists. On the contrary, they appear to be
the type of young women who would most likely be appalled and disturbed
by violent, callous racism. That said, judging from the semi- autobiographical nature of Dunham's writing, it is likely that her interactions—as well as
those of her writing staff—with Black and other non-white women have been
minimal at best. Moreover, they are likely to view non-whites and other
whites outside of their socio-economic groups as marginal—individuals to
occasionally critique from a distance or with a studious degree of indifference. As any racially astute person knows, just because a person does not
have a white hood in her closet, or a swastika in the drawer does not mean
that she is free of racism, anti-Semitism, or other forms of hatred. As those
who have been on the receiving end of hatred's venom know all too well,
racism is not always overt or blunt in nature. It can be sly, subtle, sophisticat-
ed, and unconscious.

We see a similar trend of racial marginalization in season 3 when Hannah's friend Jessa has a brief lesbian encounter with a character played by
Danielle Brooks (*Orange Is The New Black*) while they are in rehab. Jessa is
dismissed from the facility for her behavior, and we see no more of Brooks'
character after this. Similarly, Black *Daily Show* correspondent Jessica
Williams made a few appearances as one of Hannah's co-workers during the
show's third season, when both women (and a few of their colleagues) pas-
sionately discussed their literary ambitions and personal lives. Though these
women are given voices, they still exist only temporarily alongside Hannah.

Sandy, We Hardly Knew Ye!

While *Girls* producers have not openly admitted to it, negative scrutiny of the
program's racial deficiencies probably prodded them to begin the first two
episodes of the second season with Dunham romancing a Black hipster/
blipster named Sandy. These two episodes are the most notable, albeit clumsy, attempts at diversity by Dunham and her writing staff. Sandy is a fasci-

nating love interest for Hannah. He is, for all practical purposes, well adjusted, while Hannah is the poster child for indecision. She is a liberal; Sandy is a conservative Republican—a rarity among both hipsters and modern Blacks. He is attractive and in fairly good shape; Hannah is somewhat portly and aesthetically awkward. She is awkward; he is suave.

Unlike Hannah's previous boyfriends, Sandy is not violent, self-absorbed, unemployed or underemployed, bisexual, self-righteous, or confused. The two engage in several weeks of spontaneous sex, have brunch at bistros, attend movies, make out in quiet corners at bookstores, and behave like many young twenty something couples (including interracial ones). This romance comes to a grinding halt once the two get into a candid discussion on racial realities and politics. As the discussion becomes more intense, Sandy accuses Hannah of being like many typical hipster white girls who fantasize about living in the big city, hooking up with a Black man, and moving to the "gangsta" part of town.[36] Sandy then likens Hannah's behavior to that of the archetypal girl who soon learns her romanticized version of life is a fiction and grows disillusioned with reality. Hannah, in response, spouts out a comment announcing the fact that two-thirds of men on death row are Black. She then immediately accuses Sandy of racism, claiming that she "did not once see him as Black."

Hannah's last comment resorts to a form of patronizing political correctness that insults the intelligence of both Sandy and some non-white viewers. Sandy, being candid as usual, responds that Hannah's remark is "crazy" due to the fact that he is *indeed Black*. The two spar for a few more minutes, and she insults him for his political beliefs. This is somewhat perplexing as it contradicts her earlier comments to Jessa that she has come to terms with their stark political differences. Once it becomes clear that the relationship is over, Hannah gets up, looks Sandy in the eye and asks him, "Are your balls blue?" then storms out of the apartment.

Such an exchange accurately depicts the way many white liberals too often resort to responses that are awkward, if not outright offensive, when discussing race. They may not mean to offend. In the mindset of many progressive whites, not seeing race supposedly makes them enlightened and starkly distinguishes them from their more narrow-minded, conservative, and bigoted brethren. In the above scene, Hannah, a self-described white liberal, is clearly uncomfortable expressing her feelings about race, if she knows what she feels about it at all. Given her mostly white social circle, she is probably not forced to contemplate it, much less have a sincere and civilized discussion about it. Hannah's situation exposes the alarming degree of anxiety and to some degree angst that many Millennials have about race. Judy Berman from the *Atlantic* comments:

It's a credit to Dunham and the episode's writer, Jenni Konner, that the scene is so unsettling. If they had responded to the controversy over *Girls* and race by quietly casting a famous Black actor and pretending nothing more needed to be said, they might have looked just as naïve as Hannah, who claims not to see race because she's in denial about her own prejudices. Instead, they accompanied their tacit apology with a moment that challenged not only their own and their characters' privilege, but, in its deconstruction of what has come to be known as "hipster racism," that of the show's core audience. Although self-awareness pervades Dunham's work, it was surprising to see such insight from *Girls* on this particular topic. [37]

Berman further argues that despite such an effort, Dunham, as a product of white privilege, should stick to writing what she knows best, which is being white, wealthy, and well-connected. [38] In fact, it was this sort of "I don't know any Black and brown people" defense that Dunham gave in response to the diversity deficit of her show.

Hannah may not have been totally disingenuous in telling Sandy that she never noticed he was Black. Many studies conducted have found that many whites across political and economic spectrums make stark distinctions about other races, especially if they see the person in question as harboring traits different from those traditionally associated with the group in question. Conceptual artist and former Wellesley College professor Adrian Piper, a Black woman who is light-skinned enough to pass for white as well as the first Black female philosopher to receive academic tenure in the United States remarked:

> A visibly Black person may, in time, experience something very much like this unguarded friendship with a white person, if the Black person has proven his or herself trustworthy and worthy of respect, or has been a friend since long before either was taught that vigilance between the races was appropriate. But I have only rarely met adult whites who have extended this degree of trust and acceptance at the outset to a new acquaintance they knew to be Black. And to have extended it to someone who then turns out to be Black is instinctively felt as a betrayal, a violation. It is as though one has been seduced into dropping one's drawers in the presence of the enemy. [39]

Given Hannah's seemingly limited exposure to non-whites, it is plausible for her to see Sandy in a manner that defies what some progressive whites and many white conservatives would consider "authentic Blackness"—racially conscious, growing up poor or working class, elemental, filled with sexual prowess, athletically inclined (in the male's case), animated, emotional in temperament, somewhat or devoutly religious, etc. [40] On the contrary, Sandy could be viewed as a "safe and good Black person." Understandably, such a comment would be disconcerting to Sandy, or any Black person regardless of gender or skin tone, as it renders them invisible. This has been a common situation for Blacks, especially Black men. The experience recalls a passage in Ralph Ellison's 1952 novel *Invisible Man*:

> I am an invisible man. No, I am not a spook like those who haunted Edgar Allan Poe; nor am I one of your Hollywood-movie ectoplasms. I am a man of substance, of flesh and bone, fiber and liquids . . . Say, a figure in a nightmare, which the sleeper tries with all his strength to destroy.[41]

Comments such as "I never even noticed you were Black" and "I am color-blind," while intended as hip and forward-looking, are actually patronizing. There is not much difference between being colorblind and being blind. And when a person is deliberately blind, she is denying the power inherent in cultural identity. Of all the men for Hannah to date, Sandy is the most mature, relaxed, likable, and well adjusted. He has no competition, is secure in himself, knows what he wants, takes no bullshit, tells it like it is, and does not care about consequences. When Hannah says that she "did not once see him as Black," she appeared to be desperately grasping at what power she has left in the relationship before it ends.

Historically, in film, television, and much literature, Black male/white female relationships have been fraught with controversy, dysfunction, insecurity, paranoia, fear, unbridled tension, and hostility from society. Historical images have depicted Black men as wanton sexual predators—mostly well-endowed, strapping, juvenile, Mandingo-like bucks. They pose a threat to the purity of white womanhood and the sexual supremacy of the white male. In imperialist white-supremacist capitalist patriarchal culture, hatred of Black masculinity has found its most intense expression in the realm of the sexual. The dehumanization of the Black male sexual body (in a number of cases being granted with consent by Black males) is widespread and normalized.[42] In his classic, *Soul on Ice*, Eldridge Cleaver, (1935–1998), one-time radical Black panther, former expatriate, admitted serial rapist, fugitive later turned conservative Republican in the early 1980s argued that Black men embody a level of masculinity and sexual prowess that strikes fear into white men, leaving them scarred and demoralized.[43] Thus, whites, especially southern whites, employed extralegal violence—castration, lynchings, and mass incarceration—to keep "savage" Black men "in their place." For many decades, both print and electronic media promoted such dangerous stereotypes and actions.

However, in recent years, film, television, and other avenues of mainstream media have slowly yet surely refrained from projecting retrograde and racist images of Black men. While one still sees the occasional Black drug dealer, buffoon, street pimp, thug, or proud baby daddy, certain images of Black men have significantly decreased. One sees less bucking, shucking, and jiving; less childishness and callousness; less gangsta style; less demon-izing "I will bust a cap in your ass" trash talk, than before, even on the ten o'clock news. Such negative images, while not entirely departed from the screen, have been joined by more depictions of Black men as physicians, professors, attorneys, businessmen, consultants, ministers, conscientious hus-bands, good fathers, upright politicians, and generally admirable and desir-able human beings. Sandy falls into this category.

He is the antithesis of Black men such as Clay, the character from the 1964 play *The Dutchman* by Leroi Jones (perhaps better known as the Black radical, Beat poet Amiri Baraka).[44] Sandy's character is far from being vul-nerable. His persona is closer to that of Dr. John Prentice, the idealized Black man played by Academy Award-winning actor Sidney Poitier in *Guess Who's Coming to Dinner?* (1967). Sandy is more than a decade younger than Prentice and is not half so accomplished, at least not yet. He is simply a twenty-first-century hipster who knows what he wants. So, while here are two examples of characters who appear similarly strong, confident, and se-cure in interracial relationships, the difference is that in the 1960s representa-tion, the Black man had to be an internationally-accomplished physician in order to earn his relationship with a white woman, where in the millennial period, the Black man is able to simply exist as an artist dating a relatively-dysfunctional white twenty something woman who is unsure of who she is. Representations of Black men have both endured negatively and evolved positively—the clear and awkward truth.

Despite his relative "togetherness," conservative Sandy is not exactly a social conservative. He has no apprehensions engaging in recreational drug use, unabashed pre-marital sex, and other behaviors that would seem at odds with his professed conservatism. However, recent studies indicate that such beliefs and activities are commonplace and acceptable among millennial con-servatives and liberals who differ from their elder counterparts on social and cultural issues such as gay and interracial marriage and drug use.[45] Overall, Sandy's lifestyle could most accurately be described as conservative/libertar-ian. Nonetheless, he transcends Hannah's other male friends and ex-boy-friends in every manner possible, and Hannah's female friends in terms of confidence and outlook.

Notably, the show's producers were astute enough to portray Sandy as an enlightened Black man. Sandy's grounded perception of racial awareness and differences in American society starkly contrast the usual images of both Black hipsters and Black conservatives. Black liberals, the Black commu-nity, and much of the mainstream media treat both groups as political and social deviants. Sandy realizes America is no racial utopia, a point he makes clear during his breakup with Hannah. He recognizes that many on the left delude themselves into believing that we live in a post-racial nation. He has no tolerance for idealism. Sandy is no violent rebel, nor is he a nihilist. It is worth noting that Dunham and the show's creators invented a character so paradoxical, contradictory, and nonconformist—Black, hipster, Republican, and racially conscious.

Journalists and cultural critics weighed in on the Sandy/Hannah/*Girls* issue. Basketball legend Kareem Abdul-Jabbar, who had numerous NBA championships with the Los Angeles Lakers, brashly commented on the first two episodes of season 2:

> Last season the show was criticized for being too white. Watching a full season could leave a viewer snow blind. This season that white ghetto was breached by a black character who is introduced as some jungle fever lover, with just enough screen time to have sex and mutter a couple of lines about wanting more of a relationship. A Black dildo would have sufficed and cost less.[46]

Abdul-Jabbar further added that he did not see it as necessary for every program to go out of its way to include a person from every ethnic group, sexual orientation, or gender for the sake of screaming, "we have diversity." He found the addition of color to the program forced and somewhat patronizing.[47]

On the contrary, cultural critic and journalist Helena Andrews argued, "Sandy doesn't have to be Black. He just has to be the nice guy for whom Hannah isn't ready—a necessary point in the narrative of her self-discovery. A stepping-stone. But the fact that he is Black is a step in the right direction."[48] The larger question is a step in the right direction for whom? Hannah? The show's viewers? Lena Dunham and her writing staff? People of color?

Progress?

During its first three seasons, *Girls* managed to receive critical acclaim, court controversy, and spar conversations about young people's lives more than any other recent television series. Dunham's name is dropped in college dorm rooms, humanities and social sciences classes, trendy off-campus apartments, and magazine offices. Her program is a perennial topic at academic conferences and in the mainstream media. She is one of the "it" girls of the moment. Yes, the show is white in its persona, image, and values. While it would have been politically correct and idealistic to have written one of the female leads or close male friends as a person of color, for Dunham such a choice would have been intellectually dishonest and, to a degree, insulting given her actual life experiences. And yet, despite her transgressions, it would be hard to label Lena Dunham a racist. Ignorant and misguided in a bubble of privilege? Yes. Hard core bigot? No. Her past comments demonstrate what so many of her critics see as her real problem: a resistance to enter into any sort of racial discussion even when she is clearly the subject of focus. Whether the reason is confusion, awkwardness, apprehension,or disdain, it is an issue giving ammunition to detractors. [49]

While the blatant whiteness of *Girls* is undeniable and troubling, one does indeed wonder why Hannah and her group of friends do not have at least one friend of color or a love interest be it a man (or woman) of color. The show is as blunt and literal as a lighting rod. Nonetheless, in spite of these shortcomings, it is unreasonable and unfair to hold *Girls* or Lena Dunham solely responsible for addressing the issue of racial diversity in television. Television executives should handle this task. The vast majority of television is racially and economically segregated. While many people, including young people, live largely segregated social lives, there are millennials whose lives are racially integrated. *Happy Endings* (2011–2013), *How To Make It In America* (2011–2013), and *New Girl* (2011–present) are such representations of integration. Executives should make an effort to produce television series that accurately represent this demographic.

With *Girls* and race, honesty and transparency is the best policy. It is potentially dangerous to demand that people who have had minimal contact with other ethnic groups represent these groups' experiences. Such misguided ultimatums can result in disastrous art. As Ta-Nehisi Coates argues, no one can tell your story better than you can:

> In a world where the wealthy, white, well-connected Lena Dunhams always seem to end up in the spotlight, those who aren't part of her elite world shouldn't have to rely on her for representation. They need the same platform to be *their* authentic selves that she's been afforded. Until the divisions between races in America truly become meaningless, it's the only way our pop culture will ever reflect our particular patchwork of people and experiences. [50]

However, such limited social interaction and exposure does not absolve Lena Dunham and others like her who are the beneficiaries of white privilege to make a more conscious effort to promote diversity and representation for women across racial and socio-economic lines. Whether Ms. Dunham wants to acknowledge it or not, her privilege as a well-heeled, well-connected white female is evident and cannot be denied. Influential cultural critics do not define her as a "White female writer and producer" as they refer to mega successful television producer Shonda Rhimes and Issa Rae (*The Misadventures of Awkward Black Girl*) as "Black female Writers." This fact in and of itself, epitomizes white privilege. One's race is not an issue or barrier to their advancement or success. While Duhman and many of her white sisters have finally reached the mountaintop, far too many of her Black, Latina, Asian, Indian and other non-white sisters are still residing in the valley when it comes to real representation and media influence.

The fact that *Girls* provokes such passionate and heartfelt debate from so many quarters is testament to its success. Breaking down and dissecting once-taboo topics such as race, sex, mental illness, and addiction across gender, racial, social, and economic lines no matter how minimal is to be applauded.[51] Only now in her late twenties, will Lena Dunham's views on this issue likely evolve, however awkwardly and ambiguously, just as we Americans have done and will do? If so, that will be a real sign of progress.

NOTES

1. A number of mainstream and erudite publications ran multiple stories about *Girls* and the new Millennial wunderkind, Lena Dunham.

2. The *New York Times* ran, on average, a minimum of seven to one dozen articles per week about *Girls* and Lena Dunham herself.

3. *Friends* was a popular and critically acclaimed program that appeared on NBC from 1994 to 2004. The show was perennially in the top 10 in the Nielsen ratings for the majority of its duration and made household names of its stars. *Friends* also faced similar criticism, as did *Girls*, for its lack of racial and ethnic diversity.

4. http://www.entrenpreneur.com/article/230789.

5. Lena Dunham, *Not That Kind of Girl: A Young Woman Tells You What She Has Learned* (New York: Random House, 2014).

6. Upon its debut, many popular culture critics and observers made consistent comparisons between *Girls* and *Sex and the City*, another popular series that ran on HBO from 1998 to 2004.

7. Lesley Goldberg, "TCA: Lena Dunham Says HBO's 'Girls' Isn't 'Sex and the City,'" *The Hollywood Reporter*, January 13, 2012.

8. Hannah Horvath (Dunham's character), Marnie Michaels (Allison Williams), Jessa Johansson (Jemima Kirke), and Shoshanna Shapiro (Zosia Mamet) are dramatically different than Sarah Jessica Parker and her co-horts. As a side note, the characters' alliterative names are something that is interesting and perhaps intentional.

9. Francine Latour, "*Girls* in White," *Boston.com*, April 13, 2012.

10. Phoebe Robinson, "Break the Stereotypes," *Room for Debate*, www.nytimes.com/2012/04/25.

11. Kendra James, "Dear Lena Dunham, I Exist," *Racialiscious*, April 19, 2012.

12. James, *Racialiscious*, April 19, 2012.

13. Jenna Wortham, "Where My Girls At?" *Hairpin*, April 16, 2012.

14. Hilton Als, "Girls Attacked for No Good Reason," *New Yorker*, April 30, 2012.

15. Chez Pazienza, *Girls*: The Unbearable Whiteness of Being, *Banter*, May 3, 2012.

16. Jesssie Daniels, Lena Dunham and the Trouble with White *Girls*, *Racism Review*, April 8, 2014.

17. "Lena Dunham Addresses Criticism Aimed at Girls," *National Public Radio*, May 7, 2012.

18. David Rensin, "20 Q Lena Dunham," *Playboy Magazine*, March 14, 2013.

19. Robinson, "Not One of Lena Dunham's 'Girls,'" *Huffington Post*, April 19, 2012.

20. bell hooks, *Yearning: Race, Gender and Cultural Politics* (Boston: South End Press, 1990) 53.

21. Pew Research Center, "The Millenials: Confident. Connected. Open to Change," Pew Research Center, February 24, 2010.

22. Max Read, "Honky Talk Women: A Girls Writer's, Ironic Racism and Other 'White People Problems,'" Gawker.com, April 20, 2012.

23. Ibid.

24. Jon Caramanica, "Broadcasting a World of Whiteness," *New York Times*, April 25, 2012.

25. Toni Morrison, *Playing in the Dark: Whiteness and the Literary Imagination* (Cambridge: Harvard University Press, 1992) 9–10.

26. *Precious* is a 2009 movie that tells the life of obese, illiterate, sixteen-year-old Clareece "Precious" Jones, played by actress Garbourey Sidibe. Precious lives in the New York City ghetto of Harlem with her dysfunctional, abusive, unemployed mother, Mary, played by academy award–winning Mo'Nique. Precious has been raped by her father, Carl (Rodney "Bear" Jackson), resulting in two pregnancies. The family resides in a section 8 apartment and survives on welfare. Precious's first child has Down Syndrome and is being cared for by Precious's grandmother, though Mary forces the family to pretend that Mongo lives with her and Precious so she can receive extra money from the government.

27. These journalists, bloggers, and cultural critics include Max Read of *Gawker*, Gavin McInnes of *Vice*, Ta-Nehisi Coates of *Atlantic*, and Dodai Stewart of *Jezebel*.

28. Ta-Nehisi Coates, "'Girls' Through the Veil," *Atlantic*, April 20, 2012.

29. Anna Holmes, "White 'Girls'," *The New Yorker*, April 23, 2012.

30. Audre Lorde, *Sister Outsider: Essays and Speeches by Audre Lorde* (Berkeley, CA: Crossing Press, 1984) 117.

31. Ibid., 129.

32. Irene Monroe, "Remembering the Life, Love and Legacy of Audre Lorde," *The Bilerico Project*, October 17, 2014.

33. Melissa Harris-Perry, *Sister Citizen: Shame, Stereotypes, and Black Women in America* (New Haven: Yale University Press, 2011) 51–97.

34. Melisa Harris-Perry, "The Epistemology of Race Talk," *Nation*, September 26, 2011.

35. Winifred Breines, *The Trouble Between Us: An Uneasy History of white and Black Women in the Feminist Movement* (New York: Oxford University Press, 2006).

36. *Girls*, "I Get Ideas," (2:2), HBO, January 13, 2013, written by Lena Dunham, directed by Jenni Konner (New York): Jenni Konner Productions, 2013, DVD.

37. Judy Berman, "I'm A White Girl: Why 'Girls' Won't Ever Overcome Its Racial Problem," *Atlantic.com*, January 22, 2013.

38. Ibid.

39. Adrian Piper, "Passing For White, Passing For Black," *Transition: An International Review* 58 (1992): 26–27.

40. E. Patrick Johnson, *Appropriating Blackness: Performance and The Politics of Authenticity* (Durham: Duke University Press, 2003).

41. Ralph Ellison, *Invisible Man* (New York: Random House, 1952) 3–4.

42. bell hooks, *We Real Cool: Black Men and Masculinity* (New York: Routledge, 2004), 82.

43. Eldridge Cleaver, *Soul on Ice* (New York: McGraw Hill, 1968).

44. *The Dutchman* premiered at the Cherry Lane Theatre. The play won an Obie award. A more recent version of the play revived in 2007 at the same theater starring actor Dulé Hill.

45. Pew Research Center for Social and Demographic Trends, June 26, 2014.

46. Kareen Abdul-Jabbar, "*Girls* Just Wants to Have (*White*) Fun," *Huffington Post*, January 31, 2013.

47. Ibid.

48. Helena Andrews, "The Nice—and Black—Guy Gets the Girl," *Root*, January 13, 2013.

49. Zeba Blay, "Why Lena Dunham's 'N-Word' Response Isn't Good Enough," *Huffington Post*, February 24, 2013.

50. Ta-Nehisi Coates, "On Being Your Authentic Self, *Atlantic*. January 14, 2013.

51. Melissa Silverstein, "Girls, Girls, Girls," *New York Times*, April 25, 2012.

BIBLIOGRAPHY

Berg, Barbara. *The Remembered Gate: Origins of American Feminism*. New York: Oxford University Press, 1978.

Brienes, Winifred. *The Trouble Between Us: An Uneasy History of White and Black Women in the Feminist Movement*. New York: Oxford University Press, 2006.

Brown, Helen Gurley. *Sex And The Single Girl*. New York: Bernard Geis Associates, 1962.

Cleaver, Eldridge. *Soul on Ice*. New York: McGraw Hill, 1968.

Denfeld, Rene. *The New Victorians: A Young Woman's Challenge To The Old Feminist Order*. New York: Grand Central Publishing, 1996.

DuBois, W.E.B. *The Souls of Black Folk: Essays and Sketches*, 13. Chicago: A.C. McClurg, 1903.

Dunham, Lena. *Not That Kind of Girl: A Young Woman Tells You What She Has Learned*. New York: Random House, 2014. Introduction.

Ellison, Ralph. *Invisible Man*, 3–4. New York: Random House, 1952.

Friedan, Betty. *The Feminine Mystique*. New York: W.W Norton, 1963.

Harris-Perry, Melissa V. *Sister Citizen: Shame, Stereotypes, and Black Women in America*. New Haven: Yale University Press, 2011, 51–97.

hooks, bell. *Ain't I a Woman: Black Women and Feminism*, 136–37. Boston: South End Press, 1981.

———. *Yearning: Race, Gender and Cultural Politi cs*, 53. Boston: South End Press, 1990.

Johnson, E. Patrick. *Appropriating Blackness: Performance and The Politics of Authenticity*. Durham: Duke University Press, 2003.

Logan, Rayford W. *The Betrayal of The Negro*. New York: Collier, 1954.

Lorde, Audre. *Sister Outsider: Essays and Speeches by Audre Lorde*. Berkeley: Crossing Press, 1984, 117, 129.

Smuts, Robert W. *Women and Work in America*. New York: Schocken Books, 1971.

Chapter Ten

Marnye on the Ones and Twos: Appropriating Race, Criticizing Class in *Girls*

Lloyd Isaac Vayo

Though often rightly criticized for its problematic treatments of race, sex, gender, and, more particularly, class and privilege, the HBO series *Girls* does offer moments of canny insight into those same concerns. Strangely enough, many of those insightful moments occur during especially awkward situations, suggesting that it is in the uncomfortable frictions of life that our perspectives are challenged and changed. In many ways, *Girls* is Lena Dunham's baby; as creator and central protagonist, much of the show revolves around Hannah's missteps, with the other girls (Shoshanna, Jessa, and Marnie) existing as foils of sorts. Yet, at least in terms of the intersection of race, class, and privilege, it is Marnie, played by Alison Williams, who offers the most effective critique, albeit one troubled by its own contradictions.

In season 2, during the two-episode arc comprised of "It's Back" and "On All Fours," which is primarily about Hannah's mounting stress over her unfinished e-book, Marnie confronts her conflicted feelings for Charlie upon learning of his thriving app company. After getting in touch with Charlie, Marnie is invited to a celebration of a milestone for the app. This seemingly innocent invitation leads to possibly one of the most awkward moments in the series to date. Marnie, as a means of expressing both her opinion of Charlie's venture and her lingering affections for him, performs a truncated version of Kanye West's "Stronger," focusing on the second half of the first verse. By selecting this excerpt from the song, Marnie highlights West's[1] stance that others should be glad that he even makes an appearance at certain events, while also including the sexual frustration of the chorus.

Marnie's intentions in this act are relatively limited: to underline the backhanded compliment of praising Charlie's success, and also to restate her desire for him. However, Marnie's performance accomplishes much more. First, she engages in a problematic appropriation and repurposing of West's song, removing it from the mouth of an African-American[2] artist and placing it in the mouth of an especially white young New Yorker (which is redoubled by Williams's own background as the daughter of news anchor Brian Williams).[3] That appropriation is also flawed in that Marnie selectively quotes from the song, taking lines out of context and changing the song's meaning, if only through a gender reversal and her conversion of a rap song into a torch song.

Yet, at the same time, Marnie performs a critique of class and privilege, adopting the perspective of the cultural Other (West) as a means of attacking Charlie's class status and according privilege. Marnie, via West, ridicules Charlie's celebration and, by proxy, his app (meant to prevent jilted lovers from contacting their exes), challenging the swift success of the app company as akin to the boom and bust cycle of Internet startups in the late 1990s. At the same time, Marnie also offers a slight to Charlie's masculinity; with Charlie proving himself a retiring, emotional sort, Marnie adopts the insistent desire of West's song, expressing her own version of blue balls (blue boobs?) and positioning herself as the sexually assertive one, doubly insulting Charlie in the process.

Ostensibly a minor moment from a secondary character, Marnie's performance, at once a cover of "Stronger" and a remix, altering the tone and content of the song, stands as a moment of self-awareness for the series. By reflecting on the transient nature of success and the problematic nature of class- and race-based privilege, *Girls* demonstrates an awareness of its own momentary existence and uneasy relation with class and race, one that, while not always present elsewhere in the series, provides a refreshing moment of clarity here.

A further, if brief, examination of the "It's Back"–"On All Fours" episode arc is merited to contextualize not only Marnie's Kanye moment, but also the place of her relative subplot within the larger plot of the episodes. As usual, the primary focus of the episodes is Hannah, who might be thought of as the titular "girl" of the series (making a more apt title *Girl[s]*), and her struggles with the reemergence of her obsessive compulsive disorder, brought on by the stress surrounding her unfinished book. Both episodes give substantial attention to Hannah's troubles, chronicling her fixation on the number eight and accompanying repetition of all mundane acts eight times. The viewer follows Hannah through her day, especially through her encounter with her parents, who demonstrate a studied concern about Hannah's behavior that reflects the ongoing nature of her OCD. In particular, the viewer sees Hannah's misadventures with a particularly vigorous Q-Tip[4] which, when thrust to a dangerous depth into Hannah's ear, spurs a frantic call to her parents, a trip to the emergency room, and an appointment with her childhood therapist. Next in line following Hannah's saga is that of Shoshanna and Ray, whose seemingly mismatched relationship is going through something of a rough patch. Shoshanna, the hyper-anxious college student, feels some claustrophobia in her relationship with misanthropic Ray, leading to an unfortunate make-out session with a handsome doorman. Ray also registers his discontent with Shoshanna's class pretensions, as he is himself decidedly lower-middle class at best by vocation and ambition, and more accurately working class by indirect self-identification.[5] Alongside the main Hannah plotline and the Shoshanna-Ray subplot, passing reference is also made to resident free spirit Jessa and her nuptial misadventures, though she does not appear in either episode.

The true star of the "It's Back"–"On All Fours" episode arc is Marnie and, perhaps more aptly, her tenuous grip on stability and functional sanity in the wake of her separation from Charlie and subsequent sporadic relationship with eccentric artist Booth.[6] Upon learning of Charlie's successful app, Marnie expresses something close to frustration or exasperation, his continued existence in her absence being vexing enough, much less his ability to thrive. Moved to witness the phenomenon herself, Marnie pops in unannounced at Charlie's bustling office, reinserting herself into his life in a not entirely welcome manner, if only to gain clarification on the true nature of his success, though her motives soon prove to be more complex. After seeing Charlie's positive direction, and reflecting on her own stasis as a restaurant host, Marnie is moved to pursue singing after a consultation with Ray, who encourages her to follow her dreams (though he expresses some skepticism at her vocal desires). Beyond simply exercising her pipes in private, Marnie begins working on recordings, presumably for a demo tape, though no specific mention is made of efforts to that end, calling upon Ray's assistance with GarageBand[7] to produce somewhat polished material. The exact nature of their collaboration is left to the viewer's imagination, as no part of the recording process is shown, but some initial results are made evident at a celebration at Charlie's office to which Marnie was begrudgingly invited after another awkward encounter with Charlie. Commandeering the sound system and stepping to the fore, Marnie bestows her "Stronger" upon the party and the world, a performance that, while greeted as tragically embarrassing by most in attendance, seems to have a counterintuitively opposite effect on Charlie. After pulling her aside into a glass-walled office, the two rekindle their former flame, a reconciliation that extends into subsequent episodes. By reaching out to Kanye in her moment of need, Marnie establishes a bond of sorts between the two, one which extends to the level of identity, though in a distinctly racially appropriating way in Marnie's case.

Marnie's racial identity, though profoundly white at the outset, becomes somewhat blurry through her adoption of the Kanye perspective in her performance of "Stronger," shifting into a liminal space that serves to underline the privileged mobility available to her as a white woman. Throughout the series to this point and beyond, Marnie proves herself to be an almost cartoonish version of stereotypical twenty something white pseudo-affluent in New York City, a young cliché in the vein of a Carrie Bradshaw[8] in training, albeit a far less successful one. Even among the welter of privilege that is the core four of *Girls* (Hannah, Jessa, Shoshanna, and Marnie), Marnie stands out not only for her consistent polish in terms of dress and carriage, but also in terms of what might charitably be called her reserve, and less charitably be called her acute uptightness. If Marnie is capable of relaxing, the viewer sees no evidence of it, as she demonstrates herself to be tightly wound in all situations, even in comparison to Shoshanna, herself a ball of nervous energy. This overwhelming sense of propriety marks all of Marnie's interactions with others, the underlying sense of orthopraxis guiding not only her relationship with Charlie, but also with the other girls and the world at large. It is this unflinching élan that characterizes Marnie, that stands as the foundation of her personality and her identity, and that also marks her as a racial actor. Her decorum denotes not only a certain class status, hinting at a well-to-do upbringing, but also, by association, a certain racial status. Marnie's is an upper crust whiteness, that of an intense, type A go-getter fresh from a pricey liberal arts education and ready to take on whatever glass ceilings might stand in her way. Yet, that racial identity proves more unstable than Marnie's stoic consistency might first suggest, leading her to turn elsewhere to shore up her sense of self.

By the time of the "It's Back"–"On All Fours" episode arc, Marnie is at an impasse; her relationship with Charlie having failed, and her rebound with artist Booth having proven less fulfilling and exciting than first anticipated, Marnie's identity is in flux, a condition that she does not handle particularly well. A frantic energy pervades all aspects of her life, destabilizing not only her internal manner, but also her external presentation to the world, particularly in relation to her appearance. Where once Marnie was perpetually dressed to the nines, always stylish yet understated, she is now disheveled, her hair tied back into inexpert pigtails, and sweatshirts and casual wear being the order of the day. The financial status that existed as the foundation of her earlier identity has also eroded, as she finds herself as a restaurant host rather than the relatively elevated personal assistant position that she held previously. With these identity touchstones no longer present, Marnie is, in Charlie's words, "flailing,"[9] motivating her to reach beyond herself and her previous comfort zone to supplement her failing identity elsewhere. It is here that Kanye enters the picture, not only in the form of the narrator of "Stronger," but also in terms of his overall personality and presence. He is, in brief, everything that she is not; confident, affluent, sexually assertive, and in possession of a clear sense of self that Marnie is decidedly lacking. This is not to say that Marnie discards her previous identity wholesale; her Marnieness is still very much intact. However, she augments her at present less than stellar constant identity with a dash of the dashing Kanye, in the process moving away from a stagnant whiteness and adding a bit of color, in terms of both personality and racial identity.

Once she gets in touch with her inner Kanye, and once she expresses it outwardly through her "Stronger" performance, Marnie is transformed, coming out of her shell of rigid propriety, for better or worse, to become a more assertive, sexually ambitious being that bears some relation to the old Marnie, though not as much as even those close to her might expect. In her introduction to her rendition of "Stronger," Marnie identifies the song as being "really meaningful to me,"[10] underlining its centrality to her new identity permutation and adding weight to what follows. What ensues is an awkward swagger, Marnie occupying the space of Charlie's office with an uncomfortable largesse, hijacking the DJs set with her own intervention, and expressing a bodily expansiveness at odds with her standard propriety, a spreading out more akin to the wide stance of masculinity. In opposition to her usual studied reserve, Marnie throws caution (and perhaps all reason) to the wind, seizing the moment to make a thinly veiled declaration of lust, if not love, to Charlie. To consider her newfound sexual assertiveness as a product of her racial heterogeneity would put one in danger of subscribing to racist fictions of the past (and which still hold some degree of currency in contemporary discussions), and such a claim is not being made in this case. Rather, it is in Marnie's assumption of Kanye's swagger, his brash sense of self, that her racial identity expands, in a somewhat salutary way in terms of bringing her feelings for Charlie to the fore. This is not to say that Marnie's inner Kanye subsumes her overweening Marnieness; she remains herself, albeit a different version of herself, assuming a certain air of boastfulness characteristic of (and indeed in many cases a genre convention of) rap, particularly in the version offered by Kanye in "Stronger" and elsewhere. In her moment of darkness, Marnie finds solace in Blackness, a transitory and momentary racial adoption available to her without much in the way of censure, a charitable reaction not as possible for Kanye himself.

As Marnie turns to a racial mobility, a racial expansiveness as a means of at once stepping outside of and clarifying her identity, so too does Kanye consult a version of whiteness as a means of both solidifying and destabilizing his identity. To observe this process in action, it is useful to consult not only Kanye's public statements, but also and in particular his lyrical choices. It is through these lyrics that most come to know Kanye (or at least a version of him), and his lyrics also function as a kind of self-definition and self-creation for Kanye, representing both who he is and who he would like to be (or how he would like people to think of him). Early in his career, Kanye is associated more with the nebulous Blackness of rap as a genre. At first, he is known primarily as a producer, as a beatmaker to the stars, a shadowy figure whose name appears in song credits but whose profile does not extend much further than that. Even in the early days of his career as a rapper himself, Kanye is marked by a decided Blackness; his infamous "George Bush doesn't care about black people"[11] statement in the wake of the lackluster response to Hurricane Katrina positions him as an advocate of and spokesperson for Black identity and Black people, and some of his early lyrical concerns have the same effect. To take one example, the song "Diamonds from Sierra Leone" gives indirect attention to conflict diamonds and their origins,[12] complicating the bling-centric version of rap by referencing the origins of those diamonds in the suffering and exploitation of racial familiars. In these instances and elsewhere, early Kanye is a Black Kanye, commenting upon, offering incisive criticism of, and speaking through and for a notion of Black community that is not as present in his later and more recent work.

Though its particular impetus may be difficult to place (popular choices being the sudden death of his mother or his burgeoning relationship with Kim Kardashian), a distinct shift in Kanye's corpus occurs starting with *808s & Heartbreak*,[13] pausing for a moment in the momentous success of *My Beautiful Dark Twisted Fantasy*,[14] and kicking into overdrive with *Yeezus*,[15] bringing his Blackness into greater focus as that same Blackness is subject to destabilization. There are two threads to tease out here: first, the overtly masculine strain of Black identity that colors (pun intended) much of Kanye's recent work; and second, the veneer of (or perhaps more wholesale adoption of and access to) white identity that marks that same period. Turning to recent lyrical excerpts as a guide, a masculine Blackness may be found in "Monster," from *MBDTF*, where Kanye boasts of chalking up a "triple-double, no assists."[16] Given that the typical triple-double in basketball is comprised of points, rebounds, and assists, Kanye's decision to celebrate a triple-double composed of points, rebounds, and blocks is at once a singular act, with no distribution to teammates, as well as one based in physical dominance, blocks requiring a brawn in the post representative of muscular largesse and assertive performance. The choice of basketball as a metaphorical locus also hints at stereotypical notions of Blackness in the frequent, if inaccurate, association between Blackness and basketball. However, even here Kanye proves himself a complicated figure, as the song from which the above quote originates is dominated by a female version of Blackness in the person of Nicki Minaj. Sharing the track with heavyweights like Rick Ross, Jay Z, and Kanye himself, Minaj manages to steal the show with perhaps one of the greatest verses in rap history, paving the way for female adoption of the swagger characteristic of rap, if not so much Marnie's doubled white female adoption. Present in stops and starts at this point in his career, Kanye's complicated Blackness comes into greater focus on his next album, *Yeezus*.

Three songs in particular will prove instructive when looking at *Yeezus*'s treatment of Kanye's complicated Blackness: "I Am a God," "Black Skinhead," and "New Slaves," each offering a new wrinkle to Kanye's racial plurality and mobility and the consequences that it brings.[17] "I Am a God" contains a reflection on the manner in which Kanye fails to fulfill the expectations of rap observers when he states "since the tight jeans they ain't never liked you / pink ass polos with a fucking backpack,"[18] his failure to wear appropriately baggy jeans, choice of preppy, white-associated clothing, and backpack (denoting both higher education and a rap subgenre associated with more complicated and diverse lyrical concerns) invoking substantial criticism, to which he responds here. "Black Skinhead" offers a conflicted understanding of Kanye's racial simultaneity, his relationship with the nominally white Kardashian provoking observers to "call that kid King Kong,"[19] a spectacular identity that motivates audiences to "see me and my black skin,"[20] though Kanye also chastises a certain version of Blackness, calling for others to "stop all that coon shit"[21] at risk of him "black[ing] out on your ass."[22] Finally, "New Slaves" positions Kanye critically, initially invoking his mother in the statement that "my momma was raised in the era when / clean water was only served to the fairer skin,"[23] noting the hurdles placed before his fashion ambitions "unless I pick the cotton myself,"[24] and reflecting on the damned if you do, damned if you don't nature of "broke nigger racism . . . [and] rich nigger racism,"[25] all of which contribute to his appraisal of an ongoing slavery. In combination, these lyrical passages show Kanye to be at once Black and meta-Black, able to step outside of that identity and to critique it based on the mobility associated with his fragmentary and momentary whiteness, though their context within a racially identified (and at times stigmatized) musical genre adds further complexity to the discussion.

Returning to "Stronger" which, though from a slightly earlier Kanye era than the aforementioned songs,[26] is consistent with the phenomena observed therein, the song may be regarded as a sort of contemporary "race music," a historical referent that clarifies Marnie's attitude to the song and the stakes of its use. Postponing that return for a moment, the larger musical context of the episode arc adds a further layer of complexity to the ongoing discussion. When first expressing her desire to sing to a skeptical Ray, Marnie performs an abbreviated version of Norah Jones's "Don't Know Why,"[27] a song by a Black female performer that redoubles the complexity offered by the Minaj dominance in "Monster" while also presaging the sexual content of the "Stronger" selection (Jones lingering on the break between "don't know why I didn't come . . . back"[28] to hint at sexual dissatisfaction and failed performance by her partner). The episodes also contain a number of other rap songs, a snippet from Cali Swag District's "Teach Me How to Dougie" being the only male offering among songs by Rye Rye ("Boom Boom"), Santigold ("Girls") and, most notably, Angel Haze ("Werkin' Girls"), which sound-tracks the beginning of the party scene. That each of these songs is by a Black female performer is noteworthy in that it potentially points to Marnie as, in her racial adoption, a similarly minded Black performer, albeit a less polished one than those in her larger environs. The association of much of this music with the party setting also points to a carnivalesque element, an exceptional space in which the largely white party attendants may revel in an assumed Black identity that bears little relation to their day to day lives, an exceptionality that continues in Marnie's selective excerpting of "Stronger" to her own ends.

Through an especially exacting choice of verses and chorus, Marnie en-acts a racing/whitening of "Stronger," a bleaching that is further com-pounded by her delivery. Marnie's rendition begins with the opening refrain, itself sampled from the Daft Punk song "Harder, Better, Faster, Stronger" around which much of the song is based, "work it, make it, do it / makes us harder, better, faster, stronger,"[29] at once introducing the song's thematic elements while also drawing attention to the racially dense origins of the song. The Daft Punk original is itself informed by the Edwin Birdsong song "Cola Bottle Baby" which, in combination with the group's consultation of disco and dance music forms that are equally enmeshed with minority, par-ticularly Black, creators, makes Kanye's seeming appropriation of a white dance track into a reappropriation of Black art. She then moves into the first section of the chorus, calling implicitly on Charlie to "hurry up now / 'cause I can't wait much longer,"[30] progressing into chunks of the first verse. Her first excerpt, suggesting again implicitly that Charlie be "my white Kate Moss tonight," inverts the racial assignation of the Kanye original (calling for a "black Kate Moss"),[31] demonstrating a bleaching that, while certainly aimed at whitening, does not sterilize, but rather underlines Marnie's utter lack of sterility and accompanying sexual vigor. Finally, Marnie includes the boasting "you should be honored by my lateness / that I would even show up to this fake shit"[32] as a swipe at the ridiculousness of the party as a whole, trumpeting her own importance in the process. Throughout, Marnie delivers her lines in what can only be described as the opposite of flow, a halting, clipped style that removes all of Kanye's inflection and amplifies the dis-tance between her whitened version and the Black original, suggesting a relationship to Kanye's original that is akin to early twentieth-century atti-tudes towards the notion of "race music."

Referring initially to early blues 78s and gospel recordings, race music is a designation placed upon music created and performed by Black artists, with the suggestion that only Black audiences would be interested in it, though quite the opposite proves true. Under the illusion that only Black customers would be interested in this music, race records are kept in a separate section or even behind the counter so as to distance them from polite, white music. Yet, in many cases, such records are immensely popular with white audiences, either through a plain fondness for a song, a racially informed fetishism of the Black performer as almost an outsider artist or, more often, some combination of the two. It is this interest that in some ways motivates the preservation and lauding of much blues music, its very obscurity lending it a specialist air irresistible to rarity-minded music collectors. [33] Even into the early days of rock and roll, the element of danger inherent to Black music persists, requiring an Elvis to produce a whitened version to allow for mainstream acceptance. Blues being no longer of mainstream interest (though its influence on rock music persists, albeit in a largely unrecognized manner), the closest approximation of contemporary race music would be rap and hip hop. Though not necessarily subject to the same stocking restrictions as earlier race recordings, rap and hip hop maintain a cachet of danger, as demonstrated by the unlikely adoption of gangsta rap by suburban white teenagers who have little in common with the characters in the songs they love so much. This danger evinces itself in the riskiness of Marnie's use of "Stronger," as well as the overall vibe of vanilla gentrification of Charlie's party and its half-hearted stab at hipness via the DJ's music selection. "Stronger" then is a race music of sorts, in multiple senses.

In addition to the clear racial elements of "Stronger" as an example of contemporary race music, Marnie's use of the song might also be thought of as a *race* music, a music of insistence, of a limited window for desire. "Stronger" is marked by this sense of urgency; Kanye variously remarks "I need you to hurry up now," [34] "I've been waiting all night," [35] and "I need you right now" [36] as a means of emphasizing the time-sensitive nature of his desire. For Kanye, some of this urgency may be dependent on physical matters; the "harder, better, faster, stronger" [37] of the opening refrain is an indirect reference to the object of the song and her stimulation of Kanye's growing erection which, though hard and strong, cannot remain so indefinitely. Though Marnie's desire may not have the same anatomical practicalities, she shares Kanye's sense of urgency, her own mounting desire (literal and figurative) for Charlie brooking no delays beyond those already incurred. Indeed, in the wake of her performance, Marnie is able to sate that desire, embodying simultaneously the Kanye and female interlocutor perspectives by being both the subject and object of desire, feeling the hardness and strength in herself and creating it in Charlie as they have impromptu sex in an adjoining room. This sexual encounter too recalls race music in its visible invisibility; much as race music is spatially restricted yet widely known and available, so too is Marnie and Charlie's tryst kept behind the counter (in a separate space from the larger party) yet still visible and known to all (via the glass walls of the room). When Marnie expresses concern, asking "are people gonna see us?"[38] Charlie replies "who gives a fuck?"[39] making theirs an open secret. Though this particular moment may lack class, the notion of class pervades the episode arc, informing Marnie's motivations for her "Stronger" performance.

Upon hearing of the success of Charlie's app, Marnie expresses an abstract disbelief and distaste for his flourishing, one that comes into more precise focus once she encounters Charlie in his new environs. Stunned at the first mention of Charlie's new business venture, Marnie is moved into immediate action: "Charlie has a company? Sorry, I have to go."[40] The widening class divide between the former lovers is apparent from their first encounter at Charlie's office, after Marnie's unannounced pop-in, when she greets him with a "yo,"[41] which he returns with a "hi."[42] As per Marnie's forthcoming consultation of Kanye, the "yo"[43] here is racially coded, casting her as the disenfranchised other to Charlie's new franchise. Charlie draws further attention to that divide after Marnie's explanation for her unsolicited appearance at his office, when she claims "I'm just here for support."[44] His response, "from me or for me?"[45] suggests at least an emotional dependency, if not also a financial one, implying the class divide initiated by their shared salutation. Seeking clarification on the nature of the app that is bringing him such success, Charlie explains that "it prevents you from calling people that you shouldn't call . . . you were the inspiration, actually,"[46] the app charging the user $10 every time a call is placed to a blocked number. Though likely conceived as a means to put distance between Charlie and Marnie due to the painful nature of their breakup, the app also puts social and class distance between the two, casting off the now disheveled Marnie from Charlie's newfound sphere of affluence. Aghast that "Charlie is living the dream . . . I thought he was going to be broken,"[47] it is instead Marnie that is broken, or at least broke, her dire straits being met with Charlie's straight path to financial stability.

Charlie's improved state of affairs does not elude the notice of others in their shared orbit, rendering the class difference between Marnie and Charlie more than just a figment of her jealousy-fueled imagination. When accompanying Marnie to Charlie's party for emotional support, and potentially a night's diversion, both Shoshanna and Ray offer commentary on Charlie's new circumstances. Shoshanna gushes that "your office is like stupidly grown up,"[48] somewhat faint praise from a fairly naïve college student, but praise nonetheless. Her praise does not stop there; perhaps overwhelmed by the setting and a drink or two, Shoshanna remarks to Charlie that "you look amazing. You could have sex with any girl at this party, including me,"[49] a desirability that mimics that sought out by Marnie in her Kanye-infused incarnation. Ray's appraisal is somewhat less glowing; at first sight, he asserts that the office itself, as well as the overall vibe of the celebration, is "weirdly bougie."[50] Though meant as a passing smear, a swipe at the fake feel of the affluence on display, in this case marked by what Ray calls "shitty beer,"[51] artfully selected cardigans and eyeglass frames, and a studied air of detachment, Ray's choice of words also carries a much deeper class referentiality. By invoking the bourgeoisie/proletariat dichotomy central to Marx and countless others, Ray is aligning himself with the workers, his modest coffee shop job reinforcing that designation. Marnie is less interested in such an identification initially, her demeanor in much of the series prior to this episode arc hinting at both a desire for and an ability to engage in upward mobility. However, with the division between Charlie and herself in class terms being put into such stark relief, Marnie becomes more interested in a working class identity (helped also by her less than elevated status as a restaurant host). She finds a paradoxical locus for this identity in song, at once expressing class ambition in her invocation of megastar Kanye West, while also assuming Kanye's oppositional positionality to concretize her distance from Charlie.

Seeing Marnie's out-of-sorts state in the face of news of Charlie's success, the normally aloof Ray takes an interest in her, suggesting that now might be a prime moment for her to follow her dream, which she reveals as a desire to sing. Shoshanna is similarly supportive, explaining to curious parties that Marnie is "writing a song. She's following her dream,"[52] seeming to admire Marnie's bottoming out and tentative ascension. From the first, Marnie dives into her singing, demonstrating a clear vision for what she wants her sound to be in her request to Ray: "can you help me lay down this track really quickly? I want a bassoon, maybe some drums."[53] Her collaboration with Ray is instructive also; though perhaps a function of his working knowledge of GarageBand, their partnership also serves as a class alliance, Ray's self-professed proletarian status becoming Marnie's by association. The breadth and immediacy of her ambition are quickly apparent, again in a question to Ray: "on a scale of one to ten, how good is my voice . . . because I have something really special planned for tonight."[54] Her language is slightly ambiguous in this case, as Shoshanna's earlier assertion that Marnie is writing a song is proven false by the Kanye cover that ensues, though her version stands as a remix, her altered vocal tone, phrasing, and verse construction transforming the Kanye original into something else entirely. Whether Marnie's dream of vocal stardom is at all realistic is a secondary concern at best; what is important in this moment is the pulpit that her performance gives her to assert not only her newfound class identity, but also a critique of Charlie's similarly newfound class status, a critique that proves backhanded and withering.

Both the content of Marnie's version of "Stronger," as well as her prefacing and follow-up comments, produce a stinging condemnation of the pretension associated with Charlie's nebulous success, Kanye serving as a medium and a vehicle for her indictment. After commandeering the microphone and setting up her iPod for what is to come, Marnie introduces her performance by telling Charlie "how proud I am of you . . . this is such a big deal . . . to celebrate this premature success."[55] Words fail to describe the passive-aggressiveness on display here, but suffice it to say that Marnie's is not a legitimate compliment. In the performance itself, Marnie rebuffs the self-importance of the celebration with a hyperbolic self-importance of her own, or rather of Kanye's, his call to "bow in the presence of greatness"[56] asserting an importance contrary to that of the celebration. Indeed, Charlie should be pleased that Marnie "would even show up for this fake shit,"[57] as should the assembled petit bourgeoisie in attendance. Met by baffled silence at the conclusion of the song, other than Ray's overenthusiastic "fuck yeah! Wasn't that awesome?"[58] Marnie enters the moment to reinforce her backhanded praise for the company's accomplishments, saying "congrats on the twenty-thousand you guys. Really, congratulations,"[59] mocking the supposed significance of hitting twenty-thousand MAUs (monthly average users) with an artfully shit-eating grin. Through Kanye's words and her own performance, Marnie is able to establish herself firmly within the proletarian camp, a position from which she is able to express her displeasure over Charlie's success. That displeasure, while flavored with a hint of sour grapes, moves beyond mere jealousy to a more thoroughgoing critique of class. In the context of *Girls* as a whole, this is a fairly unique moment of self-awareness, further emphasizing its significance both within and outside of the episode arc.

Marnie and Kanye, or Marnye in true relationship mash-up tradition, make for an odd couple: the uptight twenty something in the city, preoccupied with her own life and its associated trivialities, and the pathologically outgoing rap star, similarly preoccupied with his own life, albeit a life far different from that of the fictional *Girl*. That said, if not peas in a pod exactly, the two have much in common in the moment captured in the "It's Back"–"On All Fours" episode arc: having been brought low by circumstances both within and outside of their control, seemingly under siege from all sides, they go on the offensive both in terms of aggression and language. By adopting an at times counterintuitive oppositional positionality (Marnie is not exactly an outsider in her apparent privilege, and Kanye leads a largely charmed, if tumultuous, life), both put the world on blast. Far from regressing into a pure me against the world stance, as the implied primitiveness of the merged episode titles ("It's Back On All Fours," quite an animalistic formulation), Marnie and Kanye's attacks are pointed, and their aim is true.

To be sure, Marnie selects a potentially problematic way of going about her critical venture: operating from a position of decided privilege, though perhaps one not as immediately apparent in the diminished circumstances in which she finds herself at the beginning of "It's Back," Marnie adopts Blackness to her own ends, using it as she sees fit and discarding it when she is satisfied with the results. This same mobility is not available to Kanye, as the consequences of his tentative racial mobility are substantially more significant (increased press attention, suggestions of his becoming a "house Negro," among others). Marnie is thereby guilty of her own Elvising, taking a Black artistic form and bleaching it of the very elements that make it unique and important, producing a bland version that is as palatable as it is boring. She may also be accused of taking another's story and making it her own, borrowing Kanye's sexual frustration and transplanting it from his context to her own.

This borrowing is not limited to Kanye; indeed, Marnie's fixation on Charlie also recalls the primary story line of the "It's Back"–"On All Fours" episode arc, Hannah's obsessive-compulsive disorder, pulling the viewer back from *Girls* to *Girl*(s). Hannah's OCD seems less a broader statement about the complexities of mental illness than a character quirk that adds to Hannah's very human, often endearing flaws. Yet, as Marnie's subplot offers a moment of insight on race and class, so too does her mirroring of Hannah's OCD. As Hannah's OCD is distinguished by counting actions in eights, Marnie too is obsessed with counting, in her case the act of counting on Charlie, assuming that he will be there at her beck and call. When Hannah becomes obsessed with an imagined blockage in her ear, to the point of abrading her eardrum to a bloody mess, Marnie too becomes obsessed with Charlie, picking at old wounds and drawing new blood, while damaging herself in the process. Where Hannah's OCD relapse is brought on by the stress surrounding her unfinished book, whose disappointing first pages are greeted by their editor with the question "where is the sexual failure?"[60] Marnie too succumbs to her own downward spiral, though hers is characterized by substantial sexual failure, both her incompatibility with Booth and her inability to re-woo Charlie. Though riven throughout with the contradictions associated with a problematic appropriation of race, Marnie's "Stronger" adds a depth of cultural critique to the "It's Back"–"On All Fours" episode arc that is not always present throughout *Girls*. Far from transcending those contradictions, the episodes revel in the mess and sculpt critique from the pieces.

NOTES

1. Though referred to somewhat formally as "West," in the bulk of the chapter Kanye West will be referred to solely via the more familiar "Kanye," his star status and outsize personality transcending the bounds of binomial nomenclature in the manner of a Madonna, though with substantially more contemporary relevance.

2. Again, more formal terminology is used at first mention, with Kanye and his racial identity elsewhere being described as "Black," a term more common to discussions of racial identification, and also one used by Kanye himself for purposes of self-description (see "Black Skinhead" among other mentions).

3. Despite his noteworthy tan, the *NBC Nightly News* anchor is decidedly white, both through the network that employs him (a favorite of older white Americans seeking generally inoffensive and sanitized versions of current events) and his overall appearance and carriage. Interestingly enough, Williams himself has a noteworthy moment of rap performance, or rather moments, as precisely arranged excerpts of his broadcasts have been arranged into renditions of classic rap songs on YouTube, including Sir Mix-A-Lot's "Baby Got Back" and Snoop Doggy Dogg's "Gin and Juice," among others.

4. An indirect reference to legendary A Tribe Called Quest member Q-Tip? Probably not, but the coincidence points towards the more familiar circulation of rap within the *Girls* universe, the Q-Tip analogy demonstrating the degree to which rap references permeate the girls' world, extending outside of the realm of performance into the everyday.

5. This assertion will receive further attention later in the chapter, but as a brief preview of the forthcoming discussion, in opposition to Shoshanna more specifically and the girls more generally, Ray positions himself as a working-class anti-hero, free of the airs that mark the behavior of the girls, with whom he is inexplicably friendly, that friendship predating his affections for Shoshanna.

6. Though initially wooed by Booth's considerable difference from the relatively bland Charlie, Booth being a well-regarded and intriguing, if diminutive, artistic talent, Booth proves himself a mere extension of other frustrations within Marnie's life, her own artistic ambitions being thwarted by Booth's inability to define the nature of their relationship and treatment of Marnie as something like a personal assistant-with-benefits.

7. GarageBand is a user-friendly piece of Apple software that enables users to create their own multi-track digital recordings, offering a more accessible entry point to a typically technologically imposing artistic realm, democratizing music production and allowing for a proliferation of professional-sounding recordings. That Ray, the resident proletarian, should demonstrate a facility with GarageBand is fitting given his class alignment.

8. The reference here, of course, is to the protagonist of the earlier HBO series *Sex and the City*, in some ways both an antecedent of *Girls* and its later incarnation. *Sex and the City* predates *Girls* in its years of existence, but may also be a vision of the future for the girls after they get their respective acts together, giving a thirty-something vision of New York life for a group of women now firmly within the professional world.

9. "On All Fours," *Girls*, directed by Lena Dunham (2013; New York: HBO Studios, 2013), DVD.

10. Ibid.

11. Kanye's incendiary (and largely accurate) statement is made during a live broadcast entitled *A Concert for Hurricane Relief*, which occurs shortly after Hurricane Katrina ravages New Orleans and other areas on the Gulf Coast. Kanye (obviously) goes off script in his harsh criticism of the Bush administration's handling of relief efforts, after which his microphone is silenced. Considerable controversy ensues, making Kanye a topic of public conversation in a way that he had not been prior to his statements, which also represent his first notable foray into cultural criticism.

12. "Diamonds from Sierra Leone" offers at best an oblique criticism of diamond sourcing, the song itself being largely concerned with Kanye's early experiences with fame. Whether the title is a trite way of addressing a matter of some geopolitical import or a canny way of backdooring critical content into a popular medium is open for debate.

13. *808s & Heartbreak* is a transitional album for Kanye, and something of an outlier in his larger catalog. Following on the heels of the college trilogy (2004's *The College Dropout*, 2005's *Late Registration*, and 2007's *Graduation*), *808s* features the heavy use of AutoTune to middling effect. The album is Kanye's first after his mother's unexpected death in late 2007, and the use of AutoTune vocal manipulation offers a frigid distance to many of the songs indicative of his mental state in that moment.

14. Kanye's 2010 return to form *My Beautiful Dark Twisted Fantasy* follows the poorly received *808s & Heartbreak*, yielding such notable hits as "Power," "Runaway," and "Monster," representing the moment of Kanye's explosion into full mainstream ubiquity, evoking comparisons to Michael Jackson in the process.

15. 2013's *Yeezus* is met with much fanfare and a fusillade of both critical adoration and disappointment, Kanye's aggressive new direction sonically being paired with a lack of the lyrical sophistication that marked his earlier work. If *MBDTF* represents Kanye's emergence into the limelight, *Yeezus* represents Kanye shrinking from the flashbulbs and lashing out at the paparazzi.

16. Kanye West, "Monster," *My Beautiful Dark Twisted Fantasy* (2010; Def Jam, 2010), CD.

17. An extremely recent examination of the complicated nature of Kanye West's racial identity may be found in Safy Hallan Farah's article "New Blackness: Pharrell, Kanye and Jay-Z and the Spectre of White Aspiration," published on the influential music website Pitchfork. The piece, though greater in scope than this analysis, offers a like-minded take on Kanye's complex identity politics.

18. Kanye West, "I Am a God," *Yeezus* (2013; Def Jam, 2013), CD.

19. Kanye West, "Black Skinhead," *Yeezus* (2013; Def Jam, 2013), CD.

20. Ibid.

21. Ibid.

22. Ibid.

23. Kanye West, "New Slaves," *Yeezus* (2013; Def Jam, 2013), CD.

24. Ibid.

25. Ibid.

26. "Stronger" dates back to 2007's *Graduation*, the moment when Kanye is on the cusp of mega-stardom, a notable hit that expands his profile within the music world, though such a profile in the world at large awaits *MBDTF* and *Yeezus*.

27. Jones's "Don't Know Why" is a leisurely, piano-led reflection on love lost, placing it firmly within Marnie's wheelhouse and presaging her makeover of "Stronger" in tone, if not content. Jones too shares Williams's burden of famous lineage, herself being the daughter of sitar master Ravi Shankar.

28. Norah Jones, "Don't Know Why," *Come Away With Me* (2002; Blue Note, 2002), CD.

29. Kanye West, "Stronger," *Graduation* (2007; Def Jam, 2007), CD.

30. Ibid.

31. Ibid.

32. Ibid.

33. Amanda Petrusich does an excellent job of tracing the role of obsessive 78 collectors in the canonization of certain blues artists in her 2014 book *Do Not Sell At Any Price: The Wild, Obsessive Hunt for the World's Rarest 78rpm Records* (Scribner, 2014).

34. West, "Stronger."

35. Ibid.

36. Ibid.

37. Ibid.

38. "On All Fours," *Girls*, directed by Lena Dunham (2013; New York: HBO Studios, 2013), DVD.

39. Ibid.

40. "It's Back," *Girls*, directed by Jesse Peretz (2013; New York: HBO Studios, 2013), DVD.

41. Ibid.

42. Ibid.

43. Ibid.

44. Ibid.

45. Ibid.

46. Ibid.

47. Ibid.

48. "On All Fours," *Girls*.

49. Ibid.

50. Ibid.

51. Ibid.

52. Ibid.

53. Ibid.
54. Ibid.
55. Ibid.
56. West, "Stronger."
57. Ibid.
58. "On All Fours," *Girls*.
59. Ibid.
60. Ibid.

BIBLIOGRAPHY

"It's Back." *Girls*. Directed by Jesse Peretz. New York: HBO Studios, 2013, DVD.
Jones, Norah. "Don't Know Why." *Come Away With Me*. Blue Note, 2002, CD.
"On All Fours." *Girls*. Directed by Lena Dunham. New York: HBO Studios, 2013, DVD.
West Kanye. "Black Skinhead." *Yeezus*. Def Jam, 2013, CD.
———. "I Am a God." *Yeezus*. Def Jam, 2013, CD.
———. "Monster." *My Beautiful Dark Twisted Fantasy*. Def Jam, 2010, CD.
———. "New Slaves." *Yeezus*. Def Jam, 2013, CD.
———. "Stronger." *Graduation*. Def Jam, 2007, CD.

Acknowledgments

The editors wish to thank Lindsey Porambo, Marilyn Ehm, and Shelby Kennedy at Lexington Books for their belief in this project, and for their successful execution and support.

Elwood Watson: Thanks to my co-editors Marc Shaw and Jennifer Mitchell for their dedication and commitment to seeing this anthology reach fruition.

Jennifer Mitchell: I am grateful to Elwood Watson and Marc Shaw.

Marc Edward Shaw: Much applause and gratitude to my co-editors. A huge thanks to those affiliated with Hartwick College for their support: especially my students and colleagues in Theatre Arts (including Ken Golden, Malissa Kano-White, and Gary Burlew) and English; to the Office of Academic Affairs (Michael G. Tannebaum, provost; Kim Noling, dean); and to the Arkell Hall Foundation.

Works Cited

"About." *Melville House*. Melville House. Web. 7 October 2014.

Adalian, Josef. "How *Friends* Decided to Pair Off Monica and Chandler." *Vulture*. 20 November 2013. Accessed 18 August 2014.

Akass, Kim and Janet McCabe, eds. *Reading Sex and the City*. London: I.B. Tauris, 2003.

Alcott, Louisa May. 1869. *Little Women*. New York: W. W. Norton & Company, 2003.

Anderson, L. V. "Girls: Bad Sex Made Great." *Slate*.

Anon. "Next Episode of 'Girls' to Feature Lena Dunham Shitting Herself during Gyno Exam While Eating a Burrito," *Onion*. March 14, 2013. Accessed July 3, 2014. http://www.theonion.com/articles/next-episode-of-girls-to-feature-lena-dunham-shitt,31661/.

Baker, Katie. 2013. "Zosia Mamet's $32,000 Folk Music Kickstarter Failed." *Jezebel*. June 10, 2013. http://jezebel.com/zosia-mamets-32-000-folk-music-kickstarter-failed-512321567.

Balfour, Ian. *Northrop Frye*. Boston: Twayne Publishers, 1988.

Beckner, Gary S., and Richard A. Posner. *Uncommon Sense: Economic Insights, from Marriage to Terrorism*. Chicago: University of Chicago Press, 2009.

Behrent, Greg and Liz Truccilo. *He's Just Not That Into You*. New York: Gallery Books, 2009.

Bell, Crystal. "'Girls' Recap: The Golden Shower Incident in 'Weirdos Need Girlfriends Too.'" *Huffington Post*. 3 June 2012. Accessed 19 August 2014.

Bellow, Saul. *Him with His Foot in His Mouth*. New York: Penguin Books, 1974.

Berg, Barbara. *The Remembered Gate: Origins of American Feminism*. New York: Oxford University Press, 1978.

Berger, Arthur. *Cultural Criticism: A Primer of Key Concepts*. London: SAGE Publications, 1995.

Blair, Elaine. "The Loves of Lena Dunham." The *New York Review of Books*. June 7, 2012. http://www.nybooks.com/articles/archives/2012/jun/07/loves-lena-dunham/.

Bloom, Harold. *The Anxiety of Influence*. Oxford University Press, 1973.

Bordo, Susan. *Unbearable Weight: Feminism, Western Culture, and the Body*. Rev. ed. Berkeley: University of California Press, 2003.

Bourdieu, Pierre. *Distinction: A Social Critique of the Judgement of Taste*. Trans. Richard Nice. Cambridge: Harvard University Press, 1984.

Brantley, Ben. "Celebrating Shaw, a Serious Optimist." *New York Times*. September 16, 2005. Accessed November 10, 2014. http://www.nytimes.com/2005/09/16/theater/newsandfeatures/16shaw.html?pagewanted=all&_r=0.

Breslaw, Anna. "Director of *Girls* Porn Slams Lena Dunham for Being Too Conservative." *Jezebel*. June 1, 2013. http://jezebel.com/director-of-girls-porn-slams-lena-dunham-for-being-too-510837480.

Brienes, Winifred. *The Trouble Between Us: An Uneasy History of White and Black Women in the Feminist Movement*. New York: Oxford University Press, 2006.

Brod, Harry. *The Making of Masculinities*. Boston: Allen & Unwin, 1987.

Brody, Caitlin. 2013. "O-M-G, You Guys. Zosia Mamet Has a Band and Tells Us All about It!" *Glamour*, July 10, 2013. http://www.glamour.com/entertainment/ blogs/obsessed/2013/07/o-m-g-you-guys-zosia-mamet-has.

Brody, Richard. "'Girls' Talk." *New Yorker*. Last modified April 5, 2012. Accessed May 15, 2014. http://www.newyorker.com/online/blogs/movies/2012/04/girls-lena-dunham.html.

Brown, Helen Gurley. *Sex And The Single Girl*. New York: Bernard Geis Associates, 1962.

Brown, Richard Harvey. "Introduction: Theorizing the Body/Self in Global Capitalism." In *The Politics of Selfhood: Bodies and Identities in Global Capitalism*, vii–xxi. Minneapolis: University of Minneapolis Press, 2003.

Bruni, Frank. "The Bleaker Sex." *New York Times*. April 1, 2012. http://www.nytimes.com/2012/04/01/opinion/sunday/bruni-the-bleaker-sex.html?pagewanted=all.

Brunsdon, Charlotte. *The Feminist, the Housewife, and the Soap Opera*. Oxford: Oxford University Press, 2000.

Burns, Jennifer. *Goddess of the Market: Ayn Rand and the American Right*. New York: Oxford University Press, 2009.

Butler, Judith. *Bodies That Matter: On the Discursive Limits of "Sex."* London: Routledge, 1993.

Caldwell, Sarah. "Girls: How are we Supposed to Feel about Adam?" *Entertainment Weekly*. 18 March 2013. Accessed 3 January 2014.

Cheah, Pheng, Elizabeth Grosz, Judith Butler, and Drucilla Cornell. "The Future of Sexual Difference: An Interview with Judith Butler and Drucilla Cornell." *Diacritics* 28, no. 1. Irigaray and the Political Future of Sexual Difference, Spring 1998. 19–42.

Cleaver, Eldridge. Soul on Ice. New York: McGraw Hill, 1968.

Collins, Wilkie. *The Woman in White*. 1859. London: Penguin, 2003.

Connell, R. W. *The Men and The Boys*. Berkeley: UC Press, 2001.

Cross, Gary. *Men to Boys: The Making of Modern Immaturity*. New York: Columbia University Press, 2008.

Daalmans, Serena. "'I'm Busy Trying to Become Who I Am': Self-Entitlement and the City in HBO's *Girls*." *Feminist Media Studies* 13.2. 2013. 359–62.

"Damage." *Oxford English Dictionary*. Accessed 3 January 2014.

Deahl, Rachel. "Melville House Has a Friend in Lena Dunham." *Publishers Weekly*. 24 April 2012. Accessed June 7, 2014.

Delaney, Janice, Mary Jane Lupton, and Emily Toth. *The Curse: A Cultural History of Menstruation*. New York: E. P. Dutton & Co., 1976.

Del Signore, John. "Ask a Native New Yorker: Why is the NYC Dating Scene So Rough?" *Gothamist*. 23 August 2013. Accessed 3 January 2014.

Denfeld, Rene. *The New Victorians: A Young Woman's Challenge To The Old Feminist Order*. New York: Grand Central Publishing, 1996.

Dolan, Jill. *Feminist Spectator as Critic*. University of Michigan Press, 1988.

DuBois, W.E.B. *The Souls of Black Folk: Essays and Sketches*, 13. Chicago: A.C. McClurg, 1903.

Dunham, Lena. *Not That Kind of Girl: A Young Woman Tells You What She's "Learned."* New York: Random House, 2014.

Ellison, Ralph. Invisible Man, 3–4. New York: Random House, 1952.

Flint, Joe. "Climax of Scene in HBO's 'Girls' a Shocker." *LA Times*. 11 March 2013. Accessed 6 January 2014.

Foucault, Michel. *Discipline & Punish: The Birth of the Prison*. Trans. Alan Sheridan. New York: Pantheon, 1978.

———. *The History of Sexuality, Vol. 1: An Introduction*. Trans. Robert Hurley. New York: Random House, 1978.

Franco, James. "A Dude's Take on *Girls*." *Huffington Post*. May 30, 2012. Accessed November 20, 2014. http://www.huffingtonpost.com/james-franco/girls-hbo-lena-dunham_b_1556078.html.

Friedan, Betty. *The Feminine Mystique*. New York: W.W Norton, 1963.

Frith, Hannah. "Labouring on orgasms: embodiment, efficiency, entitlement and obligations in heterosex." *Culture, Health & Sexuality* 15, no. 4 (2013): 494–510.

Frye, Northrop. "The Archetypes of Literature." In *The Classical Tradition: Classic Texts and Contemporary Trends*. Edited by David, 677–85. New York: Bedford St. Martins, 1989.

———. *Anatomy of Criticism: Four Essays*. Princeton, NJ: Princeton University Press, 1957.

Gallo, Phil. 2013. "'Girls' Music Supervisor Manish Raval Talks about Finding 'Cool Music.'" *Hollywood Reporter*. January 14, 2013. http://www.hollywoodreporter.com/news/girls-music-supervisor-manish-raval-412258.

Gamson, Joshua. *Freaks Talk Back: Tabloid Talk Shows and Sexual Nonconformity*. Chicago: University of Chicago Press, 1998.

Gardiner, Judith Kegan. Introduction to *Masculinity Studies and Feminist Theory*, Ed. Judith Kegan Gardiner. New York: Columbia UP, 2002.

Goble, Corban. "The 8 Best Music Moments of HBO's *Girls*." *Stereogum*. June 18, 2012. http://www.stereogum.com/1067341/the-8-best-music-moments-from-hbos-girls/franchises/listomania/.

Gorton, Kristyn. "'The Point of View of Shame': Re-viewing female desire in Catherine Breillat's *Romance* (1999) and *Anatomy of Hell* (2004)." *Studies in European Cinema* 4.2. 2007: 111–24.

Grdešić, Maša. "'I'm Not the Ladies!': Metatextual commentary in *Girls*." *Feminist Media Studies* 13, no. 2, (2013): 355–58.

Greif, Mark. "The Hipster in the Mirror." *New York Times*. November 12, 2010 http://www.nytimes.com/2010/11/14/books/review/Greift.html?pagewanted=all&_r=1&.

———. "Positions." In *What Was the Hipster? A Sociological Investigation*. Edited by Mark Greif, Kathleen Ross, and Dayna Tortorici. 4–13. Brooklyn: *n+1*, 2010.

———. 2010. "What Was the Hipster?" *New York*. October 24, 2010. http://nymag.com/news/features/69129/.

Guy, John. *A Daughter's Love*. Boston: Houghton Mifflin Harcourt, 2009.

Haddow, Douglas. "Hipster: The Dead End of Western Civilization." *Adbusters*. July 29, 2008. https://www.adbusters.org/magazine/79/hipster.html.

Haglund, David, and Daniel Engber. "Girls on HBO, 'One Man's Trash,' episode 5 of season 2, reviewed by guys." *Slate.com*. Last modified February 10, 2013. Accessed May 15, 2014. http://www.slate.com/articles/arts/tv_club/features/2013/girls_season_2/week_5/girls_on_hbo_one_man_s_trash_episode_5_of_season_2_reviewed_by_guys.html.

Hagland, David and Daniel Engber. "Guys on *Girls*, Season 2," *Slate*. February 10, 2013. http://www.slate.com/articles/arts/tv_club/features/2013/girls_season_2/week_5/girls_on_hbo_one_man_s_trash_episode_5_of_season_2_reviewed_by_guys.html.

Halberstam, Judith. *Female Masculinity*. Durham, NC: Duke UP, 1998.

Hamilton, Nikita T. "So They Say You Have a Race Problem? You're in Your Twenties, You Have Way More Problems Than That." In *HBO's* Girls: *Questions of Gender, Politics, and Millennial Angst*. Edited by Betty Kaklamanidou and Margaret Talley, 43–58. Newcastle: Cambridge Scholars Press, 2014.

Harris-Perry, Melissa V. *Sister Citizen: Shame, Stereotypes, and Black Women in America*. New Haven: Yale University Press, 2011: 51–97.

Hattenstone, Simon. "Lena Dunham: 'People called me fat and hideous, and I lived." *Guardian*. January 10, 2014. http://www.theguardian.com/culture/2014/jan/11/lena-dunham-called-fat-hideous-and-i-lived.

Hazlett, Courtney. "Lena Dunham Explains Her Thighs—And the 'No-Pants' Look." *Today.com*. October 9, 2012. http://www.today.com/entertainment/lena-dunham-explains-her-thighs-no-pants-look-1C6358990?franchiseSlug=todayentertainmentmain.

HBO. "Q&A with Manish Raval." Accessed October 25, 2014. http://connect.hbo.com/events/girls/q-manish-raval/.

Heller, Dana. "Sex and the Series: Paris, New York, and Post-National Romance." *American Studies* 46.2 (2005): 145–69.

Heller, Nathan. "That Girl." *Vogue*. January 15, 2014, 194–204.

Hermes, Joke. "Television and Its Viewers in Post-Feminist Dialogue Internet-Mediated Response to 'Ally McBeal' and 'Sex and the City.'" *Etnofoor* 1/2 (2002): 194–211.

He's Just Not That Into You. Dir. Ken Kwapis. New Line Cinema, 2009. Film.

Hess, Amanda. "Was That a Rape Scene in Girls?" *Slate*. 11 March 2013. Accessed January 3 2014.

Heti, Sheila. "Lena! Girls' Girl." *Glamour*. April 2014.

Hiatt, Brian. "Girl on Top." *Rolling Stone*. Issue 1177. February 28, 2013. http://www.rollingstone.com/movies/news/lena-dunham-girl-on-top-20130228.

Hickey, Mary C. "HBO's Girls: The Millenial Dating Scene." *AARP Blog*. 14 January 2013. Accessed 3 January 2013.

Hilton, Perez, "Howard Stern Doesn't Like *Girls* & Calls Lena Dunham 'Fat'!" PerezHilton.com. Last modified January 8, 2013. Accessed June 1, 2014. http://perezhilton.com/2013-01-08-howard-stern-calls-girls-creator-lena-dunham-fat-camera-hog#.U7BthCjMWzc.

hooks, bell. *Ain't I a Woman: Black Women and Feminism*, 136–37. Boston: South End Press, 1981.

hooks, bell. *Yearning: Race, Gender and Cultural Politics*, 53. Boston: South End Press, 1990.

Horning, Rob. "The Death of the Hipster." In *What Was the Hipster? A Sociological Investigation*. Edited by Mark Greif, Kathleen Ross, and Dayna Tortorici, 78–84. Brooklyn: *n+1*, 2010.

"Howard Stern Show Lena Denham Interview 01 16 13." YouTube, February 25, 2014. Accessed June 1, 2014. https://www.youtube.com/watch?v=9CsfmELDVaI.

Howe, Neil and Bill Strauss. *13 th Gen: Abort, Retry, Ignore, Fail?* New York: Vintage Books, 1993.

Irigaray, Luce. In *This Sex Which Is Not One*. Trans. Catherine Porter and Carolyn Burke. Ithaca, NY: Cornell University Press, 1985.

Jauss, Hans Robert. "Literary History as a Challenge to Literary Theory." New Literary History 2.1, 7-37.

Johnson, Chloé H. "Dancing on My Own: Popular Music and Issues of Identity in *Girls*." In *HBO's* Girls: *Questions of Gender, Politics, and Millennial Angst*. Edited by Betty Kaklamanidou and Margaret Talley, 186–98. Newcastle: Cambridge Scholars Press, 2014.

Johnson, E. Patrick. *Appropriating Blackness: Performance and The Politics of Authenticity*. Durham: Duke University Press, 2003.

Johnson, Liza. "Perverse Angle: Feminist Film, Queer Film, Shame." *Signs*, 30.1. *Beyond the Gaze: Recent Approaches to Film Feminisms*. Special issue edition. Kathleen McHugh and Vivian Sobchack. Autumn 2004. 1361–84.

Jones, Eileen. "The Horror of HBO's Girls." *The Exiled*. 26 April 2012. Accessed 19 August 2014.

Jung, Carl, ed. *Man and His Symbols*. New York: Dell, 1968.

Kellogg, Carolyn. "'Girls' Lena Dunham Interned at Soft Skull, Not at Melville House." *LA Times Blogs—Jacket Copy*. April 24, 2012. Accessed June 17, 2014.

Klein, Bethany. "'The New Radio': Music Licensing as a Response to Industry Woe." *Media, Culture & Society* 30, no. 4 (2008): 463–78.

Konner, Jenni. "I Get Ideas." *Girls*. Directed by Lena Dunham. HBO. January 20, 2013. DVD.

Konstantinovsky, Michelle. "Why Lena Dunham's Body Matters (And Why It's Ridiculous That It Does)." *Hello Giggles*. April 26, 2012. http://hellogiggles.com/why-lena-dunhams-body-matters-and-why-its-ridiculous-that-it-does/#read.

Kristeva, Julia. *Powers of Horror: An Essay on Abjection*. Trans. Leon S. Roudiez. New York: Columbia University Press, 1982.

Kubicek, John. "*Girls* Review: The Voice of the Worst Generation." *BuddyTV.com*. April 16, 2012. Accessed June 25, 2014. http://www.buddytv.com/articles/girls/girls-review-the-voice-of-the-45043.aspx.

Lacob, Jace. "'Girls': Graphic Content, Objectification, and That Scene." *The Daily Beast*. 12 March 2013. Accessed 6 January 2014.

Lange, Maggie. "Only Nine People Have Given to Zosia Mamet's Hipster Band Kickstarter." *Gawker.* May 29, 2013. http://gawker.com/only-nine-people-have-given-to-zosia-mamets-hipster-ba-510278912.

Lehman, Peter. "Crying over the Melodramatic Penis: Melodrama and Male Nudity in Films of the 90s." In *Masculinity: Bodies, Movies, Culture.* Ed. Lehman. New York: Routledge, 2001. 25–41.

Leland, John. 2001. "For Rock Bands, Selling Out Isn't What It Used to Be." *New York Times.* March 11. Accessed October 25, 2014. http://www.nytimes.com/2001/03/11/magazine/11SELLOUT.html?src=pm&pagewanted=1.

Lesly. "The Audacity of Lena Dunham, And Her Admirable Commitment To Making Us Look At Her Naked." *xoJane.* January 9, 2013. http://www.xojane.com/issues/lena-dunham-naked-nude.

Levine, Jesse. "Don't Shoot the Messenger: HBO's *Girls* Backlash." *Huffington Post.* April 24, 2012. Accessed June 23, 2014. http://www.huffingtonpost.com/jesse-levine/dont-kill-the-messenger_b_1443100.html.

Levy, Ariel. *Female Chauvinist Pigs: Women and the Rise of Raunch Culture.* New York: Free Press, 2005.

Lin, Tao. *EEEEE EEE EEEE.* New York: Melville House, 2007.

Lingeman, Richard. "Nader's Road to Utopia." *Nation.* October 12, 2009.

Little, Judy. *The Experimental Self: Dialogic Subjectivity in Woolf, Pym, and Brooke-Rose.* Carbondale: Southern Illinois UP, 1996.

Lloyd, Richard Douglas. *Neo-Bohemia: Art and Commerce in the Postindustrial City.* New York: Routledge, 2010.

Logan, Rayford W. *The Betrayal of The Negro.* New York: Collier, 1954.

Lorde, Audre. *Sister Outsider: Essays and Speeches by Audre Lorde.* Berkeley: Crossing Press, 1984. 117, 129.

Lorentzen, Christian. "Why the Hipster Must Die: A Modest Proposal to Save New York Cool." *Time Out New York*, May 30, 2007. http://www.timeout.com/ newyork/things-to-do/why-the-hipster-must-die.

Lunceford, Brett. *Naked Politics: Nudity, Political Action, and the Rhetoric of the Body.* Lanham, MD: Lexington, 2012.

Maciak, Phillip. "Slapstick 'Sexposition': *Girls* vs. the Body Politics of HBO." *HBO's Girls and the White Box* theme week. *In Media Res.* January 9, 2013. http://mediacommons.futureofthebook.org/imr/2013/01/09/slapstick-sexposition-girls-vs-body-politics-hbo.

Martin, Max, Rami, and Dido. "I'm Not a Girl, Not Yet a Woman." *Britney* (album). Jive Records, 2001.

Masnick, George. "Defining the Generations." *Housing Perspectives: Research, Trends, and Perspectives from the Harvard Joint Center for Housing Studies.* November 28, 2012. Accessed June 23, 2014. http://housingperspectives.blogspot.com/2012/11/defining-generations.html.

McCammon, Ross. "Lena Dunham Is Building an Empire." *Esquire.* November 13, 2012. http://www.esquire.com/features/americans-2012/lena-dunham-interview-1212?link=rel&dom=buzzfeed&src=syn&mag=esq.

McDonough, Katie. "TV critic mad because the nudity on 'Girls' doesn't titillate him." Last modified January 10, 2014. Accessed June 1, 2014. http://www.salon.com/2014/01/10/tv_critic_mad_because_the_nudity_on_girls_doesnt_titillate_him/.

McNutt, Myles. "*Game of Thrones*: "The Night Lands" and Sexposition." *Cultural Learnings.* April 8, 2012. http://cultural-learnings.com/2012/04/08/game-of-thrones-the-night-lands-and-sexposition/.

Miller, Jon. "Active, Balanced, and Happy: These Young Americans are not Bowling Alone." *The Generation X Report: A Quarterly Research Paper Report from the Longitudinal Study of American Youth*, no. 1-1 (2011): 1–8.

Molloy, Tim. "Judd Apatow and Lena Dunham Get Mad at Me for Asking Why She's Naked So Much on 'Girls.'" *TheWrap.com.* Last modified January 9, 2014. Accessed June 1, 2014. http://www.thewrap.com/judd-apatow-lena-dunham-get-mad-asking-shes-naked-much-girls/.

Moore, Madison. "5 Reasons Dating in New York City is Exhausting." *Thought Catalog*. 26 November 2013. Accessed 3 January 2014.

Mulvey, Laura. "Visual Pleasure and Narrative Cinema." *Screen* 16.3. Autumn 1975. 6–18.

Nussbaum, Emily. "Hannah Barbaric." *New Yorker*. February 11 & 18, 2013. http://www. newyorker.com/magazine/2013/02/11/hannah-barbaric.

———. "It's Different for 'Girls'." *New York Magazine*. 25 March 2012. Accessed 19 August 2014.

———. "It's Different for *Girls*," *New York Magazine*. March 25, 2012. Accessed June 20, 2014. http://nymag.com/arts/tv/features/girls-lena-dunham-2012-4/.

Oakes, Kaya. *Slanted and Enchanted: The Evolution of Indie Culture*. New York: Holt Paperbacks, 2009.

Paglia, Camille. *Sexual Personae, Art and Decadence from Nefertiti To Emily Dickinson*. Vintage Books, 1991.

Paskin, Willa. "Why Girls Got So Dark." *Salon*. 17 March 2013. Accessed 6 January 2014.

Penn-Terborg, Rosalyn. *African American Women in the Struggle for the Vote*, 1850–1920. Bloomington: Indiana University Press, 1998.

Prange, Gordon W. *At Dawn We Slept: The Untold Story of Pearl Harbor*. New York: Penguin, 1981.

"Q&A with Lena Dunham." *HBO Connect*. Accessed May 28, 2014. http://connect.hbo.com/ events/girls/lena-dunham/.

Rakow, Lana F. "Feminist Approaches to Popular Culture: Giving Patriarchy Its Due." *Feminist Critiques of Popular Culture: A Special Issue of the Journal Communication* 9, no. 1 (1986): 19–42.

Rand, Ayn. *The Fountainhead*. New York: Plume Books, 1994.

Reality Bites. Directed by Ben Stiller. 1994. Hollywood, CA: Universal Studios, 2004. DVD.

Reeser, Todd W., and Steven D. Spalding. "Reading Literature/Culture: A Translation of 'Reading as Cultural Practice.'" *Style* 36, no. 4. 2002. 659–76.

Rensin, David. "20Q Lena Dunham." *Playboy*. March 14, 2013. http://www.playboy.com/ playground/view/20q-lena-dunham.

Richter, David, ed. *The Critical Tradition: Classic Texts and Contemporary Trends*. New York: Bedford St. Martins, 1989.

Roberts, Saroya. "Naked If I Want to: Lena Dunham's Body Politic." *Salon*. February 9, 2013. http://www.salon.com/2013/02/09/naked_if_i_want_to_lena_dunhams_body_politic/.

Robinson, Sally. "Pedagogy of the Opaque: Teaching Masculinity Studies." In *Masculinity Studies and Feminist Theory*. Ed. Judith Kegan Gardiner. New York: Columbia UP, 2002.

Roiphe, Katie. *The Morning After: Fear, Sex and Feminism*, Boston: Bay Back Books, 1994.

Rosenberg, Alyssa. "5 Productive Ways to Ask Lena Dunham about the Nudity on 'Girls.'" *Think Progress*. January 10, 2014. http://thinkprogress.org/alyssa/2014/01/10/3148721/ lena-dunham-girls-nudity/.

Rosin, Hanna. "*Slate*'s Guys are so Wrong about *Girls*." *Slate.com*. February 11, 2013. Accessed on June 29, 2014. http://www.slate.com/blogs/xx_factor/2013/02/11/slate_s_guys_ on_girls_what_they_get_wrong_about_one_man_s_trash.html.

Rowe, Kathleen. *The Unruly Woman: Gender and the Genres of Laughter*. Austin: University of Texas Press, 1996.

Ruiz, Michelle. "The Booth is Back: Jorma Taccone on Returning to *Girls* . . . " *Cosmopolitan*. Jan 27 2013. Accessed November 15, 2014. http://www.cosmopolitan.com/entertainment/ celebs/news/a4163/jorma-taccone-girls-interview/.

San Filippo, Maria, et al. *HBO's Girls and the White Box* theme week. *In Media Res*. http:// mediacommons.futureofthebook.org/imr/theme-week/2013/02/hbos-girls-white-box-january-7-january-11-2013.

Sepinwall, Alan. "Review: *Girls*–'One Man's Trash': Dancin' with Mr. Brownstone." *What's Alan Watching? Inside Television*, February 10, 2013. Accessed on June 28, 2014. http:// www.hitfix.com/whats-alan-watching/review-girls-one-mans-trash-dancin-with-mr-brownstone.

Shaw, Marc E. and Elwood Watson. Introduction to *Performing American Masculinities: The 21st-Century Man in Popular Culture*. Bloomington: Indiana UP, 2011.

Silver-Fagan, Alexandra. "Dating in New York: Right Swipe or Left." *Huffington Post*. 18 September 2013. Accessed 6 January 2014.

Smith, Dodie. *I Capture the Castle*. New York: St. Martin's Press, 1948.

Smuts, Robert W. *Women and Work in America*. New York: Schocken Books, 1971.

Sommers, Christina Hoff. *Who Stole Feminism?: How Women Have Betrayed Women*. New York: Simon & Schuster, 1994.

Stanley, Alessandra. "There's Sex, There's the City, but No Manolos." *New York Times*. April 12, 2014. Accessed June 20, 2014. http://www.nytimes.com/2012/04/13/arts/television/lena-dunhams-girls-beginsonhbo.html?_r=0.

Stasi, Linda. "New Girl on Top." *New York Post*. January 24, 2013. http://nypost.com/2013/01/04/new-girl-on-top/.

Stein, Joel. "Millennials: The Me Me Me Generation." *Time.com*. May 20 2013. Accessed June 25, 2014. http://www.fandm.edu/uploads/media_items/stein-2013-megeneration.original.pdf.

Talley, André Leon. *A.L.T. 365+*. New York: Powerhouse Books, 2005.

Thornton, Sarah. *Club Cultures: Music, Media, and Subcultural Capital*. Cambridge, UK: Polity Press, 1995.

Tiffany, Kaitlyn. "Lena Dunham, Make Me a Pop Star." *The Cornell Daily Sun*, April 15, 2014. http://cornellsun.com/blog/2014/04/15/tiffany-lena-dunham-make-me-a-pop-star/.

Tolentino, Jia. "The Right to a Sexual Narrative: On the Lena Dunham Abuse Claims." *Jezebel*. November 4, 2014. http://jezebel.com/the-right-to-a-sexual-narrative-on-the-lena-dunham-abu-1654187731.

Trask, Stephen. "Midnight Radio." *Hedwig and the Angry Inch: Original Cast Recording*. Atlantic Records/WEA, 1999.

Unterberger, Andrew. "Is 'Girls' Finally Gonna Make a Hit Out of Icona Pop's 'I Love It'?" *Pop Dust*. January 28, 2013. http://popdust.com/2013/01/28/girls-icona-pop-i-love-it-soundtrack/.

VanDerWerff, Todd. "*Girls*: 'Weirdos Need Girlfriends, Too.'" *Onion*. June 3, 2012. http://www.avclub.com/tvclub/girls-weirdos-need-girlfriends-too-75587.

Verizon Wireless. "Droid Turbo. 'The Fall' with James Franco [one-minute version]." *YouTube.com*. October 30, 2014. Accessed November 8, 2014.

"The Video Generation." *Newsweek*. December 30, 1985. 44.

Vogel, Kristofor. "Perceptions of Subversion: The Formulation of a Pop-Subculture." Master's Thesis, University of Texas at Arlington, 2013.

Wagner, David. "Proof that Lena Dunham Has the Power to Make Hip Songs into Huge Hits Now." *The Wire*. January 15, 2013. http://www.thewire.com/entertainment/2013/01/girls-soundtrack-sales-numbers/61035/.

Watson, Elwood, ed. *Generation X Professor Speak: Voices from Academia*. Toronto: Scarecrow Press, 2013.

Williams, Alex. "Riding the Wave of 'Girls.'" *New York Times*. March 19, 2014. http://www.nytimes.com/2014/03/20/fashion/girls-television-cameos-new-york-city.html?_r=0.

———. "The End of Courtship?" *New York Times*. 11 January 2013. Accessed 6 January 2014.

Williams, Linda. *Hard Core: Power, Pleasure, and the 'Frenzy of the Visible'*. Expanded ed. Berkeley, University of California Press, 1999.

Winerip, Michael. "Boomers and Millennials Feel a Need to Care for One Another." *New York Times*. December 20, 2012. Accessed July 2, 2014. http://www.nytimes.com/2012/12/20/booming/ boomers-and-millenneals-feel-a-need-tocare-for-each-other.html?_r=0.

Woolf, Virginia. *A Room of One's Own*. London: Penguin Books, 2000 (1928).

Index

About the Contributors

Jocelyn L. Bailey is a PhD candidate in American literature at the University of Arkansas at Fayetteville. Her dissertation work focuses upon representations of the female body in nineteenth-century American sentimental literature. In addition to academic work, she is a freelance editor and writer.

Yael Levy is a teaching fellow at the Department of Film and Television in Tel Aviv University. Her research fields include television studies, feminist theories, and textual temporalities. The chapter included in this anthology is part of her PhD research, which focuses on the feminist politics of textual temporalities in turn of the millennium women-led US TV drama.

Jennifer Mitchell, visiting assistant professor at Union College, obtained her PhD from The Graduate Center, City University of New York. Her work about queer theory and bisexuality, children's and adolescent fiction have appeared in the *Journal of Bisexuality Studies*, *Bookbird*, and the *Journal of the Fantastic in the Arts*. She has written several articles and book chapters about modernism, masochism, and psychoanalysis.

Tom Pace is associate professor of English and director of core writing at John Carroll University, where he teaches a variety of writing and literature courses. He also directs the English department's Professional Writing Track. His areas of interest include style, the history of writing instruction, and popular culture. He has published articles on style and audience and is the co-editor of *Refiguring Prose Style: Possibilities for Writing Pedagogy*. More recently, he has published on the rhetoric of Generation X in *Mad Men* and has presented research at national conferences on *The West Wing*, *Gilmore Girls*, and *Breaking Bad*.

Maria San Filippo is author of *The B Word: Bisexuality in Contemporary Film and Television* (Indiana University Press, 2013), a Lambda Literary Award winner and one of *Slant*'s top 10 film studies books of 2013. She is an assistant professor at University of the Arts in Philadelphia and professor and director of the film and media studies. She is the author of *The B Word: Bisexuality in Contemporary Film and Television*(Indiana University Press, 2013). She has taught at Harvard University, MIT, UCLA, and Wellesley College, where she was the 2008–2010 Mellon Postdoctoral Fellow in Cinema and Media Studies. Her articles and reviews have been published in *CineAction, Cineaste, Cinema Journal, Cinephile, English Language Notes, Film History, In Media Res, Journal of Bisexuality,* the *Quarterly Review of Film and Video, Senses of Cinema,* and in the anthologies *Global Art Cinema* (Oxford, 2010) and *Millennial Masculinity* (Wayne State, 2013). She writes on twenty-first-century film and film-going on her blog, *The Itinerant Cinephile* (www.itinerantcinephile.com), and on Twitter.

Marc Edward Shaw is the Arkell Hall Chair in the Arts and Associate Professor in Theatre Arts, Hartwick College, Oneonta, New York. He is co-editor of *Performing American Masculinities: The 21st-Century Man in Popular Culture* (Indiana University Press, 2011), and his writing appears in *Salon.com, Theatre Journal, Shakespeare Bulletin*, Rodopi Press, McFarland Press, Wiley & Sons, *Modern Drama,* and *Theatre Topics.* Shaw's theatre directing credits include *FringeNYC* (Wish We Were Here), *Highways Performance Space* (A Singular Event, also co-creator/performer), *UC Santa Barbara Main Stage,* and *Summer Theater Lab.* He is the founding artistic director of the popular weekly comedy show *Improvability* which has run since 2004 at UCSB. Recent artistic training includes Improbable in London (Phelim McDermott), MICHA (Michael Chekhov Technique), SITI Company, Christopher Bayes. Shaw has presented research at the national conferences of PCA/ACA, Comparative Drama, ATHE, ASTR, & MLA (Pinter Society).

Lloyd Isaac Vayo is a lecturer in cultural studies and comparative literature at the University of Minnesota-Twin Cities. He has written extensively on 9/11 and terrorism, popular music, and literature. With Todd Comer, he edited the 2013 volume *Terror and the Cinematic Sublime: Essays on Violence and the Unpresentable in Post-9/11 Films* (McFarland).

Elwood Watson is professor of history, gender studies and African American studies at East Tennessee State University. He is the author of *Outsider Within: Black Women in the Legal Academy after Brown v. Board* (Rowman and Littlefield). His edited collections include *Performing*

American Masculinities: The 21st Century Man in Popular Culture (Indiana University Press, 2011), *Pimps, Wimps, Studs: Thugs and Gentlemen: Essays on Media Images of Masculinity* (McFarland, 2009), *The Oprah Phenomenon* (University Press of Kentucky, 2007), *Searching the Soul of Ally McBeal: Critical Essays* (McFarland, 2006), and *There She Is, Miss America: The Politics of Sex, Beauty and Race in America's Most Famous Pageant* (Palgrave Macmillan, 2004), *Mentoring Faculty of Color: Essays on Professional Development and Advancement in Colleges and Universities* (McFarland, 2012), *Generation X Professors Speak: Voices From Academia* (Scarecrow Press, 2013), *Overcoming Adversity in Academia: Stories From Generation X Professor*s, (University Press of America, 2014), and *Beginning a Career in Academia: A Guide For Graduate Students of Color* (Routledge Press, 2015). He has published numerous articles about race, gender, and American culture in national newspapers and magazines and is a blogger for *Diverse Education, Huffington Post, The Good Men Project, X/Y Online* and *The Black Past.org*

Hank Willenbrink is an associate professor of theatre at the University of Scranton where he serves as Director of the theatre program. He received his PhD from the University of California, Santa Barbara in 2009. Hank has articles in *Theatre Journal, Contemporary Theatre Review*, and *Theatre Forum*. He co-edited *Palabras: Dispatches from the Festival de la Palabra* for No Passport Press. Hank's play *The Boat in the Tiger Suit* was published by Original Works Publishing.

Laura S. Witherington holds a PhD in English literature and is an assistant professor of English at the University of Arkansas at Fort Smith. Her research interests include nineteenth-century landscape writing, economic criticism, pedagogy, and popular culture. Her interest in HBO's impact on culture includes a Marxist reading of *Girls* in *HBO's* Girls: *Questions of Gender, Politics, and Millennial Angst*. She is currently researching the impact of public park development in England and the United States during the late nineteenth century.

www.ingramcontent.com/pod-product-compliance
Lightning Source LLC
Chambersburg PA
CBHW030646110726
47901CB00002B/593